D0079580

THE GREAT DEPRESSION AND THE NEW DEAL

**Other Titles in the Greenwood Press Guides
to Historic Events of the Twentieth Century**
Randall M. Miller, Series Editor

THE GREAT DEPRESSION AND THE NEW DEAL

Robert F. Himmelberg

Greenwood Press Guides to
Historic Events of the Twentieth Century
Randall M. Miller, Series Editor

Greenwood Press
Westport, Connecticut • London

Library of Congress Cataloging-in-Publication Data

Himmelberg, Robert F.
    The Great Depression and the New Deal / Robert F. Himmelberg.
       p.   cm.—(Greenwood Press guides to historic events of the twentieth century,
    ISSN 1092–177X)
    Includes bibliographical references (p.   ) and index.
    ISBN 0–313–29907–2 (alk. paper)
      1. United States—History—1919–1933. 2. United States—History— 1933–1945. 3.
    Depressions—1929—United States. 4. New Deal, 1933–1939. I. Title. II. Series.
    E806.H56   2001
    973.92—dc21   00–042224

British Library Cataloguing in Publication Data is available.

Copyright © 2001 by Robert F. Himmelberg

All rights reserved. No portion of this book may be
reproduced, by any process or technique, without the
express written consent of the publisher.

Library of Congress Catalog Card Number: 00–042224
ISBN: 0–313–29907–2
ISSN: 1092–177X

First published in 2001

Greenwood Press, 88 Post Road West, Westport, CT 06881
An imprint of Greenwood Publishing Group, Inc.
www.greenwood.com

Printed in the United States of America

The paper used in this book complies with the
Permanent Paper Standard issued by the National
Information Standards Organization (Z39.48–1984).

10 9 8 7 6 5 4 3 2 1

Copyright Acknowledgments

The author and publisher gratefully acknowledge permission for the use of the following material:

Garet Garrett, "Great Works," *The Saturday Evening Post* 211 (April 8, 1939), 5–7, 86–88. Reprinted from The Saturday Evening Post 1939.

Geoffrey T. Hellman, "Mrs. Roosevelt: Her Admirers Have Their Own 1940 Platform: A New President But the Same First Lady," *Life* 8 (February 15, 1940), 70–72, 78–80. Geoffrey Hellman/Life Magazine © Time Inc. Reprinted by permission.

Cover photos: 1932 breadline (front); FDR in a 1935 "fireside chat" (back). FDR Library & Digital Archives.

ADVISORY BOARD

Michael Adas
Professor of History, Rutgers University

Ross E. Dunn
Professor of History, San Diego State University

Howard Spodek
Professor of History and Urban Studies, Temple University

Contents

CONTENTS

A photo essay follows page 80

Series Foreword

As the twenty-first century opens, it is time to take stock of the political, so-cial, economic, intellectual, and cultural forces and factors that made the twentieth century the most dramatic period of change in history. To that end, the Greenwood Press Guides to Historic Events of the Twentieth Century presents interpretive histories of the most significant events of the century. Each book in the series combines narrative history and analysis with pri-mary documents and biographical sketches, with an eye to providing both a reference guide to the principal persons, ideas, and experiences defining each historic event, and a reliable, readable overview of that event. Each book further provides analyses and discussions, grounded in both primary and secondary sources, of the causes and consequences, in thought and ac-tion, that give meaning to the historic event under review. By assuming a historical perspective, drawing on the latest and best writing on each subject, and offering fresh insights, each book promises to explain how and why a particular event defined the twentieth century. No consensus about the meaning of the twentieth century emerges from the series, but, collectively, the books identify the most salient concerns of the century. In so doing, the series reminds us of the many ways those historic events continue to affect our lives.

Each book follows a similar format designed to encourage readers to consult it as both a reference and a history in its own right. Each volume opens with a chronology of the historic event, followed by a narrative over-view, which also serves to introduce and examine briefly the main themes and issues related to that event. The next set of chapters is composed of topi-cal essays, each analyzing closely an issue or problem of interpretation introduced in the opening chapter. A concluding chapter suggesting the long-term implications and meanings of the historic event brings the strands of the preceding chapters together while placing the event in the larger historical context. Each book also includes a section of short biographies of the principal persons related to the event, followed by a section introducing and reprinting key historical documents illustrative of and pertinent to the event. A glossary of selected terms adds to the utility of each book. An annotated bibliography—of significant books, films, and CD-ROMs—and an index conclude each volume.

The editors made no attempt to impose any theoretical model or historical perspective on the individual authors. Rather, in developing the series, an advisory board of noted historians and informed high school history teachers and public and school librarians identified the topics needful of exploration and the scholars eminently qualified to examine those events with intelligence and sensitivity. The common commitment throughout the series is to provide accurate, informative, and readable books, free of jargon and up to date in evidence and analysis.

Each book stands as a complete historical analysis and reference guide to a particular historic event. Each book also has many uses, from understanding contemporary perspectives on critical historical issues, to providing biographical treatments of key figures related to each event, to offering excerpts and complete texts of essential documents about the event, to suggesting and describing books and media materials for further study and presentation of the event, and more. The combination of historical narrative and individual topical chapters addressing significant issues and problems encourages students and teachers to approach each historic event from multiple perspectives and with a critical eye. The arrangement and content of each book thus invite students and teachers, through classroom discussions and position papers, to debate the character and significance of great historic events and to discover for themselves how and why history matters.

The series emphasizes the main currents that have shaped the modern world. Much of that focus necessarily looks at the West, especially Europe and the United States. The political, commercial, and cultural expansion of the West wrought largely, though not wholly, the most fundamental changes of the century. Taken together, however, books in the series reveal the interactions between Western and non-Western peoples and society, and also the tensions between modern and traditional cultures. They also point to the ways in which non-Western peoples have adapted Western ideas and technology and, in turn, influenced Western life and thought. Several books examine such increasingly powerful global forces as the rise of Islamic fundamentalism, the emergence of modern Japan, the Communist revolution in China, and the collapse of communism in eastern Europe and the former Soviet Union. American interests and experiences receive special attention in the series, not only in deference to the primary readership of the books but also in recognition that the United States emerged as the dominant political, economic, social, and cultural force during the twentieth century. By looking at the century through the lens of American events and experiences, it is possible to see why the age has come to be known as "The American Century."

Assessing the history of the twentieth century is a formidable prospect. It has been a period of remarkable transformation. The world broadened and narrowed at the same time. Frontiers shifted from the interiors of Africa and Latin America to the moon and beyond; communication spread from mass circulation newspapers and magazines to radio, television, and the Internet; skyscrapers reached upward and suburbs stretched outward; energy switched from steam, to electric, to atomic power. Many changes did not lead to a complete abandonment of established patterns and practices so much as a synthesis of old and new, as, for example, the increased use of (even reliance on) the telephone in the age of the computer. The automobile and the truck, the airplane, and telecommunications closed distances, and people in unprecedented numbers migrated from rural to urban, industrial, and ever more ethnically diverse areas. Tractors and chemical fertilizers made it possible for fewer people to grow more, but the environmental and demographic costs of an exploding global population threatened to outstrip natural resources and human innovation. Disparities in wealth increased, with developed nations prospering and underdeveloped nations starving. Amid the crumbling of former European colonial empires, Western technology, goods, and culture increasingly enveloped the globe, seeping into, and undermining, non-Western cultures—a process that contributed to a surge of religious fundamentalism and ethno-nationalism in the Middle East, Asia, and Africa. As people became more alike, they also became more aware of their differences. Ethnic and religious rivalries grew in intensity everywhere as the century closed.

The political changes during the twentieth century were no less profound than the social, economic, and cultural ones. Many of the books in the series focus on political events, broadly defined, but no books are confined to politics alone. Political ideas and events have social effects, just as they spring from a complex interplay of non-political forces in culture, society, and economy. Thus, for example, the modern civil rights and women's rights movements were at once social and political events in cause and consequence. Likewise, the Cold War created the geopolitical framework for dealing with competing ideologies and nations abroad and served as the touchstone for political and cultural identities at home. The books treating political events do so within their social, cultural, and economic contexts.

Several books in the series examine particular wars in depth. Wars are defining moments for people and eras. During the twentieth century war became more widespread and terrible than ever before, encouraging new efforts to end war through strategies and organizations of international cooperation and disarmament while also fueling new ideologies and instruments of mass persuasion that fostered distrust and festered old national rivalries. Two world wars during the century redrew the political map, slaughtered or uprooted two generations of people, and introduced and hastened the development of new technologies and weapons of mass destruction. The First World War spelled the end of the old European order and spurred communist revolution in Russia and fascism in Italy, Germany, and elsewhere. The Second World War killed fascism and inspired the final push for freedom from European colonial rule in Asia and Africa. It also led to the Cold War that suffocated much of the world for almost half a century. Large wars begat small ones, and brutal totalitarian regimes cropped up across the globe. After (and in some ways because of) the fall of communism in eastern Europe and the former Soviet Union, wars of competing cultures, national interests, and political systems persisted in the struggle to make a new world order. Continuing, too, has been the belief that military technology can achieve political ends, whether in the superior American firepower that failed to "win" in Vietnam or in the American "smart bombs" and other military wizardry that "won" in the Persian Gulf.

Another theme evident in the series is that throughout the century nationalism continued to drive events. Whether in the Balkans in 1914 triggering World War I or in the Balkans in the 1990s threatening the post–Cold War peace—or in many other places—nationalist ambitions and forces would not die. The persistence of nationalism is yet another reminder of the many ways that the past becomes prologue.

We thus offer the series as a modern guide to and interpretation of the historic events of the twentieth century and as an invitation to consider how and why those events defined not only the past and present but also charted the political, social, intellectual, cultural, and economic routes into this century.

Randall M. Miller
Saint Joseph's University, Philadelphia

Preface

This book on the Great Depression of the 1930s and the New Deal will, I hope, prove interesting and useful, both for students taking courses on the subject and general readers. The book contains a narrative text, a set of biographies of a number of the leading figures of the period, a selection of important documents from the period, a glossary, and an annotated bibliography. The text begins with an introductory chapter that reviews the central story and issues of the period, the Great Crash of 1929, the continuous decline of the economy for four long years afterward, President Hoover's embattled and unsuccessful attempts to reverse this long plunge into an economic abyss, and the gradual improvement in the nation's economic fortunes that accompanied the New Deal of President Franklin Roosevelt. This introductory chapter is followed by four topical chapters dealing, successively, with the economics of the depression, with the nature, purposes and effects of the New Deal, with the political revolution of the 1930s, and with the depression's impact on American society and culture. A final chapter sums up and attempts to evaluate the longer range impact of the depression and New Deal on American life.

Within the limits of a compact narrative, I have endeavored to convey a sense of what I regard as the most cogent current scholarship on a number of the major issues involved in interpreting the period. Readers may therefore find that some topics, such as the connection between the Great Crash and the depression, why the depression was so stubbornly long, and what the effects of the New Deal's policies were, are interpreted in a way new to them. Questions such as these never receive final answers, of course, and scholars writing on the period continue to disagree about many of them. Space, and the nature of this book, prevented me from lengthy discussions of views alternative to those presented, but this is compensated for, I believe, by the lengthy and up-to-date annotated bibliography. I hope this will serve well the reader who wants to explore the issues further.

The biographies furnish the more detailed information about the leading personalities of the epoch that would have slowed the narrative too much but will interest many readers. As for the documents section, I hope all readers will enjoy its contents as thoroughly as I enjoyed designing it. The documents furnish the reader with an opportunity to examine the issues and arguments of the 1930s directly. The intention in making the selections was to include items representative of as many different points of view from the period as possible. Another intention was to find documents that would convey a feel for the period, a sense of the way people spoke and communicated, the way they presented themselves and their ideas, in the 1930s. The print medium can at best accomplish this purpose only partially, of course. Photographs, such as those included in this book, are essential for developing one's historical sensibility. Many readers will want to supplement what they find here by viewing more of the photographic record and sampling the abundant film footage from the period. These, as well as the sounds of the period's voices, are readily available nowadays through videocassettes, a number of which are referenced at the end of the bibliography and will amply repay viewing.

The general editor of the series of which this book is a part, Randall Miller, was extraordinarily patient and helpful in overseeing my project. I would like to thank also a number of people, graduate assistants and others from Fordham University's Graduate School of Arts and Sciences, who helped with library searches, document reproduction, and all the other multifarious tasks involved in producing this book, including Jill Budny, John Alikpala, Dominique Gerard, Paul Seaton, and Megan Alvis.

Abbreviations

AAA	Agricultural Adjustment Administration
AFL	American Federation of Labor
BEF	Bonus Expeditionary Force
CCC	Civilian Conservation Corps
CIO	Committee for Industrial Organization (later, Congress of Industrial Organizations)
CPA	Communist Party of America
CWA	Civil Works Administration
FAP	Federal Art Project
FDIC	Federal Deposit Insurance Corporation
FERA	Federal Emergency Relief Administration
FHA	Federal Housing Administration
FSA	Farm Security Administration
FTP	Federal Theater Project
LNPL	Labor's Non-Partisan League
NAACP	National Association for the Advancement of Colored People
N.I.R.A.	National Industrial Recovery Act
NLRB	National Labor Relations Board
NRA	National Recovery Administration

NYA   National Youth Administration

PWA   Public Works Administration

RA   Resettlement Administration

REA   Rural Electrification Administration

RFC   Reconstruction Finance Corporation

SCS   Soil Conservation Service

SEC   Securities and Exchange Commission

TNEC   Temporary National Economic Committee

TVA   Tennessee Valley Authority

UAW   United Auto Workers

UMW   United Mine Workers

USHA   United States Housing Authority

WIB   War Industries Board

WPA   Works Progress Administration

Chronology of Events

1928

November   Herbert Hoover, Republican, wins presidential election over Al Smith, Democrat.

1929   Year of record prosperity; real GNP (value of all goods and services, adjusted for price changes) is up 38 percent over 1922; unemployment rate is 3.2 percent of work force, an all-time low; common stock values have tripled since 1922.

September 3   Values on New York Stock Exchange peak; they have doubled since July 1926.

October 29   Black Tuesday; after several trading days of decline, stock market falls disastrously. By year's end market has lost one-third of its value at the peak.

1930   Real GNP falls by 10 percent; unemployment rises to 9 percent; common stocks fall to half their value in September, 1929.

Smoot-Hawley Act substantially increases U.S. tariffs on imports.

1931   Real GNP falls by another 8 percent; unemployment rises to 16 percent; common stocks continue to fall.

April   Congress passes Bonus Bill, providing partial payment of sums due veterans at later date, over Hoover's veto.

May	Credit-Anstalt, the Austrian central bank, fails, triggering European financial crisis.
June	Hoover proposes year-long moratorium on inter-governmental debt payments; final agreement not secured until August.
September	England abandons gold standard.
October–November	American banking system increasingly threatened; Hoover proposes and bankers establish National Credit Association.
1932	Real GNP declines to 71 percent of 1929; unemployment rises to 24 percent; common stocks fall to approximately 15 percent of value at 1929 peak.
January–February	Hoover proposes and Congress enacts Reconstruction Finance Corporation (RFC) and other measures to bolster banking and financial system.
July	Emergency Relief and Construction Act provides federal money to states for unemployment relief and federal public works.
	Bonus Expeditionary Force (BEF) routed from Washington by General Douglas MacArthur.
November	Franklin Delano Roosevelt (FDR) wins presidential election by wide margin over Hoover.
1933	Real GNP declines slightly; unemployment at 25 percent; stock values rise to one-third of 1929 level. The bottom year of the Great Depression.
February	Congress enacts Twenty-First Amendment, repealing prohibition of alcoholic beverages and sends to states for ratification.
February–March	Runs by depositors threaten to bring on collapse of banking system nationally; governors declare bank holidays.
March 4	FDR inaugurated; promises bold leadership and declares he will ask Congress for emergency powers as in wartime if necessary.
March 5	President calls Congress into special session for March 9.
March 6	Roosevelt declares national bank holiday.
March 9	The "One Hundred Days" begin as Congress assembles; Emergency Banking Act swiftly passed at president's request, restoring confidence in banks and enabling government to reopen most of them almost immediately.
March 12	Economy Bill enacted, signaling Roosevelt's New Deal will be fiscally responsible.

March 31   Civilian Conservation Corps created to provide employment in conservation projects for young men.

May 12   Federal Emergency Relief Administration created; provides $500 million to states for unemployment relief.

May 18   Tennessee Valley Authority established to provide low-cost hydroelectric power and aid economic development of Tennessee River valley.

May 27   Securities Act enacted to compel Wall Street disclosure of information concerning new stock issues.

June 13   Home Owner's Loan Corporation created to prevent home foreclosures; will lend over $3 billion over next three years to refinance home mortgages.

June 16   President signs National Industrial Recovery Act (N.I.R.A.), creating National Recovery Administration (NRA) empowered to approve industrial codes that stabliize prices and wages; Section 7(a) guarantees workers right to organize.

June 16   Glass-Steagall Act divorces investment from commercial banking and creates Federal Deposit Insurance Corporation (FDIC).

July– August   NRA administrator Hugh Johnson stimulates national wave of marches and rallies supporting NRA codes and hope of quick industrial recovery.

November   Civil Works Administration (CWA) created to provide direct federal work relief for unemployed; 4 million men will be employed before CWA is dismantled in spring of 1934.

1934   Real GNP rises marginally and unemployment declines to 22 percent; stock values up by 9 percent.

Year of mounting political unrest and vocal opposition to Roosevelt program; Huey Long founds Share Our Wealth Society advocating radical redistribution of income and wealth; Fr. Charles Coughlin, the popular "radio priest," breaks off support of New Deal and forms National League for Social Justice; Dr. Francis Townsend's plan for extravagant old-age pensions attracts widespread support.

Labor unrest grows; over 2,000 strikes erupt, many involving confrontation and violence.

July   General strike in San Francisco.

September   Textile workers strike from Maine to Georgia.

November   Minnesota Farmer-Labor Party reelects Floyd Olson as governor; Philip LaFollette elected governor in Wisconsin as third-party candidate; in California, socialist Upton Sinclair narrowly defeated for governor after winning Democratic primary; nationally, Democrats sweep midterm congressional elections.

1935   Real GNP up to 87 percent of 1929; unemployment down to 20 percent; stock values steady.

April   Emergency Relief Appropriation Act provides $4.8 billion for relief; president creates Works Progress Administration (WPA) under Harry Hopkins, which will provide work relief for millions of the unemployed over the next several years.

May 27   Supreme Court declares NRA unconstitutional.

June   FDR abandons NRA approach to recovery and reform; the "Second Hundred Days" begin in which legislation shaping a "Second New Deal" emerges.

                National Labor Relations Act, authored by Senator Robert Wagner of New York, establishing the National Labor Relations Board (NLRB) empowered to protect workers' right to organize and bargain collectively, becomes law.

July–
August   Social Security Act creates federal old-age pensions through a payroll tax; joint federal-state system created for unemployment compensation and aid to the dependent.

                Wealth Tax Act sharply raises tax rates on high personal incomes and large inheritances and on corporate profits.

                Public Utility Holding Company Act, requiring reorganization of inefficient utility "pyramids," under threat of "death sentence," becomes law.

                Banking Act centralizes control of Federal Reserve System in presidentially appointed Federal Reserve Board.

September   Huey Long assassinated.

November   Committee on Industrial Organization (CIO), later named the Congress of Industrial Organizations, formed; will spearhead organization in mass production industries.

1936   Real GNP climbs to 97 percent of 1929; unemployment down to 17 percent; stock values soar by one-third to 60 percent of 1929 level.

                Supreme Court rules AAA unconstitutional.

Fr. Coughlin, Dr. Townsend and Gerald L. K. Smith, Huey Long's heir, form Union Party and nominate William Lemke as presidential candidate.

November — FDR wins smashing victory over Alf Landon, Republican presidential candidate, by taking 61 percent of popular vote; "New Deal Coalition" has been created.

December — United Auto Workers (CIO union) begins "sit-down" strike against General Motors.

1937 — Real GNP equals 1929 level; unemployment still high, at 14 percent; stock market is steady.

January — FDR, believing recovery is at hand, begins cuts of federal spending; WPA rolls cut in half by summer.

February — FDR, fearing Supreme Court will throw out New Deal reforms, submits plan giving him control of it disguised as plan for federal court reform; quickly becomes known as "court-packing" plan.

March–May — In reversal, Supreme Court majority forms that approves state minimum wage law and upholds Wagner Act and Social Security Act.

Court-packing bill defeated in Congress as many Democratic congressmen join with Republicans to form a "conservative coalition," which endures to defeat FDR proposals subsequently.

March — UAW wins recognition from GM, initiating wave of victories for CIO unions.

August — Stock market sharply declines, signaling steep downturn of output and employment that continues into 1938; unemployment rises sharply until recovery begins in mid-1938.

November — FDR calls Congress into special session but fails to secure passage of wage-and-hour bill and other important New Deal proposals.

1938 — Real GNP falls by 5 percent; unemployment rises by 5 percent, to 19 percent; stock values plunge by 25 percent.

March — FDR appoints Thurman Arnold head of Antitrust Division.

April — FDR asks Congress for emergency work relief funds and asks for investigation of monopoly power, signaling new policy— deliberate deficit spending to bolster employment together with renewal of antitrust policy.

May — Congress establishes Temporary National Economic Committee to investigate concentration of economic power.

June   FDR secures congressional approval of Fair Labor Standards Act, setting minimum wage and maximum hours in industry.

November   Republicans rebound in congressional elections; FDR's attempt to "purge" conservative Democrats in primaries largely fails.

1939   Real GNP surpasses 1929 by 7 percent; unemployment falls to 17 percent; stocks improve only slightly.

September   World War II begins in Europe as Germany attacks Poland.

1940   Real GNP rises to 113 percent of 1929; unemployment falls to 15 percent; stocks down.

September   Roosevelt aids England with "destroyers-for-bases" deal. Congress passes Selective Service Act.

November   Roosevelt elected for a third term, defeating Republican Wendell Wilkie.

1941   Real GNP is 130 percent of 1929 level; unemployment falls drastically to 10 percent, but stocks decline again, to 38 percent of 1929 level.

THE GREAT DEPRESSION AND THE NEW DEAL EXPLAINED

1

The Great Depression and the New Deal: An Overview

Unforeseen and unexpected, inexplicable and inexorable, the Great Depression was a traumatic experience for many of the men and women of the 1930s and exercised a profound influence on the generation that lived through it. In its duration and magnitude, it was infinitely more severe than any other episode of "hard times" in American national life and was unquestionably the dominant force molding the nation's history during the long decade reaching from mid-1929 through 1940. The depression brought great hardship and suffering to millions of Americans. It also created a political and social atmosphere fertile for major changes across the entire range of economic, political, and social institutions and policies. The depression made a strong impact on people's everyday lives because so many suffered from economic hardship and insecurity. The majority of Americans escaped actual unemployment or loss of farm or home, but all felt their lives shaped by the depression to some degree because they lived in fear that it might directly engulf them too.

The most important and evident change the depression introduced was the New Deal, the series of new departures in the federal government's economic and social policies brought about through the leadership of the period's key figure, Franklin Delano Roosevelt (FDR), the Democratic president first elected in 1932 in the depths of the depression. By the decade's close many New Deal partisans asserted that, out of the crisis of the depression, the Democratic Party under Roosevelt's leadership had wrought a virtual "revolution" in American life. Under FDR the government, they claimed, had instituted measures to bring about recovery and guard against future depressions, and taken steps to secure help for the unemployed and better the lives of the bottom third of American society.

This scenario, or something like it, lives on, dimly reflected in the historical consciousness of Americans to this very day. Somehow, many Americans would say, President Roosevelt took strong and innovative steps to rescue the economy from greedy hands, to promote recovery from the depression, and to provide jobs and security for the unemployed and the helpless. Partisan commentators challenged this story when it was fashioned, of course. Historians, too, have long debated its elements and are far from concluding the argument. It is clear today that not all the New Deal's economic and social programs and reforms actually promoted recovery or economic growth and that they fell far short of substantially changing the pattern of income distribution and wealth-holding between the social classes. Yet it is also clear that many of the New Deal's reforms significantly strengthened the business system's stability and promoted positive economic and social change. Many of those whom the American system had marginalized politically, socially, and economically had been empowered and their condition greatly improved.

The aim of this chapter is to provide a survey of the depression era, of how the depression came, how it affected the lives and livelihood of so many Americans, how it influenced social behavior, and how it led to sweeping changes in American politics and in governmental economic and social policies. Later chapters describe and assess these topics in detail and depth.

PRELUDE TO THE GREAT DEPRESSION: AMERICA IN THE 1920s

The onset of the Great Depression came, as most people at the time saw it, with shocking suddenness. In the space of a few days in October 1929, values on the New York Stock Exchange abruptly collapsed, wiping out the heady optimism of the "great bull market" of 1928–1929 and the seeming invincibility of Republican prosperity. Stock values had risen steadily and with a nearly unbroken pace since 1922, as the nation moved away from a sharply felt but brief postwar depression that began in 1920. World War I had placed great demands on the American economy, even before direct American participation began in 1917. Excessive demand led to a steep inflation of prices and set the economy up for an equally sharp deflation when the high rate of government spending, though continuing for a time after the Armistice of November 1918, rapidly slackened by 1920. Unemployment for millions of industrial and other workers ensued, but hardship extended

to the middle class as well. Farmers were hit especially hard because many
of them had borrowed heavily at high rates during the war to increase their
output. Now agricultural prices and farm income collapsed, and foreclosures on farm property soared. But recovery from this postwar depression
came promptly and swiftly. By late 1921, the signs of recovery were clear.
A long period of prosperity had begun, marred only by brief slowdowns in
the growth trend and by the failure of certain sectors of the economy, such
as agriculture, to keep pace.

The people of the 1920s, especially those nearer the top of the economic
ladder, came to see the era as one of fabulous prosperity. This fable of a
golden age of prosperity had much support in reality, though less than the
mythmakers believed. For the professional and managerial classes and for
many clerical and blue-collar workers too, times were indeed good. Production and consumption of the goods that are the stuff of a modern industrial
economy came into their own in this decade.

It was the newer, highly innovative industries that fueled the expansion
of the 1920s. During the decade auto registration rose from 9 to 27 million
as the automobile industry, led by Henry Ford's highly affordable Model T,
put ownership within the reach of a mass market. Electrical goods too
flooded markets from new American factories as refrigerators replaced the
"ice-box" in a high proportion of urban homes, brooms gave way to vacuum
cleaners, and radios brought entertainment, sporting events, and news into
the home. The enormous increase in such products and the rapid expansion
of the automobile indicated that higher incomes and more modern consumption patterns were filtering down from the well-to-do through the middle class and the working class.

The disposition of Americans to adjust their consumption patterns and to
accept new products often needed little encouragement, but it was assisted
and heightened by a thriving advertising industry that adopted the newer
and more high-powered techniques for manipulating consumers we are familiar with today. Madison Avenue persuaded consumers to buy an ever
widening array of products by implying their use, or possession, would improve one's status or attractiveness, as in the campaign to persuade people
to buy Listerine to combat "halitosis." A wider availability of consumer
credit, "buying on the installment plan," was still another reason for the propensity of most Americans to spend at a high rate on consumer goods during
the 1920s.

The prosperity of the decade had its limits. National income grew rapidly, but the share of the increase going to those in the upper two-fifths of the
income scale was far higher than for those lower down on it. Blue-collar
workers enjoyed relatively stable employment, but their wages grew only

modestly, and the income of family farmers did not grow commensurately with that of the urban middle class. Moreover, farming was not the only industry whose participants failed to share in the prosperity of the twenties. A number of older, basic industries, especially soft-coal mining and cotton textiles, for a variety of reasons suffered from overcapacity and the shift in production and consumption. That is, the capital and labor employed in the industry could supply so much output that prices were endemically too low to provide a normal return on capital and to give workers regular work through the year at a decent wage. In the long run, in situations like this, capital and labor leave the industry and go elsewhere for employment. But such adjustment takes time, and in some cases, for reasons peculiar to the industry, change is stubbornly slow. These industries, with their low wages and semiemployed workers, were a drag on the economy and in the depression decade became an even more serious problem. Still, though important currents of discontent ran strongly among some groups, political and social reform proved secondary during the 1920s to the well-nigh universal preoccupation with enjoying the fruits of prosperity.

For Americans who had reached maturity before the 1920s, the decade often appeared a time of rapid social and cultural, as well as economic, change. Clearly it was, though it is equally clear that to include all the younger generation within the "flaming youth" category would be a gross exaggeration. Many young Americans of college age, however, did lead a more liberated life than their parents had led, and their behavior did trickle down to high school youths. Many younger women, still in school or working in offices, as they did in ever increasing numbers during the decade, adopted less restricting and chaste apparel, "bobbed" their hair, and smoked and drank like men. Attitudes toward premarital sexual experience became much less restrained among younger men and women and young married couples. Contraception became more widely practiced, and the birthrate declined as middle-class women, and men too, rejected large, burdensome families that prevented living the high-consumption, urban life-style that was becoming the national aspiration.

These changes in national moral and cultural attitudes resulted from the fact that America was ever increasingly an urban-industrial society, a society in which people moved frequently from place to place in response to job opportunities. Thus they depended less and less on family and community ties for a livelihood and lost the immediacy of family and community traditions. The transition witnessed during the 1920s toward attitudes that are eminently familiar to us today were assisted and driven by the particular circumstances of that decade. The automobile gave young people far more mobility and privacy than ever before, and respect for authority was perhaps eroded somewhat in the eyes of many people by the decade's "Noble experiment," as President Herbert Hoover called it, that is, the prohibition of alcoholic beverages. Introduced in the aftermath of World War I, opponents of Prohibition saw it as the imposition of a certain form of Protestant morality, which, in fact, in great measure it was. Evasion of Prohibition was widespread. While politicians argued over Prohibition's merits, a criminal industry controlled by often warring rival gangs provided a steady flow of "bootleg" liquor for the "speakeasies" and hip flasks for which the 1920s are notorious. The widespread political and law enforcement corruption that accompanied Prohibition degraded respect for authority and tradition.

Paralleling these changes in mores and another sign that America was rapidly becoming an urbanized, mass consumption society departing in many ways from its social traditions was the growing public preoccupation with, and the insatiable public desire to identify with, celebrity figures. The reach of radio and movies grew with astonishing speed during the 1920s, providing the basis for participation by all Americans in a new popular culture. Adulation of such film stars as Rudolph Valentino and Mary Pickford, such sports heroes as Babe Ruth, and such adventurous spirits as Charles Lindbergh became a national pastime in which Americans of all classes enthusiastically shared.

THE GREAT CRASH AND THE DEPRESSION'S COURSE, 1929–1932

The soaring stock market became the symbol of prosperity, seeming to signify the endless capacity of the American economy for wealth production. Though limited by modern standards, the number of Americans drawn into stock market speculation grew rapidly and was far greater by the late 1920s than ever before. Thus, when the crash came, it had a stunning impact on the confidence of consumers and investors. This no doubt exacerbated the economic downturn, which became more and more visible in the months after the collapse of the market. Contemporaries in fact tended to blame the depression above all on the market crash, but here they exaggerated. The stock market crash signaled the end of an era. It wiped out the savings and confidence of many Americans. But it alone did not explain the failure of the American economy. The economy actually peaked during the second quarter of 1929, well before the crash, and the reasons why the economy turned down so disastrously for years in a row once the decline began go well beyond its influence.

That the downturn of 1929 would become a severe depression, let alone the beginning of a decade-long period of economic decline and stagnation, was not immediately apparent or even imagined by the direst Cassandras of 1929. Opinion makers, whether drawn from the ranks of politicians, businessmen, or journalists, tend to diagnose economic problems and base their policy prescriptions on experiences from the recent past. The most recent depression, after World War I, had been deep but brief in duration. The thinking from 1929 through much of 1930 was that this depression too would be brief, and to be grateful that the downward trend of the economy was so much more moderate than it had been during the previous episode of depression. There also had developed a deeply engrained belief, especially in business circles, that the modern economy, with its immense production and consumption of so great a variety and volume of consumer goods, had become virtually depression-proof.

These beliefs and hopes proved vain. Unemployment rose steadily throughout 1930; consumer spending and production of goods and services fell relentlessly, even though gradually; the stock market continued its decline; farm prices collapsed; and many banks, squeezed by the inability of borrowers to repay loans, approached the brink of failure. American exports, moreover, declined sharply as depressed conditions appeared in Europe soon after the American crash in late 1929. Germany was the worst affected. A steady inflow of American loans had helped Germany maintain economic stability during the 1920s, but after the crash the loans stopped and the ability of the German government to pay its war debts and meet other obligations was immediately impaired. As the depression spread throughout the Continent, European markets for American goods fell off, creating still more unemployment. The new Smoot-Hawley tariff, more protective than the previous one, passed by the Republican-dominated Congress in 1930, was castigated at the time as responsible for the fall off in American exports, and thus a key factor in worsening the depression in America, because it provoked the European governments to raise their own tariffs in retaliation. This probably was an exaggeration. As modern economic historians have pointed out, exports fell off only proportionately to the decline of the European economies and thus appear to have been declining simply because of falling European buying power rather than because of retaliatory tariffs. Regardless, the decline of the European economies aggravated the depression in America, because it narrowed the market for American exports and put pressure on the American financial system.

During the latter part of 1930, two things occurred that created dire foreboding about the economic future. One was a natural disaster, a drought in the south-central states, especially in Arkansas, which brought acute suffering to an already greatly afflicted agricultural region. It was the beginning of a dry period that extended over the next several years throughout

Oklahoma, Kansas, and the other states of the Great Plains, creating conditions that made the region into what contemporaries called the "Dust Bowl." It was as though nature herself was conspiring with unknown economic forces to create a period of unbearably hard times. The other occurrence was a number of bank failures, caused in part by an erosion of public confidence in banking that led to "runs," large-scale withdrawals of cash by depositors, until banks were forced to close and declare bankruptcy.

Unemployment and evidence of widespread dislocation and suffering multiplied during 1931. Conditions in Europe rapidly deteriorated, compounding the American economic crisis. The German economy sagged precipitously. The British and French economies proved substantially more resistant to unemployment during the early 1930s than either the American or German, but by mid-1931 the banking and monetary systems of all three European countries were under severe pressure because of falling international trade, lowered government revenues, and the continuing necessity of making large payments on the huge international debts created during World War I. By September 1931, financial pressure forced Britain to abandon the gold standard, a step that traditional financial thought in America believed would destabilize international trade and finance even more.

THE DEPRESSION BECOMES A CATASTROPHE, 1931–1933

By late 1931, America's economic condition had become desperate, and it only worsened during the next year. When the depression bottomed, a staggering number of workers, one out of four, had no employment at all, and many of those still with jobs had only part-time work. Large numbers of Americans, unable to make mortgage payments, lost their homes, and even more lost their savings as the banking system came under increasing pressure. The rate of bank failures mounted rapidly during 1930 but rose to epidemic proportions in 1931. In that year conditions forced 2,294 banks, holding deposits worth $1.7 billion, to close, with depositors losing much of their money.

Statistics tell the same saddening story wherever we look. Farm prices dropped by 55 percent between and 1929 and 1932, drastically lowering farm income and worsening the burden of fixed debt most farmers were carrying. As a result, foreclosures occurred with frightening frequency, and a very high proportion of farmers, perhaps as many as one-third, lost their land and livelihood. In manufacturing, the rate of unemployment rose even higher than the national average as output dropped by half between 1929 and 1932, and in some industries, such as automobiles, by nearly three-quarters. In many of the great industrial cities such as Detroit, Toledo, and Cleveland, half or more of the blue-collar workers were unemployed by 1932. Signs of destitution and the utter disruption of ordinary life patterns afflicted the lives of countless people, old and young. Hundreds of thousands of farm families, many from the Dust Bowl states, lost their farms and became migratory farm workers. Many families from Oklahoma and Arkansas, known derisively as the "Okies" and "Arkies," were forced into this condition. Their miserable plight was memorialized by John Steinbeck's *The Grapes of Wrath*, the novel that, more than any other literary product of the depression years, captured the bewilderment of those who lost their livelihood, and, despite their best efforts, were never to recover a secure place in American life. Signs of grave dislocation abounded. The number of hoboes, men (and some women too) who wandered the country "riding the rails" and living by begging or through intermittent labor, numbered in the millions. It was commonplace for housewives in cities and towns along the railways to find ragged men knocking at their back doors asking for food, a request that was more often granted than not. Many of these hoboes were among the large number of men who, shamed and beaten down by prolonged inability to provide for their families, deserted them.

Pessimism about what was to come grew during these worst years of the depression. Two of the most important social indicators, the marriage rate and birthrate, fell sharply between 1930 and 1932 as young people shrank from family formation. The trend reversed in 1933 and 1934 and the later years of the decade, indicating that many Americans had regained a measure of faith in the future.

Americans on the whole proved remarkably patient through the ordeal of the early 1930s. In these worst years of the depression, they were for the most part even passive. But a few events contradicted this passivity. The most notable of them was the encampment in the nation's capital during the spring and summer of 1932 of the Bonus Expeditionary Force (BEF), when thousands of unemployed veterans came to Washington to lobby for immediate payment of a bonus for wartime service, only to be routed out by the U.S. Army and a government fearing social unrest. Most Americans who lost jobs and property, however, in accordance with the deeply engrained belief that individual effort determined personal prosperity and success, appear to have blamed themselves rather than the system. In addition they initially tended to believe the reassurances they received, for they had long entrusted the success of the economy to Republican presidents and to big business leaders. Paradoxically, it would only be later, after the Democrats had taken control of the presidency and Congress and recovery had begun from the depths of the depression that workers would adopt a more militant stance in their dealings with employers and that middle Americans would begin to listen attentively to the irresponsible preachments of demagogic figures such as Fr. Charles Coughlin (the "Radio Priest") or Senator Huey Long of Louisiana, who would make "every man a king" through a radical redistribution of income and wealth from the few to the many.

The faith of the people in the Republican Party, which most of them had regarded as the custodian of prosperity, and in the Republican president, Herbert Hoover, by 1932 had reached the vanishing point. Governmental efforts to stem the tide of depression had failed. As the situation grew worse, expectation of strong action in Washington had grown everywhere except among rigid conservatives such as the secretary of the treasury, Andrew Mellon, who advised the president to "liquidate, liquidate, liquidate," to let the depression run its course without doing anything. President Herbert Hoover would go out a beaten man, his once-sterling reputation as a humanitarian and the nation's best problem solver tarnished almost beyond redemption by his failure to reverse the depression.

Hoover was elected in 1928 by a large popular majority over his Democratic opponent, Al Smith, the first Catholic presidential candidate. Hoover had hoped to preside over a continuation of Republican prosperity. Unlike his Republican predecessors of the decade, Warren Harding and Calvin Coolidge, Hoover believed in using government actively to solve, and to encourage the various economic organizations and groups to solve, the country's endemic economic and social problems. In 1929, before the depression became apparent, he set out to do just this, for example, by encouraging Congress to adopt a farm program that had potential for stabilizing farm prices and improving farmers' income. The crash and the depression soon pushed this and other attempts at fundamental reform aside. Hoover attempted to meet the challenge of the depression, his policies becoming more vigorous as the depression worsened. The program he pushed through Congress early in 1932, most notably the Reconstruction Finance Corporation (RFC), a federal agency empowered to support financial institutions by lending them large sums, stemmed the banking crisis for the moment. Hoover, however, believed strongly that stimulation of businessmen's confidence, together with his program for financial stability, held the key to recovery and strongly resisted proposals for large spending from the federal treasury for public works and unemployment relief despite their great popular appeal.

Not until late in his term did he agree on a compromise with the Democratic Congress on these issues. By that time his critics had fixed firmly in the public mind the picture of a callous president who refused to act when local and state relief funds for the jobless were exhausted or utterly inadequate. Despite his unprecedented efforts to use the power of the central government to arrest the downturn, it defeated him. In desperation, voters turned away from the Republican Party in the election of 1932.

FRANKLIN D. ROOSEVELT AND THE FIRST NEW DEAL, 1933–1935

The worst came in the winter of 1932–1933, as the nation awaited the transition in the presidency that would come on March 4, 1933, when Franklin Delano Roosevelt (FDR), who had won the election on the promise of a "New Deal for America," would take the oath of office. The inauguration came in the midst of a frightening economic crisis. Hoover's initiatives, especially the creation of the Reconstruction Finance Corporation, had shored up the banks and slowed the tide of failures, but, in the winter of 1932–1933, with economic indicators registering no progress, public confidence again collapsed and runs on the banks broke out everywhere, now affecting even the stronger institutions. Unwilling to act without President-elect Roosevelt's agreement to join him in affirming certain principles, including, in effect, maintaining the gold standard, Hoover did nothing when Roosevelt declined to limit his options after he would take office. As the presidential inauguration date approached, governor after governor declared bank holidays in their states. With the banks closed, commerce and industry began to grind to a halt. Roosevelt's swearing in would be in the midst of mounting fear and panic.

FDR's inaugural address was a masterpiece in the art of taking command. He promised to act swiftly and surely, assuring Americans, the great majority of whom were listening to him over the radio, that "the only thing we have to fear, is fear itself." Rescue and recovery proposals moved promptly from the White House to Capitol Hill, and, initially at least, Congress promptly enacted them. A measure of confidence returned to the nation as Roosevelt first boldly closed the banks while Congress enacted a reform measure, the Emergency Banking Act, and then reopened most of them, declaring them sound. In another early and extremely important move, Roosevelt took the country off the gold standard and shortly afterward endorsed the Thomas amendment, an addition that Congress was preparing for the new agricultural measure that would empower the president to inflate the currency. This raised expectations that prices of commodities would go up and initiated hopes for an economic upturn. Additional recovery measures followed through the spring months of 1933, the period of the "One Hundred Days," measures creating new governmental agencies intended to restore fair prices for farm goods (the Agricultural Adjustment

Administration), to provide flood control and cheap electricity for the people of the South (the Tennessee Valley Authority), to put young men to work at conservation projects (the Civilian Conservation Corps), and to restore and stabilize the industrial economy and pay better wages to workers (the National Recovery Administration).

The National Recovery Administration (NRA) became the centerpiece of this "First New Deal," as the recovery and reform program of 1933 became known. Roosevelt appointed to head it Hugh Johnson, a flamboyant and colorful personality who had helped fashion the draft during World War I and had learned much about American industry working during the 1920s for Bernard Baruch, a wealthy Wall Street speculator. Baruch had headed the War Industries Board, the agency that had controlled industry during World War I, and had served for many years as a major financial prop of the Democratic Party. The basic program of the NRA was simple. The government would allow business and industry to "stabilize" prices, that is, fix them, through "codes of fair competition." In return, workers would get higher wages and their right to organize and bargain collectively would be recognized. Believing the NRA program could boost the economy rapidly into a recovery pathway, Johnson barnstormed the country by airplane, a somewhat perilous undertaking in those days, persuading businessmen to complete their codes promptly or to sign the "blanket code" under which they promised to raise wages. The NRA adopted the "Blue Eagle" as the symbol of cooperation. Theoretically, businessmen who failed to abide by the NRA program would be shorn of the right to display the Blue Eagle and shamed by buyers and consumers into compliance. During the summer of 1933, the NRA program became a national preoccupation. Torchlight parades and other exhibitions of public support were organized in many cities, with hundreds of thousands of marching citizens participating.

Whether these innovations of the First New Deal initiated recovery or it came despite them is a question long debated and one a later chapter addresses. In any case, the economy did begin to rebound during the later months of 1933, although that year was on the whole the worst in the depression era in terms of unemployment and national output. The recovery continued at a rate that was impressive in percentage terms but all too slow in terms of reducing unemployment to tolerable levels. Unemployment in 1935 remained high, at 20 percent of the labor force, and gross national product (GNP) remained far below the 1929 level.

The slow pace of recovery, together with the restoration of hope for better times that Roosevelt and the New Deal had imparted, created conditions for the rapid rise of political and social unrest during 1934 and early 1935. The National Industrial Recovery Act had promised workers higher wages and, in the law's Section 7(a), protection of the right to form labor unions. Wages, however, rose little during 1933–1934, and the New Dealers did less to uphold collective bargaining. Strikes blossomed during 1934, as workers sought directly through their own efforts to gain the benefits Section 7(a) had promised. Hundreds of strikes erupted in a number of basic industries, making 1934 a banner year in American history for labor unrest.

Meanwhile, citizens throughout the nation, middle as well as working class, increasingly lent their attention to the messages of figures that Roosevelt and other established political leaders regarded as unprincipled and dangerous demagogues. The most impressive of these was Senator Huey Long, a spectacularly popular and ruthless Democrat whose political machine had dominated Louisiana politics for a decade. Long now was using his Senate seat to embarrass and humiliate Democratic congressional leaders and was reaching out to voters through nationwide radio broadcasts in which he advocated his "Share Our Wealth" program, a plan for a radical redistribution of income through confiscatory taxation of the wealthy. Two other such figures were capturing a national following also, Fr. Charles Coughlin of Royal Oak, Michigan, the "Radio Priest," who advocated nationalization of banks and other radical reforms, and Dr. Francis Townsend of California, whose theme was creation of generous old-age pensions, so generous in fact that adoption of Townsend's plan would have been ruinous to the economy. Equally troubling to Roosevelt and the political lieutenants he relied on, such as James Farley, his postmaster general and key distributor of political jobs and rewards to loyal followers, was the emergence of third-party movements. In Minnesota, for example, the relatively radical Farmer-Labor Party was gaining strength rapidly and threatening to undercut Roosevelt's popular following.

FDR AND THE SECOND NEW DEAL

Responding to this popular discontent, in 1935 Roosevelt and the Democratic Congress pushed through a new, more reformist, and even, in the eyes of many contemporaries, radical program. This "Second New Deal" in many respects parted with the recovery tactics of 1933. The two premier programs of the First New Deal, the NRA and the Agricultural Adjustment Administration (AAA), were based on the supposition that the market economy had failed and was incapable of restoring prosperity to industry and agriculture. They represented, to some extent, experiments with a form of economic planning, the notion that economic stability and prosperity could be achieved by regulating production. By 1935 the NRA had attracted much criticism, and the Supreme Court in any case early in 1935 declared it unconstitutional, making government-regulated planning for industry across the board appear a less viable option than previously. For this reason, but more importantly because of the pressures for new directions that were building up among the people, the emphasis of the Second New Deal would be different from its predecessor.

The planning approach of the First New Deal did not disappear after 1935. Various measures were enacted, or continued, after the fall of the NRA with the purpose of regulating output and prices in certain industries, including coal, oil, and trucking. The First New Deal policy of raising farm income by limiting the production of staple crops also continued, though the methods employed changed. The AAA during the First New Deal paid farmers for reducing acreage under cultivation, raising the necessary funds through a tax on food processors. A Supreme Court ruling in 1936 found the law unconstitutional, but Congress continued the policy of limiting agricultural production with the Soil Conservation and Domestic Allotment Act, under which the government paid farmers for reducing acreage devoted to soil-depleting crops. When this measure failed to limit production of cotton and other commodities to the extent desired, a new Agricultural Adjustment Act was enacted in 1938 which authorized the imposition of production quotas. The fundamental policy, of planning agricultural production to fit demand and thus raise farm prices, was thus consistently maintained. The Tennesse Valley Authority (TVA) also continued robustly throughout the 1930s to build dams, furnish cheap electricity, and coordinate resource use in the Tennessee River Valley, as it had been charged to do at its creation in 1933. Moreover, a substantial volume of energy went into activities that can be seen as economic planning, if the term is defined as government providing services and products that the private, market economy was perceived by the New Dealers as not able to provide. These activities ranged from building public housing to teaching Great Plains farmers to practice soil conservation.

The Second New Deal abandoned emphasis on regulation of industrial production and stressed instead direct improvement of the income and security of the unemployed, blue-collar workers, the aged, and the dependent. This new direction clearly was a response to the political turmoil of 1934 and early 1935, although in part it represented reforms that Roosevelt had probably intended to introduce, when political conditions were right, from the outset of his term.

The Second New Deal had work relief and support for labor unions as its centerpieces. The relief measure of the First New Deal, the Federal Emergency Relief Administration (FERA), had to a great extent simply continued the type of federal relief program started in 1932 while Hoover was still president, a program that provided federal money to allow the state relief agencies to provide a "dole" for the unemployed. The funds provided were more generous than before, but were still pitifully inadequate, though the relief payments they provided averted actual starvation for millions of unemployed workers. Roosevelt's "Minister of Relief," Harry Hopkins, had lobbied from the outset of Roosevelt's term for providing jobs at reasonable wages for the unemployed, arguing that the dole not only was inadequate for maintaining families but also robbed jobless workers of self-respect. When Congress in 1935 appropriated a large sum for relief, FDR created the Works Progress Administration (WPA) to provide the kind of program Hopkins advocated. By 1936 the WPA was directly employing nearly one million men and by the close of the 1930s nearly seven million of the unemployed would have held a job through it. Much of this was pick-and-shovel work, in some cases resulting in the construction of durable improvements, such as LaGuardia Airport in New York City, whereas in others it amounted to little more than "leaf-raking," as the WPA's numerous critics often insisted. But in Hopkins's vision, the national government would to the extent possible furnish employment appropriate to a worker's skills and training. This resulted in a remarkable efflorescence of WPA programs such as the Federal Theatre Project, which gave employment to actors and free performances to the people, and the Federal Arts Project, through which unemployed artists adorned public offices and other public structures with murals, paintings, and statuary, generally on American themes and subjects.

Several other highly significant measures defined the shape of the Second New Deal that emerged from Congress during the summer of 1935. The Wagner Act (the National Labor Relations Act) responded to the militancy that had taken hold among workers during the New Deal years. The measure created the National Labor Relations Board (NLRB) to protect the right of workers to bargain collectively, and it spurred an immense growth of labor unions, both the traditional craft unions of the American Federation of Labor and the new industrial unions in the steel and automobile industries of the Congress of Industrial Organizations (CIO). Another very important measure of the Second New Deal was the Social Security Act, which established a system of old-age pensions and unemployment insurance that endures to this day, and still another was the Public Utility Holding Company Act, which created the basis for a much more forceful federal regulation of the electric power industry.

By the fall of 1936, FDR could boast of an impressive degree of recovery and reform, and he was swept back into office by one of the widest margins in presidential electoral history. The election of 1936 was a key moment in

American political history for it created what became known as the "New Deal coalition," a rearrangement in which organized labor, minorities (especially blacks), and white southerners, in varying degrees of commitment, stood behind FDR and the Democratic Party in a supportive relationship that would endure for many years. In short, voters at the lower end of the economic scale, the blue-collar workers and the "ethnics," the predominantly Catholic and Jewish immigrants from southern and eastern Europe who had poured into America during the age of mass immigration in the thirty years before World War I, and their children, now aligned solidly behind the Democrats. The big industrial cities of the Northeast and Midwest, which had been Republican strongholds through the 1920s, now produced huge Democratic majorities. Social as well as economic considerations motivated these voters, for Roosevelt had extended political recognition and political appointments to Catholics and Jews at a rate vastly surpassing the Republican administrations of the preceding era. Together with the traditionally Democratic southern states, the industrial states of the North delivered a popular majority of over 60 percent to FDR in 1936 and reduced the Republicans in Congress to a small and seemingly powerless minority.

THE LAST PHASE OF THE NEW DEAL, 1937–1940

Despite his popularity, political turmoil marked Roosevelt's second term more than success in advancing a reform agenda. The New Deal was vulnerable to political attack because, above all, its economic success was limited. Though production of goods and services during 1936 and 1937 rose sufficiently to match the level of 1929, unemployment remained far too high, at about 15 percent of the work force. This high unemployment rate in the face of high output resulted from two factors, growth in the size of the labor force and technical improvements in some industries that reduced the demand for labor. Although most Americans felt gratitude for the return of a measured prosperity, all felt the pressure of the economy's relative stagnation. After a decade of travail, the economy still stumbled under a burden of excess labor. The huge number of unemployed workers depressed wages and retarded the renewal of the robust spending on consumption that was needed to initiate the rate of economic progress each decade that the nation had known previously for a hundred years and more.

Division within the Democratic Party also made Roosevelt vulnerable to attack. Many Democratic senators and congressmen deeply distrusted the direction the New Deal had taken in 1935. Largely from southern and western states, they feared the growing predominance of urban Democrats and the policies they advocated of weighting the New Deal toward benefits for industrial workers and the problems of the urban North.

Early in 1937, FDR, his political acumen perhaps dulled somewhat by the sheer size of his recent electoral victory, made two serious mistakes: One was political, the other economic. The first was his insistence that Democratic leaders in Congress introduce and pass a bill for changing the composition of the Supreme Court that its enemies soon would call the "court-packing plan." Dominated by conservative jurists, the Court had found several important New Deal measures unconstitutional, and Roosevelt, fearing the Wagner Act and other key measures might be rejected, now insisted on this measure that would in effect give him the power to appoint additional justices to the Court and thereby control it. Characterizing it as an attack on the separation of powers, opponents could trounce the court-packing plan as an assault on the Constitution itself and darkly hint of the danger of dictatorship it implied. The bill furnished an opportunity for conservative Democrats in Congress to oppose the president and form a coalition with Republicans. This "conservative coalition" in Congress defeated the court-packing plan and, worse for Roosevelt, continued to operate to some degree in opposing other measures he favored.

Roosevelt's second mistake of 1937 was to cut back on spending for work relief and other New Deal programs. FDR was in many ways a traditionalist and had never ceased to believe that deficit spending, government spending in excess of tax revenue, was bad policy. Substantial deficits had marked the previous years of the New Deal, but Roosevelt had justified these on the basis of the absolute need to provide relief. Now, prodded by Secretary of the Treasury Henry Morgenthau, his longtime friend and advisor, and a fiscal conservative, FDR decided recovery had progressed enough to warrant reducing the budget deficit. The ensuing cut in public spending probably helped initiate a sharp downturn. Late in 1937 the weak economy tumbled and the depression reappeared. The stock market again declined violently, and unemployment spiraled during 1938, rising to 19 percent of the work force for that year and threatening to reach the depths of 1932 and 1933. Recovery came in 1939 and 1940, thanks in part to a renewal of heavy spending on work relief. The revival of political opposition, however, as well as a shift in the nation's mood, meant that the period of dramatic introduction of new measures of reform and welfare had largely ended. The most important reform measure of this period was the Wage and Hour Law of 1938. It established a federal minimum wage and the forty-hour week, but FDR's supporters pushed it through Congress only after a long and bitter fight.

After a period of uncertainty, Roosevelt and his circle, spurred by Marriner Eccles, the head of the Federal Reserve Board and now an influential advisor, settled on deficit spending, together with a renewal of antitrust prosecutions, as the central policy of this phase of FDR's presidency. Sheer necessity justified renewal of heavy government outlays, but a new factor bolstered the case for deficit spending. The work of the British economist John Maynard Keynes, especially his *General Theory of Employment, Interest and Money,* published in 1936, by this time was exercising a strong influence over economic thought in America. Keynes's great contribution was to argue convincingly that, contrary to traditional economic theory, conditions could arise in which natural economic forces, such as the availability of cheap raw materials and labor, could for long periods fail to persuade businessmen to invest in new plants and equipment. Without large investment spending, only large increases in spending on consumption could raise national income and employment, and only government could provide for that increase in spending.

As a further step toward economic revival, the Justice Department's Antitrust Division, under the leadership of Thurman Arnold, a former Yale law professor, initiated dozens of prosecutions under the antitrust laws against business practices that tended to prevent competition from lowering prices. Arnold's aim was not "trust-busting" (the break-up of large, dominant corporations) but outlawing practices, formal or informal, which reduced competition within the consumer goods and construction industries, kept prices artificially high, and thus reduced consumption. These years, 1938–1940, are sometimes referred to as the Third New Deal.

A solid prosperity did not return until 1941, when governmental spending on defense mounted rapidly as the United States became the "arsenal for democracy" in a world at war. In Europe, World War II had broken out in September 1939 when Adolf Hitler attacked and subjugated Poland, and Great Britain and France declared war on Germany in response. France fell to German might in June 1940, leaving Great Britain fighting alone until Hitler made the monumental mistake of attacking Russia in May 1941, exposing Germany to a two-front war. Roosevelt felt, along with many others, that America could not stand by while Great Britain fell, and he knew that American relations with Japan might deteriorate to the point of war because of U.S. refusal to accept Japan's subjugation of China and its moves toward further imperial expansion in the Far East. Not until 1941, however, was resistance on the part of isolationists, those who strongly advocated noninvolvement in these conflicts, overcome and large-scale defense spending begun. By the close of that year, the depression had vanished, and the war years would witness soaring production, labor shortages, and rising prosperity.

Economic recovery during 1939–1941 and the return of full employment during World War II led Americans and their political leaders to move rapidly to the political center. Promptings toward further serious change in social or economic institutions or the pursuit of greater economic and social equality now had less appeal in public discourse. The great reforms of the New Deal, the taming of the stock market, the aid for farmers, the recognition of labor unions, the minimum wage and social security, were now part of the system and accepted by nearly everyone, but further interest in reform fell into abeyance. To maintain a progressively more animated consumerist economy was now the central mission of economic policy. This was the aim of the last phase of the New Deal, and its most important bequest to American life.

2

A Decade of Depression, 1929–1941: Theories of Cause and Cure

THE UNIQUE SEVERITY OF THE DEPRESSION

Why was there a Great Depression, and what should have been done to overcome it? To this day no one has formulated answers to these questions that command general consent. To its contemporaries, the Great Depression was a vast and menacing enigma, an unprecedented and inexplicable catastrophe. Economic depressions, periods of unemployment, falling prices, failing banks, and much increased human insecurity and misery were of course no strangers to American national life. They had on the contrary played an important role in shaping political and social life since the earliest days of the Republic and became all the more influential after the Civil War as the pace of industrialization quickened, and the number of wage workers dependent on large corporations for a livelihood rapidly expanded. Each of the decades of the late nineteenth century experienced an economic downturn, the depression of the 1890s being the most severe. Indeed, the Panic of 1893, as the 1890s depression was known, was so severe that it too, like the Great Depression, touched off major political changes and a period, the Progressive era, of fundamental change in the relationship between government and economic and social life.

The Great Depression differed from preceding depressions because it was deeper and longer and reached worldwide. Not only was the devastation wrought by the economic decline from 1929–1933 without precedent in American history, but the anemic quality of the recovery, which began late in 1933 and extended through much of 1937 was also without parallel.

The year-to-year growth of employment and industrial output was in itself quite impressive, averaging 10 percent, but the overall result proved disappointing. After four years of recovery, the output of goods and services finally regained its 1929 level, but the recovery of output failed to generate anything like full employment or general prosperity. In 1937, at the peak of the recovery, approximately 15 percent of the industrial work force still was unemployed. So large a mass of job seekers created downward pressures on the incomes of many who were employed. The incomes of a large proportion of American families—those whose breadwinners were among the unemployed, or had jobs offering only intermittent employment, or were still afflicted by depression-level pay rates—were very low. The recovery peaked and then reversed late in 1937 when a new stock market crash heralded a retreat. Unemployment again soared and production fell as the depression struck with renewed force. The recovery that followed in 1939 displayed considerable shallowness. Production recovered, but unemployment remained high. The economy began to show real strength only after the nation began seriously to prepare for war in 1941.

Many people escaped the direct hardships of the depression. One of the paradoxes of the 1930s is that life went on with little interruption for the well-to-do and for those lesser souls fortunate enough to have jobs that were relatively depression-proof. Workers with seniority; workers and managers in such industries as the retail food trade, which remained relatively stable in volume of business and employment throughout the depression years; or workers who benefited from the government's efforts after 1933 to boost wages in fact enjoyed a quality of life that actually was better than ever. The price of consumer goods remained low, and those households with relatively favorable incomes lived well. But people also lived uneasily, knowing how many others were in distress, and knowing that the paralysis of the economy might easily reach them as well. A great majority of Americans thus heard the ring of truth in President Franklin D. Roosevelt's famous evocation, in his second inaugural address in March 1937, that "one third of a nation [remained] ill-housed, ill-clad, ill-nourished." It seemed a true representation of reality to the millions who daily felt, or observed, the continuing misery of so many Americans.

EARLY THEORIES ABOUT THE DEPRESSION

Nothing in previous economic experience had challenged the explanatory ingenuity of economists, businessmen, and financial or political leaders, as did the Great Depression. Early explanations for the depression emphasized the 1929 Great Crash of the stock market in October 1929. To many commentators at that time, the Great Crash represented a judgment on what they now saw as the speculative excesses of the 1920s. Recent analyses are less severe. It appears that stock values, at least until the last stages of the rising market of the 1920s, were not excessively high in terms of prices relative to earnings, compared with those in later periods.

As the economy declined during 1930 and 1931, explanations that emphasized financial and trade dislocations were offered. In the wake of the market crash and downturn of 1929, the United States experienced a major fall-off in exports to European and other markets abroad that intensified during 1930 and 1931. Thus, many commentators focused on the dislocative effects of the burden of international debt payments among the major European countries and between them and the United States. This burden, it was argued, imposed intolerable strains on the international monetary system and impaired normal international trade after 1929, thus broadening and multiplying the impact of the economic downturn that inevitably followed the stock market crash of 1929.

The burden of paying international debts, together with the worldwide decline in trade, eventually made it impossible for the major European nations to maintain the gold standard, and this too, in the eyes of most conventional commentators in America, harmed international trade and further dampened business confidence. Most American financiers and businessmen regarded the gold standard as the essential condition for the flourishing international trade, which was thought to play a major part in maintaining the prosperity of the major economies. Under the gold standard, nations equate a unit of currency to a fixed amount of gold. Adherence to the gold standard had for a long time been regarded as both a moral and practical obligation by the world's major governments. This was because it was accepted that a system in which national currencies were redeemable in terms of a fixed amount of gold was the only way in which traders across national boundaries could be assured debt would be honored in money of predictable value. The gold standard was also valued by the middle and upper classes of Europe and America, because it assured protection against governmental manipulation of the value of money, especially against inflation. During World War I, the European governments had been forced to leave the gold standard and had returned to it only gradually during the 1920s. Containing inflation during the immediate postwar years had been a major problem both in America and Europe. In Germany inflation had soared to ruinous levels, disrupting the economy and wiping out the accumulated wealth of much of the middle and upper classes. The fear of inflation, induced or permitted by government, was thus the nightmare of the monied classes, even in the context of the depression. Conventional opinion in America emphasized the bedrock importance of maintaining the gold standard, even as Britain and the other major European economies abandoned it. Herbert Hoover echoed this opinion and, until the end of his presidency in March 1933, fought resolutely to maintain American adherence to it.

LATER THEORIES: UNDERCONSUMPTION AND OVERPRODUCTION

By 1931 and 1932, however, the depression had become so profound and so prolonged that previous explanations for its cause began to seem shallow and inadequate. Soon even more sophisticated and seemingly more fundamental explanations in public discourse found a ready reception. Two major theories emerged: It was "underconsumption" or "overproduction," or perhaps both, that accounted for the depth and tenacity of the depression. Franklin Roosevelt and the people he relied on for advice found these explanations appealing, as did many others who had a role in making policy during the 1930s. They exercised considerable influence as the New Dealers under Roosevelt sought to formulate and justify programs they hoped would restore prosperity.

Two amateur economists, William T. Foster and Waddill Catchings, originated and popularized the underconsumption theory in the 1920s. The theory taught that, contrary to mainstream economic theory, the American economy would become unable to generate sufficient "purchasing power" to buy the flood of goods it was creating. The reason for this, according to Foster and Catchings, was that too great a share of national income went to high-income receivers who saved a good deal of their money rather than spending it. The solution, they held, would be redistribution of income downward on the economic ladder.

After 1930, as conventional economic theory proved unequal to the task of diagnosing and prescribing for the worsening failure of the economy, the underconsumption theory gained a wide acceptance despite its unorthodoxy. The theory had another equally popular and influential version that identified dislocations in the structure of prices between sectors of the economy as the cause of underconsumption. This version emphasized the disparity, which had become excessive during the depression, between the high, stable prices maintained by manufacturing corporations and the deflated prices of farm goods and raw materials. The producers of foodstuffs and other primary products had gradually become impoverished and unable to buy the products of the industrial sector. As in the first version, the remedy was redistribution, but in this case accomplished mainly through raising the prices received by the deprived sector. Obviously underconsumptionist arguments served well the agendas of the politicians and interest group leaders who were clamoring for measures to boost farm prices and thus raise farm income, or who championed the cause of unemployment relief, or argued for governmental support for higher wages for industrial workers.

The underconsumption idea claimed to have found the cause of the depression in a glaring flaw in the very structure of the American capitalist economy. So, too, did the other unorthodox but greatly popular conception about the depression that had become very influential by the eve of the New Deal—namely, that the economy endemically produced more than could be consumed, that it inevitably ran to "overproduction." Widely embraced in business and financial circles, but also by many intellectuals who had lost faith in the self-regulating economy envisioned by orthodox economic theory, this "overproduction" viewpoint argued that runaway production in both agriculture and manufacturing had led to a crisis of profitability and thus to the depression. Overcapacity had fed competitive forces that depressed prices and wages. Those who held this or a similar point of view usually pointed to the need for some kind of planning by the members of industries acting collectively, whether by themselves or under governmental guidance, with the goal of achieving balance and stability.

The theories of "underconsumption" and "overproduction" were a major influence during the years from 1933 to 1937, when much of the New Deal legislation was enacted. If overproduction made it impossible for businessmen and farmers to earn a profit, then it was logical to conclude that it had caused the depression and that only limitation of production could restore prosperity. The impact of this conclusion is visible in much of the economic intervention undertaken by the Roosevelt administration. Its influence was especially profound during the First New Deal of 1933–1935. Indeed, its two most important programs, the NRA, for businessmen, and the AAA, for farmers, clearly were predicated substantially upon it.

The overproduction thesis led many observers, and in some moods FDR himself, to speculate that American economic growth had reached its limit, that the day of unfettered entrepreneurial capitalism had ended. Prosperity in the future would come through planning, or at least partial planning, of what and how much the economy should produce, a process in which government would be required to play a major role.

THE EMERGENCE OF KEYNESIANISM

The underconsumption and overproduction concepts both identified fundamental flaws in the very structure of the American economy as the cause of the depression, flaws that could be removed only through structural remedies such as planning. By the late 1930s, however, economic opinion was falling under the spell of a new theory whose proposed remedies might not require anything more profound than having the government spend a great deal of money in excess of tax revenues. The new thinking was inspired by John Maynard Keynes, the British economist whose importance in the history of economic thought most members of his profession would rate second only to that of Adam Smith. Keynes published his *General Theory of Employment, Interest and Money* in 1936, and it quickly attracted the attention and influenced the convictions of economists everywhere. Keynes took up the same issues that traditional economic thought appeared utterly unable to address and for which the underconsumption and overproduction theses had offered attractive but ultimately unsatisfactory solutions. They were unsatisfactory because on examination by professional economists they proved naïve. Keynes's answers were unconventional too, but they were as compelling as the others were unsophisticated. Keynes's analysis overturned the engrained conclusion of traditional economic theory that the competitive forces of the market economy would inevitably create sufficient demand to buy all that was produced and provide for full employment of resources. Keynes argued that the volume of investment in new plant and equipment was the key variable for maintaining full employment. Circumstances could arise, he held, in which savings would not be translated into investment over a long period and that the result could be a situation, like the depression, of protracted underemployment of resources. Keynes's analysis provided the theoretical underpinning for the policy that most conventional economic opinion had continued to reject, that the continued state of depression mandated heavy government spending through borrowing.

Some American Keynesians found in the new theory of the British economist reason to believe that American capitalism had become fundamentally flawed. Alvin Hansen, an American disciple of Keynes, was one of these. In 1938 he published "Economic Progress and Declining Population Growth" in the *American Economic Review*, a famous article that occasioned much debate. In it, he coined the phrase "secular stagnation" to delineate the state of the American economy. Hansen's application of Keynes to the American situation drew gloomy conclusions. America was in the grip of "secular stagnation" because investment had failed and could not recover. The volume of investment would never again be sufficient to create full employment because the major stimuli that had promoted investment historically—the need to develop the frontier and a booming birthrate—had now disappeared. The frontier had closed, and the birthrate was falling.

Large-scale government deficit spending could provide for employment, but economic controls to prevent interest groups from taking advantage of rising prosperity and causing inflation would be necessary. Deficit spending might cure unemployment, but the cost would be the abandonment of a considerable degree of the freewheeling entrepreneurial capitalism America had always known and relied on. As Hansen saw it, the day of bureaucratic control of the economy was dawning.

The next few years proved to most observers that Keynes was right. Defense spending grew rapidly during 1940 and 1941 but vaulted to previously unimaginable levels after the Japanese attack on Pearl Harbor on December 7, 1941, drew a united America into World War II. Federal spending on war production now soared. Unemployment vanished, and the standard of living rose, despite wartime scarcity of some consumer goods. By 1944 the total production of goods and services had nearly doubled relative to 1937.

The surging economy of the war years served to emphasize the tragic extent of the losses economic stagnation had inflicted on the nation during the Great Depression. To many observers, it demonstrated that America could have escaped those losses. Clearly it was massive government expenditures that brought the economy to life after 1939 and ended the years of economic doldrums. For those who had called for large increases in government borrowing and spending as the way out of depression, the economic expansion and prosperity of the war years was a vindication.

The economic revival, moreover, continued after World War II. After a brief postwar recession, the American economy set off on a long period of steady growth, which, with some lapses, as during the highly inflationary and intermittently depressed 1970s, has extended to the present day. High-volume governmental spending continued throughout this period. But most economists attribute postwar growth to a revived capitalism, the processes of economic innovation, and private investment in new industries and new products. American experience during and after World War II seemed to indicate that, first, deficit spending could effectively stimulate employment and, second, that American capitalism was still capable of steadily producing economic growth and a high level of employment of resources.

Why was the vigorously expansionist government spending policy adopted to win the war not applied much earlier to conquer the depression? Today economists and the informed public accept as axiomatic the Keynesian prescription for recovery from a downturn, partly because America's experience during World War II demonstrated its cogency, but partly because his pathbreaking analysis of how the economy worked was so persuasive. Many voices before Keynes's book had argued urgently for heavy and prolonged deficit spending, but none had offered arguments for it convincing enough to puncture the broad consensus among mainstream economists, businessmen, financiers, and political leaders, that is, that the national government could contribute to recovery best by maintaining a balanced budget.

WHY WAS THERE A FAILURE OF INVESTMENT?

If it is true, as Keynes held, that it was failure on the part of businessmen to invest in new plants and equipment that kept the economy mired in depression, it remains to explain why they would not invest. Investment means spending on housing and other construction and on new industrial plants and equipment. Such spending did indeed collapse during the downturn of 1929–1933 and recovered only weakly thereafter. In fact, this persistent failure of investment during the 1930s accounts for the weakness of the recovery. But the reason investment lagged so seriously remains a matter of dispute. Answers range from the classic belief among conservatives that New Deal reforms are to blame because they frightened businessmen so much that they kept their pocketbooks closed, to more recent speculations that the structure of American industry was at a particularly vulnerable juncture at the end of the 1920s when the depression began. This latter view stresses that the makeup of the industrial structure is in constant flux. Older, well-established industries reach a limit of expansion, and unless new industries with strong growth potential rise to provide opportunities for profitable investment and thus for industrial growth, investment lags and the economy slows or recedes. Many of the older industries that had matured during the 1920s, such as the primary metals, textile, lumber, and leather goods industries, showed little capacity to grow during the 1930s. A number of newer industries, or old industries with an array of new products, such as the chemicals, glass, petroleum and petroleum products, processed food, rubber, and plastics industries, displayed a surprising capacity during the 1930s to absorb investment capital and maintain a robust growth rate. But growth of sales and investment in these industries were not sufficient to compensate for the lagging investment in the major fields that largely lacked growth opportunities. New Deal policy may have been partly to blame because it tended to support and prop up some of these major but stagnant industries rather than focus on policies designed to promote innovation, technological change, and new enterprise. It probably erred, too, by attempting, in accordance with the underconsumption viewpoint, to drive wages up. Raising the cost of labor was not the best way to encourage employers to put the unemployed back to work.

In any case, government spending could have compensated for the failure of investment. But unfortunately both depression-era presidents, Hoover and Roosevelt, accepted the authority of the balanced budget dictate and tried to obey it. Hoover's fiscal policy was thus consistently restrained, except for 1931, when Congress enacted over the president's veto a bill providing for the immediate payment of part of the bonus veterans were scheduled to receive under earlier legislation, in 1945. Roosevelt also practiced a restrained fiscal policy, although he acquiesced in modest deficit spending during 1933–1936 to fund unemployment relief and other programs of recovery. The modest deficits of those years stemmed not from a deliberately expansionary fiscal policy but were incidental to the creation of programs intended to alleviate the depression's impact. The magnitude of this deficit spending was sufficient to exert some positive force on the economy but fell far short of sparking full recovery. By 1937–1938, however, when the recovery halted and reversed, Keynes's ideas had taken root and the spending policies of the late New Deal years were influenced by them.

THE MONETARY FACTOR

Although the failure of investment is a convincing explanation for why the economy performed so anemically once recovery began in 1933, much current economic thought stresses another factor entirely for the dramatic downturn of 1929–1933. No firm consensus exists generally among economists and economic historians even at this late date about the causes for the depression, but the work of the economist Peter Temin, probably the best known and most persistent student of the causation issue, is widely accepted. In his most recent work, Temin attributes the downturn of 1929, and the ensuing descent into the economic abyss, to bad governmental monetary policy. In 1928 and 1929, the Federal Reserve banks, concerned about the soaring stock market speculation, adopted interest rate policies that exerted deflationary pressures on the economy. America's banking authorities, in other words, set interest rates at a level that slowed the pace of healthy borrowing for business purposes and limited growth of the supply of money below the real needs of the economy. None of this deterred the stock market boom, which during the first half of 1929 became more dangerously speculative than before, but it did succeed in slowing down the economy. This in turn led, in October 1929, to the Great Crash. The downward trend of the economy, once set in motion, had a momentum of its own and was aggravated by a number of circumstances, such as those mentioned earlier in this narrative. Another fundamental factor was the development of the expectation among consumers and investors that the bad times would continue indefinitely, a self-fulfilling expectation that led to the withholding of spending on both consumption and investment in new business activities. But the central problem during the downturn was the continuation of a deflationary monetary policy, a policy that kept interest rates too high and the money supply too low.

The reasons why this policy held sway are complex. In part, high interest rates and general reluctance to lend was a result of the fearfulness of the banking community generally; in part it was the result of the policy of the Federal Reserve. A root cause, however, was the overriding determination in banking and government circles to maintain the gold standard at all costs. Low interest rates in the United States might have led to a drain of American gold abroad and to gold hoarding, and this, it was feared, could force the nation off the gold standard.

More flexible ideologically than Hoover, Roosevelt proved to be more open to unorthodox economic ideas and more willing to experiment with new policies. Respecting fiscal policy, Roosevelt remained, at least until the closing years of the 1930s, in principle as convinced as Hoover was that a balanced budget was the sound road to recovery. He was somewhat more willing to incur deficits than Hoover, but only because they were absolutely required to relieve the suffering of the unemployed. Even after the downturn of 1937–1938, Roosevelt remained cautious about deficit spending. But respecting monetary policy, he was, compared with Hoover, a radical. The wing of the Democratic Party made up of western and southern agrarians, upon which Roosevelt had relied to secure his party's nomination in 1932 and upon whose members of the House and Senate he relied, had, since the days of William Jennings Bryan, favored expansionist or downright inflationist monetary policies. Influenced by this tradition and also by the arguments of certain maverick economists, Roosevelt took the country off the gold standard in 1933, enabling him to experiment with policies intended to diminish the value of the dollar in terms of other nations' currencies and decrease its worth within America, as well. Terming it "reflation," FDR set out to bring about inflation of the price level, hoping especially to inflate the extremely depressed prices of agricultural commodities and other raw materials. Many commentators who held to traditional economic beliefs hotly opposed going off gold and reflation. They believed that these policies ran counter to reestablishing international trade and to the general revival of the capitalist world of the West, both of which they believed were preconditions for American recovery. Roosevelt's monetary policy was indeed intensely nationalistic and did part company with traditional wisdom, but it succeeded in initiating a rise in American prices. More importantly, the policy worked to reverse the expectation of further deflation that had taken such strong hold in business and financial circles. Roosevelt's departure from the gold standard and attempts to bring about inflation sent a strong signal to decision makers in the economy that the government was now pursuing expansionary rather than deflationary policies, and they began to react accordingly. Investment spending on new enterprises revived somewhat during 1933 and the following years, as did consumer spending. Some of this renewal is perhaps attributable to certain other steps the New Deal took, but much of it probably stemmed from this reversal of expectations held by businessmen and consumers.

3

America's Struggle Against the Depression, 1929–1940: From Hoover to Roosevelt and the New Deal

America's struggle against the Great Depression began with Herbert Hoover, on whose watch the depression began, but reached epic proportions under Franklin Roosevelt and his New Deal. These two men epitomized much of the best of the American political tradition, and both deeply and single-mindedly committed themselves to restoring prosperity and thereby saving the nation from the political extremes that massive unemployment might create.

HOOVER'S "NEW DAY"

Hoover's efforts failed, and he is to this day held up to contempt as one who could not escape the bounds of the past and offer the inspired, experimental leadership that Roosevelt is credited with giving. This contempt stems from the bitterness many depression-generation Americans felt toward one whose standing and accomplishments promised so much when the nation elected him by a landslide majority in 1928, but whose leadership during the massive economic downturn of 1929–1932 offered such paltry results.

In the decades following the depression, historians portrayed Hoover as a conservative in the tradition of the mainstream politicians who dominated the Republican Party, and national politics, during the 1920s. Hoover did rely, as the conservatives did, on the principles of low taxes, budget control, and minimal government regulation of business, but, unlike Warren Harding and Calvin Coolidge, the Republican presidents of the 1920s, whom he served as secretary of commerce, Hoover believed the national government should play a major and active role in enhancing the economic and social welfare of the people.

Hoover's vision of this role, however, was not that of the "progressives" found within both the Republican and Democratic Parties. These liberal critics of Republican policies challenged them as a do-nothingism that favored those who already possessed wealth and did little to help those who were struggling to achieve it. "Progressive" senators and congressmen represented mostly southern and western constituencies whose economies were still largely dependent on production of foodstuffs and raw materials. They had gained less from the industrially based prosperity of the 1920s than the manufacturing core of the nation, the heavily urbanized region stretching from the northeastern states out through the Midwest to Chicago, that was then the stronghold of Republicanism. Many political leaders from the less successful, agrarian regions, Democrats and Republicans alike, believed the national government should act to correct the imbalance.

Progressives could not, however, dismiss Hoover as credibly as they had Harding and Coolidge. In the first place, Hoover's feats of organization and management during World War I, when he served first as head of the Allied effort to save the starving people of Belgium, then as head of the wartime Food Administration in America, and finally as head of the American food relief effort in eastern Europe, after the war, had given him heroic status in the American imagination. In the second place, Hoover's career as secretary of commerce under Harding and Coolidge had situated him in American politics as a new kind of progressive. Though he often fought hard against the proposals that progressive congressmen put forward during the 1920s that involved direct governmental intervention to deal with farm income and other such problems, Hoover dissented profoundly from the view that the government should stand aside from the workings of the marketplace and have little or nothing to do with economic and social problems. Hoover's stance represented something rather new in American thinking about the intersection between government and the economy. The correct position, he thought, was between the two extremes of governmental minimalism and expansion of governmental regulation of the economy. Government's role, he believed, was to energize the people, through their social and economic organizations, and to provide the scientific and economic knowledge and the stimulus to help people to cooperate among themselves to solve the great problems of the day. The best known of Hoover's efforts to apply this ideology during the 1920s was his Commerce Department's promotion of trade associations. Hoover preached the gospel of associationism, arguing that through such practices as standardization of product sizes and quality, trade associations could promote industrial efficiency and productivity and a rising standard of living for all. Business cooperation through trade associations could, he insisted, even flatten out the business cycle. By providing accurate information on an industry's prices and market conditions, trade associations could persuade businessmen to avoid the overexpansion of production that typically occurred during periods of peak prosperity and, as Hoover and many of his contemporaries believed, led to an overheated economy that then crashed.

When he ran for president in 1928, the electorate regarded him as the nation's "Great Engineer" and leading problem-solver. Hoover's campaign theme in 1928 was the "New Day," a vision of a new American era in which the problems of cyclical depression, poverty, and social distress would be solved through a cooperative partnership between government, science, and private sector groups. The depression crushed this vision and dethroned Hoover as an American hero. He left the presidency in 1933 discredited and reviled, remembered not for his efforts to fight the depression but for his failure to reverse it.

HOOVER VERSUS THE DEPRESSION

When the stock market collapsed in October 1929, Hoover attempted to prevent the crash from dampening business activity, wages, and spending. He adopted two strategies. Relying on his familiar belief in the power of business-government cooperation, he called business leaders from the major industries to Washington and exhorted them to continue with planned industrial spending and to maintain wage rates and the volume of employment. In a second maneuver designed to maintain overall national spending, Hoover persuaded Congress and many state governments to increase expenditures. Thanks to this prompting, federal and state government spending during 1930 substantially increased. The effect was positive but fell far short of reversing the downward swing of the economy.

Hoover's attempt to ward off a depression rather than simply waiting for the economy to readjust represented a major new departure in American public policy. His tactics, however, proved insufficient, and the depression gradually worsened during 1930. Hoover's standing with the electorate began to crumble, partly for this reason, partly because of political and personal factors. Hoover failed to give the Republicans, who held a majority in both houses of Congress, effective leadership during 1930, resulting in a protracted struggle over tariff revision that made them highly vulnerable to

Democratic attacks. Unfortunately for Hoover, this happened at just the moment when the national machinery of the Democratic Party had fallen under the control of an effective organizer, the new chairman of the party's National Committee, John Jacob Raskob. Using his own wealth, Raskob created an efficient Democratic propaganda bureau in Washington that mercilessly attacked the Republican Congress and Hoover. Stung by criticism and loss of public approval, Hoover proved remarkably inept in dealing with the Washington press corps. The result was an upset in the 1930 congressional elections that gave the Democrats control of the House for the first time since the elections of 1918.

The economic statistics early in 1931 gave Hoover some grounds for hoping his recovery tactics finally were working, but these hopes soon evaporated. The depression had afflicted the European countries too. In the late spring of 1931, a crisis threatened to destroy the major banks and the monetary systems of several of them and bring down American banks with them. In June, Hoover intervened with a proposal, thought daring at the time, for a year-long moratorium on all intergovernmental debt payments. Though accepted by the major governments after some delay, the moratorium failed to stem the European financial crisis that now spread to America. Faced in the last months of 1931 with rapidly rising unemployment and a banking system on the brink of collapse, Hoover embarked on a new strategy. When Congress convened in December, he demanded prompt enactment of a far-reaching recovery program intended principally to save the American banking and financial system from total collapse. His program's central feature was the Reconstruction Finance Corporation (RFC), a new federal agency authorized to lend on a large scale to banks and other financial institutions. The measure represented a striking new development in the government's role. Never before, except in wartime, had the federal government intervened so directly and extensively into the economy as Hoover now proposed it should do.

With the presidential election looming in November, many Democrats, who previously had cooperated with Hoover, grew restive. They regarded Hoover as the representative of eastern big business and finance and began to assert the progressive and populistic themes that had characterized the southern and western wings of the party since the turn of the century. In March 1932, a political battle erupted between the president and the Congress, first over the plan, tentatively agreed on by Hoover and the Democratic Speaker of the House, John Nance Garner of Texas ("Cactus Jack," as he was known), to balance the budget through a national sales tax. The Democrats demanded steeper income tax rates on the higher income brackets instead. Soon the battle was joined also over the Veterans Bonus Bill, a measure providing for payment of the remainder of a bonus granted veterans by Congress in 1931. Above all, the Democrats demanded spending for relief of the unemployed. Hoover had strongly opposed federal relief spending as pressure for it had mounted during 1931 and 1932. Now critics bitterly assailed him for being willing to lend hundreds of millions of dollars to banks, through the RFC, but to provide nothing to relieve the suffering of the unemployed and their families. This was a weighty charge. It permanently damaged Hoover's reputation. To him, the argument against federal relief spending was sound. His aim was economic recovery. This, he thought, depended on the restoration of business confidence because, he believed, borrowing and spending by businessmen was the only way to achieve recovery. Opening the door to federal spending on relief would signal to businessmen the onset of heavy government borrowing and heavy taxation, the very signals that would further erode business confidence. The logic, to Hoover, was inescapable; to his critics, it was cruel and misguided.

After weeks of bitter maneuvering, Hoover and the Democrats agreed on a relief measure providing federal loans, totaling $300 million, to the states, together with a measure providing for large-scale spending on public works. Meanwhile a situation was developing in Washington whose outcome gave the final blow to Hoover's reputation as a humanitarian. Through the spring and summer, tens of thousands of unemployed veterans flocked to Washington to lobby for the Bonus Bill and camped there as the Bonus Expeditionary Force (BEF). Hoover had tolerated this and even allowed local authorities to issue army supplies for their encampment. Many BEFers, however, remained in Washington after the defeat of the Bonus Bill, some of them living in buildings on Pennsylvania Avenue near the Capitol that were slated for demolition to make way for a large-scale federal construction project. Tension mounted, and fighting between the police and some of the veterans broke out. Hoover ordered General Douglas MacArthur, the army's chief of staff, to use troops to force those occupying the buildings back to the main BEF camp in Anacostia Flats, near the Potomac. MacArthur exceeded his orders and drove the veterans out of Washington altogether, burning their encampment to the ground. Even though MacArthur had disobeyed his orders, Hoover acquiesced in what the general had done and let the responsibility fall to himself. The nation's press, and the greater part of public opinion, soon came to see the rout of the BEF as unnecessary, heartless, and even brutal, and Hoover's reputation never recovered.

FDR AND THE COMING OF THE NEW DEAL

National leadership now passed to Franklin Delano Roosevelt. Born to privilege, the son of a wealthy Hudson River landowner, Roosevelt was educated at Groton and Harvard and rapidly attained high visibility in Democratic politics, partly because of the illustrious name that connected him to his popular (though Republican) relative, Theodore Roosevelt. Named assistant secretary of the Navy after Woodrow Wilson's upset victory in the presidential election of 1912, Roosevelt gained enough public exposure during World War I to be named his party's vice-presidential candidate in 1920. Stricken by polio in 1921, Roosevelt spent much of the 1920s in a futile attempt to regain use of his legs, but he still maintained a substantial presence in Democratic national affairs and laid plans for an eventual run for the presidency. Running for governor of New York in 1928, Roosevelt was elected in a year that witnessed the trouncing of the Democratic presidential candidate, fellow New Yorker Al Smith.

Now well positioned to bid for the presidential nomination, Roosevelt enjoyed widespread support from Democrats in the southern and western states but faced strong and well-organized conservative opposition from the leading figures and political bosses of most of the eastern and midwestern states. In fact he only narrowly avoided defeat at the Democratic convention in Chicago. Once nominated, however, Roosevelt immediately demonstrated the selfconfidence, assurance, and capacity for innovation that would typify his presidential persona. He flew to Chicago from New York, in itself a daring undertaking in those early days of aviation, in order to break a long-standing tradition of nominees waiting on the party to bring the nomination to them, and read his acceptance speech before the convention before it dissolved. Unable to repudiate him without repudiating themselves, Republicans nominated the unpopular Hoover. Roosevelt defeated him by a substantial margin in the 1932 election.

As the March 1933 transition of presidential power approached, the economy fell into a state of utter disaster. The rate of bank failures surged during February, and in the last days of Hoover's presidency, one state governor after the other declared bank holidays. Meanwhile farmers desperate to force up prices declared "farm holidays," destroying crops and produce to keep them from the market, and an assassin tried to kill the president-elect in Miami. An ugly mood of despair hung over the nation, even as the promise of a new administration dawned. The day Roosevelt was sworn in (March 4, 1933), the banking system was at a standstill, and the economy was grinding toward a complete halt.

In his inaugural address, FDR radiated self-assurance and confidence in his ability to deal with the crisis, a sharp contrast with what had become Hoover's haggard and defeated mien. The temper of the people demanded, he declared in his masterful inaugural address, bold innovation. He promised strong leadership to find the way out of the economic morass that had engulfed the country and challenged the American people to realize that "the only thing we have to fear is fear itself."

THE FIRST NEW DEAL, 1933–1935

Roosevelt's dramatic performance in the three months following his inauguration on March 4, 1933, is unrivaled in the history of the presidency. Taking advantage of an arcane provision in a law dating from World War I, FDR immediately declared a national bank holiday and within days rushed legislation, the Emergency Banking Act, through a willing Congress, now controlled by large Democratic majorities. The measure enabled the government swiftly to close banks endangered by failure and to reopen those deemed stable. Their fears allayed, depositors regained confidence in the banking system. The tendency to hoard cash diminished rapidly, panicky withdrawals ended, money returned to checking and savings accounts, and the banking system stabilized. Within weeks, further measures to strengthen the banks, among them the creation of the Federal Deposit Insurance Corporation (FDIC), emerged from Congress at Roosevelt's behest.

Many measures aimed at recovery and reform soon appeared on the congressional agenda, most of them at Roosevelt's urging, and quickly were enacted. Spurred on by a Washington press corps that reveled in excited reporting about the lively pace of change that had overtaken the capital, the people took heart. The president radiated confidence and communicated it to the people by explaining his actions in frequent, chatty, radio talks (the "fireside chats") and through twice weekly press conferences in which his friendly and bantering style charmed reporters. Hope, for the time being at least, replaced despair, critics fell silent, and Americans of all classes and condition, from business moguls to dirt farmers, rallied around what the newspaperpeople, and soon everyone, called "the New Deal." In a word play that compared Roosevelt's first three months with Napoleon's mobilization of the French nation in 1814, reporters dubbed this period the "One Hundred Days."

Thanks again to the newspapers, which naturally endowed the political scene with as much drama as they could muster, contemporaries, tended to see FDR and his circle of close advisors as the center from which everything emanated. The most visible and important of these advisors were three Columbia University professors Roosevelt had recruited a year before as idea men and speechwriters. The so-called "Brain Trust" of three professors—Raymond Moley, Rexford G. Tugwell, and Adolf A. Berle—contributed substantially to the shaping of the program that emerged during the One Hundred Days and would become known as the First New Deal. The First New Deal, however, was far from being a unified program, a blueprint for recovery and reform drawn up by university intellectuals. Nor was it the product of a consensus among Roosevelt's other major set of advisors, the departmental secretaries who composed the Cabinet. They were a mixed group: some chosen simply to reward or placate the older generation of Democrats; some, principally Harold Ickes, in an effort to reach out to progressive Republicans; and some, like Frances Perkins, the secretary of labor, and the first woman to serve in the Cabinet, and Henry A. Wallace, the secretary of agriculture, because FDR thought they would be useful in helping him devise the means to carry out important policies he wanted to pursue.

All the numerous new agencies and programs of the One Hundred Days were justified by the New Dealers in terms of economic recovery and reform, but it is difficult to discern any coherent economic theory behind them. In retrospect, in fact, in terms of their actual effects, they often appear in some respects economically contradictory, although Roosevelt and his supporters would have vehemently claimed otherwise. Political necessity rather than economic theory provided much of the impetus for the key measures of the One Hundred Days as the president had little choice, if he wished to provide the public with bold innovation, than to cooperate with the agendas of the major interest groups and their political representatives.

Political necessity, obedience to the will of the strongest political forces, the best-organized and most influential interest groups, though a powerful force, was not the sole influence on Roosevelt in shaping the First New Deal. Although closely attuned to the getting and keeping of political power, FDR did have deeply held convictions and dispositions about the depression, the economy, and reform. One guiding conviction FDR held that influenced much of the First New Deal was the importance of "reflating" the economy. He believed prices, especially agricultural and raw materials prices, but all seriously depressed prices, had to rise. This was a common conviction among Democrats, especially the western and southern Democrats on whom Roosevelt had depended for his nomination and with whom he had forged ties through the previous ten years.

Almost immediately after taking office, Roosevelt, again invoking the wartime Trading with the Enemy Act, as he had in closing the banks, prohibited export of gold from the United States, in effect taking the country off the gold standard. A few weeks later, the president agreed to accept the Thomas Amendment to the Farm Relief Bill. This measure, which he used cautiously during succeeding years, empowered him to inflate the dollar through any of six methods. Reflation also served as an important, if unspoken, motive for many other measures, including the two premier initiatives of the First New Deal, the creation of the Agricultural Adjustment Administration (AAA) and the National Recovery Administration (NRA).

A second major conceptual influence was Roosevelt's conviction that "overproduction"—the tendency of what he regarded as an overly competitive, market-driven economy to run to excessive production and to radical imbalances among the economic sectors—was a fundamental cause of the depression. It was a conviction held by his key Brain Trust advisors, all of whom thought that only national economic planning, in some form and to some degree, could create lasting economic stability. Roosevelt discussed these ideas repeatedly with the Brain Trusters during the precampaign months and even devoted a key campaign speech (the Commonwealth Club address in September 1932) to speculate whether the closing of the frontier meant that striving for boundless economic growth should give way to a search for economic balance and stability.

Still another conceptual influence on FDR was the memory, held by everyone of his generation, of how the nation had handled its last great emergency, in 1917–1918, when America joined the Allies in war against Germany. The economic problem then was rapid economic mobilization to provide the materials of war. It had been successfully accomplished through a degree of governmental regulation never undertaken before in America. During World War I, the economic problem had been management of an overheated economy, not revival of one mired in depression. The memory of large-scale governmental regulation of industry and agriculture during one crisis, however, lent credibility to proposals for similar efforts during the new crisis of depression.

Less readily defined ideas and motivations in Roosevelt's makeup also help to explain his actions. By temperament, he simply was more given to an experimental mode than most political leaders of his generation, more willing to try policies and measures that conventional economic beliefs condemned as unsound. He was, moreover, inclined toward social reform, to continuing the movement toward improving the conditions under which the marginal participants in American capitalism lived and labored that many states had begun under progressive governors before World War I and in a few cases, notably in New York under Al Smith, continued during the 1920s.

Finally, there were visionary elements in Roosevelt's personality that sometimes led him to endorse and support measures that even his most loyal and more liberal advisors thought were impractical. A good example was the Civilian Conservation Corps (CCC), a program concocted largely by Roosevelt himself during the 1932 campaign, for putting large numbers of young men to work in the national forests. Ridiculed by the Republicans and frowned on by his own advisors, even Rexford Tugwell, the most left-leaning of the Brain Trusters, the CCC, set up during the One Hundred Days, continued through the entire New Deal era with ever-growing popularity and impact.

The AAA, created in May 1933, is the most evident example of how political necessity and the wish to raise prices, especially of commodities, influenced the president's proposals. The measure stemmed from the campaign that farm organizations and farm state congressmen had waged since the early 1920s to create a federal mechanism to raise the prices of farm commodities. Hoover had conceded substantially to this movement by asking Congress, in 1929, to create the Federal Farm Board, an agency endowed with considerable capital and power to fund farm cooperative selling agencies and, in emergencies, to buy and temporarily withhold farm products from the market as a means of preventing the decline of commodity prices. This agency expended large sums after the depression began in an effort to stabilize prices but failed to achieve stabilization. Most farm leaders viewed Hoover's program as a pale substitute for the program for whose enactment they had lobbied for years, the plan embodied in the McNary-Haugen Bill. This proposal provided for direct federal manipulation of farm prices through the purchase of commodities to an extent sufficient to drive up their prices, this "surplus" to be disposed of by dumping it on overseas markets.

Under FDR, the long campaign by farm representatives to obtain higher farm prices through federal regulation of the market was successfully concluded. The New Deal's AAA, however, provided for an alternative mode of enhancing farm income—namely, subsidies to farmers in return for their limiting acreage under cultivation—and this mode of operation, the so-called domestic allotment, was used with the goal of raising farm prices to a supposedly fair or "parity" level, putting them higher relative to the prices of manufactured goods. Indeed the New Deal was so anxious to put the plan into operation that it began domestic allotment payments to farmers as quickly as possible, in the fall of 1933. This meant that in the summer farmers, to qualify for payments, had to plough under a large share of crops planted in the spring and now nearing harvest and to slaughter large numbers of that year's newly birthed livestock. Some 10 million acres of cotton were ploughed under and approximately 5 million pigs slaughtered and disposed of. By destroying food and fiber crops in the midst of so many millions of people short of food and clothing, the New Dealers risked and received a good deal of ironic comment from those who could not appreciate the farm program's stated goal of establishing the kind of a balance between production and consumption of farm products that would provide better prices and an appropriate standard of living for the nation's farmers. In this instance, the needs of one powerful interest group, farmers, overruled the interests of other groups.

The political need to meet the demands of powerful interest groups also accounts for the other two most memorable innovations of the First New Deal, the Tennessee Valley Authority (TVA) and the National Recovery Administration (NRA). The creation of the TVA acknowledged the newly powerful position in Congress of the southern and western Democrats whose demands for federal construction and operation of a vast hydroelectric project in the valley of the Tennessee River the Republican-dominated presidency and Congress had rejected for over a decade. The NRA, enacted in May 1933, conceded to demands that many sectors of the business community had been making for many years, and with increasing vehemence during the depression, to relax the federal antitrust laws. The NRA permitted the members of a broad array of industries to draft industrywide codes regulating, and oftentimes seriously limiting, competition among them. Once such codes were accepted by the president, they would have the force of law. As a concession to workers, the law creating the NRA, the National Industrial Recovery Act (N.I.R.A.), mandated that the codes establish standards for minimum wages and maximum work hours within an industry and guaranteed, in Section 7(a), the right of workers to organize and bargain collectively, that is, to form unions. Believing that allowing businessmen to stabilize or increase prices would promote recovery, and hoping they could be persuaded to raise wages, another step toward increasing purchasing power and promoting recovery, Roosevelt invested much promise in the NRA. To run the program, which FDR hoped would swiftly codify American business and thus initiate a rapid move toward prosperity, the president appointed Hugh Johnson, an associate of wealthy Wall Street speculator Bernard Baruch, who had bankrolled the Democratic Party for many years. Johnson seemed a dramatic and energetic administrator. He adopted as an emblem a design known as the Blue Eagle and, threatening to withhold the right to display it from those who did not cooperate, and so subject them to public boycotts for their un-American behavior, managed to codify nearly all of American business within a few months. He proved unreliable and inconsistent, however, once this phase was over. He was unable to deal with the accusations consumer representatives and progressive congressmen soon made that the NRA system was, by stifling competition, raising prices but having little positive effect on recovery, and had to be removed.

Despite the swift, varied, and very substantial expansion of governmental regulation and guidance of economic affairs during 1933 and 1934, much of the First New Deal adds up to what was a profoundly conservative program. Though the New Dealers argued that the premier measures, the AAA and the NRA, would increase purchasing power, raise prices, and break the downward spiral of the depression, their first and direct impact was simply to improve the income and profits of property-owning farmers, businessmen, and industrialists at the expense of unorganized workers and consumers. Tenant and sharecropping farmers suffered under the AAA because property-owning farmers, needing to cut down acreage under cultivation, turned them out. Workers gained some but little immediate advantage from the wage provisions of the NRA codes and were disappointed by the agency's failure to enforce Section 7(a)'s pledge to protect the right to form unions. Nor, though they did foster economic recovery and stability, could one find much of social reform in such measures as the Federal Deposit Insurance Corporation (FDIC), or the Securities and Exchange Commission (SEC), designed to oversee and prevent future debacles of the stock market, or the Home Owners Loan Corporation (HOLC), intended to promote the ability and disposition of banks to refinance the mortgages of borrowers threatened with foreclosure on their homes and to extend mortgage loans to prospective home buyers. Though they proved effective and in many cases have endured to the present day, such measures were intended to, and did, prop up and maintain the existing economic and social structure and did not introduce alterations in the relationships between the social groups who possessed more, and less, of income, security, and status. A conservative bent governed the relief measures of the First New Deal as well. Federal relief under FDR's Federal Emergency Relief Administration (FERA) continued to be essentially a dole and was still distributed through state agencies, as it had been under Hoover, though it is true that the New Dealers expended appropriated funds at a much faster clip than had the previous administration. Spending on public works through the Public Works Administration (PWA) headed by the secretary of the interior, the vinegary Harold Ickes, also proceeded in the early years of the New Deal at a slow and careful pace. It was true, though, that for a few months during the harsh winter of 1933–1934 the Roosevelt administration did create a very large and costly federal work relief agency, the Civil Works Administration (CWA), through which the federal government directly provided jobs to hundreds of thousands of the unemployed. The CWA was a harbinger of the more aggressive relief policy that came later in the New Deal, but in 1933–1934 it was an anomaly.

THE COMING OF THE SECOND NEW DEAL

In 1935 a fresh spate of New Deal legislation was rushed through Congress when it became evident that the policies and programs of the First New Deal were inadequate to the task of regaining prosperity and meeting the demands of the people. This Second New Deal, produced by Congress within the space of a Second Hundred Days, as the reporters of the day named it, moved the reform and recovery effort in new directions and in certain respects introduced changes more profound than the earlier outburst of reform in 1933. Yet, in terms of fundamental purposes and intentions, there was substantial continuity between the First and Second New Deals.

Political necessity in large part drove FDR and other Democratic leaders toward another engagement with reform. Recovery from the depression did begin late in 1933. Americans gave the First New Deal credit for the upswing, but, though the rate of recovery was in fact relatively impressive, the economy had fallen so low that the impact on job growth was initially scarcely discernible, especially to the millions who remained unemployed. Disappointed at what seemed the slowness of recovery and yet perhaps emboldened by the very fact that the government's activism seemed to be yielding results, the temper of many of those still afflicted by privation and insecurity became more restive and assertive. For the most part, Americans had remained patient, almost passive, during the depression, waiting for the established political and business leaders to find its remedy. The tradition of self-reliance was deeply engrained, and many of the unemployed were more ashamed than angry, convinced that somehow they, not the system, had failed. The rank and file of the American people were little disposed toward radical departures from the economic and political system they felt had served them well historically. Many intellectuals by this point had turned leftward, becoming members of the Communist Party of America or at least adopting much of its radical critique of American capitalism and American government, but most of the people continued to eye this kind of radicalism suspiciously. In 1934 and 1935, however, a more assertive attitude overtook hopelessness. The dispossessed, and the millions more who feared joining them, began to demonstrate a disposition to follow new and unorthodox ideas and leaders and a new willingness to act to save themselves.

This new assertiveness showed itself above all in the wave of strikes that swept over American industry during 1934 and 1935. After rapid expansion under governmental protection during World War I, labor unions had suffered decline during the 1920s and early depression years. Unions with any real influence existed only within the ranks of the skilled trades, the traditional province of the American Federation of Labor. Emboldened perhaps by the promise of Section 7(a) of the N.I.R.A., which guaranteed the right of workers to organize, but which the Roosevelt administration did little to enforce, workers all over America participated in an immense wave of strikes during 1934 and 1935 whose goal was recognition of the right to organize and bargain, as much as it was immediate wage gains. To a major extent, the strikes involved unskilled workers, largely unorganized, in the mass production industries and signaled a new labor militancy in the industrial sectors where the managerial class had assumed almost complete control over the shop floor.

A newly assertive mood was also evident in the large, and growing, following of three popular figures who offered direct and immediate remedies and novel promises of economic salvation. The Catholic priest, Fr. Charles E. Coughlin of Royal Oak, Michigan, used his radio programs, broadcast from the Church of the Little Flower, to skewer FDR as a stooge of the bankers and to call for a radical reform agenda that ranged from nationalization of the banks to a guaranteed annual wage for workers. Coughlin later in the decade veered into anti-Semitism and flirted with fascism in his ideas, leading to his final silencing by church authorities, but he enjoyed a huge audience in the mid-1930s, especially among listeners of Irish descent. Francis E. Townsend of California had been moved by the plight of the impoverished elderly and proposed a federally funded program of very generous old-age pensions that recipients would have to spend monthly, thereby stimulating the economy. Townsend clubs sprouted across the country as older Americans and their families rallied to this appealing but extremely expensive panacea. The most important and politically dangerous critic of the New Deal was Huey P. Long, former governor of and now U.S. senator from Louisiana. As a very popular governor, Long, the "Louisiana Kingfish," had showed his capacity for using ruthless methods to maintain political control of his state, while bringing a truly populist agenda of education, roads, and other benefits to poor people. Like Fr. Coughlin, Long made skillful use of national and regional radio hookups, preaching the gospel of "Share Our Wealth," by which the government would redistribute wealth by taxing the rich at very high rates to underwrite an annual income and other benefits for all. Every man would be a king. Very popular and influential in the states of the lower Mississippi Valley, Long posed a genuine threat to FDR's reelection if, as it appeared he planned to do, he ran as a third-party candidate for president in 1936. In that event, many Democratic voters might well turn to Long, throwing the race to the Republicans.

By the spring of 1935, FDR realized that the mood of the electorate, and of many of his Democratic supporters in Congress, required a fresh effort at reform and recovery. Inaction meant he risked losing control of the popular will and leaving the political initiative to men such as Long, men whom he considered to be dangerous demagogues. But what should the agenda be? The First New Deal had pinned much of its hopes for recovery on the NRA, which Roosevelt had portrayed as a "partnership" between government and business to improve wages and stabilize prices and thus reverse the downward spiral of the depression. But by the end of 1933, critics asserted that business was in fact using the NRA codes to stifle competition and raise prices while doing little to improve wages. As criticism mounted, FDR eased Johnson out and created a committee to run the NRA and reform the codes, but little was accomplished. But what alternatives were there to the policy of cooperation with business, a policy several of Roosevelt's most trusted advisors had urged on him in 1933 and which it was his own inclination to follow? The people themselves—workers by demanding the right to unionize, others by giving so much heed to the extremist proposals for redistribution of wealth trumpeted by such irresponsible leaders as Huey Long—had supplied answers. Arguments for taking a new direction had come also from other voices on whom Roosevelt relied heavily for advice, such as Felix Frankfurter, the extraordinarily influential and highly respected Harvard law professor who had supplied Roosevelt with many of the lawyers, known as the "happy hotdogs" for their enthusiasm, who staffed the New Deal agencies. Two of these, Benjamin Cohen and Thomas Corcoran, who acted as speech writers and legislative drafters for FDR, had become especially influential with him and were among those urging that the New Deal lessen its dependence on cooperation with business and try a different tack toward reforming and revising the economic system.

THE SECOND NEW DEAL

In May 1935, the Supreme Court handed down a decision in a case involving the NRA codes, *Schechter v. United States* (known as the "sick chicken" case because it involved a poultry wholesaler), that found the N.I.R.A. unconstitutional. The Court held that Congress had improperly delegated legislative power to the executive branch by giving it authority to approve codes that had the force of law. Although ways possibly existed to rewrite the law and continue the NRA's policies, the decision appears to have helped turn Roosevelt decisively in a new direction. By the end of the summer, a series of measures had become law, some at FDR's prompting, some merely with his consent and little more, which represented a Second New Deal. To some extent, the measures added up to a shift in ideology, a change in fundamental ideas about how to reform and promote the American economic and social system, but it would be mistaken to emphasize this point too much. Although this Second New Deal dropped cooperation with business as a central theme and instead adopted what most businessmen regarded as a prolabor and antibusiness bias and endorsed far more aggressive relief and welfare policies than the First New Deal, FDR's goal still was to revive and promote American capitalism, not to undermine it and replace it with a state-directed economy.

The premier reform of the Second New Deal was the National Labor Relations Act, or Wagner Act, which established the National Labor Relations Board (NLRB), an agency endowed with ample authority to enforce the right of workers to form unions of their own choosing. Its author, Senator Robert Wagner of New York, was representative of the new influence and power of Democratic congressmen from the urban-industrial states, whose number had greatly increased through the elections of 1932 and 1934. The Wagner Act played an important role in what became during the next several years a veritable revolution in the relative power of labor unions and the corporations. The conservative and tradition-bound leaders of the American Federation of Labor (AFL), long the dominant labor organization in America and composed of skilled workers in craft unions, had failed thus far to channel the worker militancy of 1934 into the formation of new unions. They feared that a rapid organizing of the workers in the great mass production industries such as steel, automobiles, and clothing would result in the rise of industrial unions which enlisted all workers in a particular industry, skilled and unskilled, and lead to the decline of craft unionism. In 1935 a new labor organization appeared, the Committee for Industrial Organization (later the Congress of Industrial Organizations). The CIO was led by John L. Lewis of the United Mine Workers, the one major industrial union in America. Lewis, one of the most skilled and formidable leaders in the history of American unionism, made the CIO into a major force in the American economy and political arena. With the backing of the NLRB during the New Deal era, the CIO created unions with a membership totaling nearly 4 million workers in the mass production industries. It also introduced militant tactics, as in the great "sit-down" strike against General Motors in 1937, in which workers stayed in the factories and threatened to destroy the machinery unless management met their demands for recognition and collective bargaining.

Equally dramatic was the new relief policy, the Works Progress Administration (WPA). The WPA represented a fundamental policy shift regarding relief in that the agency would offer work rather than a handout to the unemployed. The brainchild of Harry Hopkins, FDR's relief administrator throughout the decade, by 1936 the WPA was giving work to over one million unemployed Americans. Though the work done by WPA workers was often derided by critics as "leaf-raking," a good deal of it led to durable results, such as LaGuardia airport in New York City. The WPA provided more than pick-and-shovel jobs, as Hopkins also strove to help unemployed artists, writers, and actors. Through the Federal Arts, the Federal Writers, and the Federal Theatre Projects, a multitude of murals appeared in public buildings and free dramas played in the parks and streets of America, as well as theaters, throughout America. Through the WPA the New Deal made perhaps its most direct and appealing impact on the lives of the people.

A related innovation, clearly a response to Townsend's crusade, but a measure that became one of the New Deal's most enduring reforms, was the Social Security Act that initiated a federal welfare system. The centerpiece was old-age pensions, administered directly by the federal government. Other elements of the system, such as unemployment insurance and aid for dependent people, would be partly funded and administered by the states under federal guidelines. Though the levels of support envisioned by the initial legislation were modest, the effect was to undercut the appeal of the grandiose schemes of Townsend and others of his kind. Most importantly, however, the basis had been created for the more generous "entitlement"system that developed after World War II.

The program created by Roosevelt and Congress in 1935 differed substantially from the program of 1933. The Second New Deal abandoned the NRA and with it the aim of creating prosperity by encouraging a species of planned industrial economy through business self-regulation under the mild supervision of government bureaucrats. The disappearance of the NRA only attenuated the New Deal's flirtation with the concept of economic planning, however; it by no means ended it entirely. The AAA's policy of limiting, or planning, agricultural production, also a major policy of the First New Deal, continued throughout the 1930s, even though the methods used had to be changed under new legislation in 1936 and 1938, after the Supreme Court found the original Agricultural Adjustment Act unconstitutional. Moreover various measures such as the Guffey Act continued or were enacted after the fall of the NRA with the purpose of restricting the output of oil, coal, and other basic commodities. The concept that planning of some kind was required to meet at least some of the economic problems that ailed America also continued robustly during the Second New Deal under the TVA, which was charged with the task of building up the prosperity of the Tennessee Valley, not only by furnishing it with cheap hydroelectric power but also by coordinating all its resources.

Even a number of new measures enacted during the years of the Second New Deal could be regarded as economic planning, though in a different meaning of the term than in the case of the NRA and the AAA. The Resettlement Administration (RA), created by executive order in 1935 and placed under Rexford Tugwell's direction, sought to help landless and impoverished tenant farmers, by establishing them, in some cases, in farm cooperatives that, to conservative critics, looked all too much like the agricultural communes of communist Russia. Its successor, the Farm Security Administration (FSA) of 1937, however, focused instead simply on lending money to help low-income farmers improve the efficiency of their operations. The Soil Conservation Service (SCS), created in 1935 to teach farmers new cultivation methods less destructive of farmland, represented New Deal planning, as did the far-flung effort of the Forest Service to build a "shelterbelt" of trees stretching across the Great Plains from south to north to break the force of windstorms. Many New Dealers tried to promote planning in still another sense by advocating that the government provide what the private sector was not providing during the 1930s—new housing. Tugwell dreamed of the New Deal constructing ideally planned suburban communities, and his RA actually did build three such "greenbelt" towns. The PWA constructed some 50,000 housing units before 1937. Then Senator Wagner's housing bill created a United States Housing Authority (USHA) that built over 100,000 public housing units by the close of the New Deal era.

POLITICAL OPPOSITION AND POLITICAL TRIUMPH: THE ELECTION OF 1936

Many business leaders perceived the Second New Deal's labor and work relief policies as antibusiness and were equally appalled by the tax bill of 1935, which raised tax rates somewhat on higher personal and corporation incomes. But the Public Utility Holding Company Act seemed the worst threat of all. This act, mandating the breakup of electrical utility holding companies (companies that held control of large numbers of operating companies that actually produced electricity) unless they could demonstrate the efficiency of their operations sufficiently, passed Congress by only a narrow margin and then only after acrimonious opposition in which many of the more conservative Democrats in Congress had participated. Already much of the business community had bitterly criticized the New Deal as antibusiness and socialistic, thinking of the TVA and certain other lesser programs of the First New Deal. The reforms of 1935 drove most business leaders, for the time being at least, into bitter opposition to Roosevelt and the New Deal. Indeed, in some circles the "rich" would not even speak FDR's name, referring to him contemptuously as "that man."

The great majority of the people, however, endorsed FDR's Second New Deal enthusiastically. Buoyed by a rising economy and a substantially reduced unemployment rate, and with farm income on the upswing, Roosevelt carried the presidential election of 1936 by a landslide majority against an ineffective moderate Republican, Alf Landon of Kansas. Roosevelt had tied together the traditional base of the Democratic Party in the southern and western states with the working-class populations of the industrial states of the eastern and midwestern states. This "New Deal Coalition" would dominate national government for decades. With this degree of personal popular support and both houses of Congress controlled by overwhelmingly Democratic majorities, FDR believed he could press on with additional social-economic reform, such as federal minimum wage legislation, an item he had long wanted to put on the New Deal's agenda, and governmental reforms that would reorganize the executive branch and strengthen its ability to administer national programs efficiently.

REACTION AND DECLINE—THE NEW DEAL'S LAST PHASE

Roosevelt thought that before there could be legislative progress the threat to the New Deal posed by recent decisions of the Supreme Court had to be eliminated. Relying on constitutional doctrines that had for years sharply limited the authority of the federal government to regulate economic and social affairs, the Court had in 1935 and 1936 declared a number of New Deal measures, including the NRA and the AAA, unconstitutional. Roosevelt feared that the Court might strike down the Wagner Act and still other key measures, and thus early in 1937, he sent to Congress a proposal to "reform" the Court with the intention of making it more amenable to New Deal measures. This proposal, which its numerous opponents labeled the "Court Packing bill," would have allowed the president to appoint an additional justice to the court for every sitting justice over seventy years of age who failed to retire, to a maximum of six such appointments. As none of the sitting justices was young and six of them were older than seventy (critics had described the Court as the "Nine Old Men"), the bill patently represented an attempt by the president to control the Supreme Court. The proposal, to which Roosevelt clung despite mounting opposition, gave moderate and conservative Democrats an opportunity to oppose the president openly, something they had been hesitant to do before. Joining with the Republicans, these Democrats defeated the measure.

An important factor in the defeat of the Court Packing bill was the "switch in time that saved nine," as one newspaper wag put it. In the midst of the struggle in Congress over the Court Packing bill, the Court handed down a decision upholding the Wagner Act, signaling a fundamental shift in its interpretation of the powers of the Congress under the Constitution. From this point onward, in its review of challenges to New Deal legislation the Court deferred almost entirely to Congress in the realm of economic regulation, abandoning constitutional doctrines that had sharply limited congressional authority for decades. The New Deal thus had achieved liberation from constitutional challenges, but it proved a costly victory. The "conservative coalition" in Congress that formed during the fight over the Court Packing bill, once created, took on a life of its own and thereafter would often block, or at least force, the attenuation of FDR's plans for further reform.

Prospects for a "Third New Deal" diminished further in the fall of 1937 when a serious business recession abruptly ended the upward trend of the economy. Faced with rising unemployment and taunted by critics that this was a "Roosevelt Recession," FDR found it increasingly difficult to keep the loyalty of the voters and to control Congress, yet was unsure what course to take to restore prosperity. Within the administration a major debate over policy developed. FDR's trusted friend Henry Morgenthau Jr., the secretary of the treasury, urged a conservative policy of balanced budgets and cooperation with business; others in a similar vein pushed for revival of the NRA approach.

In the end, two quite different policies, new to the New Deal, won out. The first was the renewal of heavy governmental spending for work relief and other programs, even though this would mean large budget deficits. Roosevelt was deeply traditionalist by instinct, despite his remarkable capacity to respond to the nation's needs and demands with innovative policies, and throughout his presidency had sought to limit deficit spending as much as possible. The New Deal's budgets had been out of balance in order to accommodate relief and public works spending, but this was only because of need, not on the theory that the government could promote prosperity by spending beyond its revenues. A growing number of Roosevelt advisors (Marriner Eccles, the chair of the Federal Reserve Board was the most influential), however, now vigorously argued for purposeful, heavy deficit spending as the key to recovery. These voices now claimed credibility because of the recently published writings of the British economist, John Maynard Keynes. Keynes's work offered an entirely new theory of the causes of the depression. It argued persuasively that deficit spending was the only way to lift the economy from the doldrums and was rapidly replacing older economic thinking in the minds of American economists. The second new major policy direction was the renewal of antitrust enforcement, on the supposition that the suppression of competition through monopolistic agreements and behavior was keeping prices for consumers' goods artificially high and that this had retarded recovery and brought on the recession. Congress did approve large-scale spending for work relief early in 1938 and also launched a well-staffed and ultimately very illuminating study of business and its monopolistic practices through the Temporary National Economic Committee, under the chairmanship of Wyoming Senator Joseph C. O'Mahoney. Meanwhile, Roosevelt's new appointee as assistant attorney general for antitrust, Thurman Arnold, launched a spectacular series of cases intended to promote competition. Arnold's aim was not to break up large corporations but to prevent anticompetitive behavior, whether on the part of large corporations or small, and thus to reduce prices to the consumer.

FDR's political strength, however, had ebbed. His Fair Labor Standards bill did pass Congress in 1938, but only after overcoming strong opposition. Republicans made major gains in the November congressional elections that year, and it was clear that an era of reform was over. Economic recovery returned in mid-1938, and production gradually increased until it was surpassing the 1929 rate, though unemployment remained high until the country went to war late in 1941. It is likely too that the capacity of many Americans to support economic and social change of the magnitude they had witnessed during the First and Second New Deals simply was exhausted. With the return of relative prosperity, many Americans wanted to concentrate again on consumption and entertainment and travel. They wanted to marry, start families, go to school and do the other things postponed by and during the depression. Despite its travail, American industry had not stagnated during the 1930s, and the range and quality of consumers' goods available to American households, from vacuum sweepers to automobiles, had increased substantially by this time. This was even truer of popular entertainment. Radio had come of age and, with its serial "soap operas" during the day and dramas, comedy hours, talent shows, sports broadcasts, and serious musical presentations in the evening, had now become for most families what television would become for later generations. Vacation travel had become almost obligatory for Americans of any means at all; automobile trips across the mountains and deserts of the West were very popular, especially for midwesterners.

In any case, FDR and the nation were increasingly preoccupied by developments in Europe and the Far East. Nazi aggression in Europe set off a new world war in 1939, and the depression ended as beleaguered western democracies bought food and manufactures from America. By 1940, with the threat of involvement in the European conflict looming and the likelihood of war with Japan ever more real, American defense spending was mounting and the era of depression disappearing.

4

The Great Depression and American Politics

Nowhere was the impact of the Great Depression upon America more profound than in the realm of politics and political institutions. As it had in other periods of stress and crisis, the American constitutional and political system proved remarkably adaptable and flexible when circumstances demanded rapid change and adjustment. Although sorely tested by potentially disruptive political forces and figures, the traditional system proved capable of transforming political unrest into a new version of party politics, one that was capable of providing reforms that successfully met the demands of an electorate disillusioned with leaders and policies that now seemed utterly inadequate and worn-out.

The outcome might have been less positive. The Great Depression severely tested democratic government everywhere. In Europe it fared badly. Unemployment and business failure in Germany so radicalized much of the electorate that by 1932 a large majority of voters had swung to the support of either the Communist or National Socialist parties, each of which in a different way represented revolutionary extremes. A National Socialist, or Nazi, electoral victory in 1933 soon led to Adolf Hitler's dictatorship and set Germany on a course of rearmament and expansion, and, finally, in 1939, to a war in Europe war that soon became worldwide. Representative democratic government survived in Britain and France, but the depression so sharpened class conflict and enmity between political parties, in France especially, as to weaken gravely the government's capacity to deal with the growing threat from Germany.

REALIGNMENT—THE NEW DEAL COALITION

Economic adversity struck America as hard as it did Germany, but the political changes it produced represented shifts and adjustments within the existing political system rather than its overthrow. During the 1930s the American political-constitutional system grew measurably and evidently more representative and democratic, more responsive to the wishes and needs of social classes and groups that until then had enjoyed only a sharply limited presence in America's national politics.

To be specific, the central political change of the 1930s was the transformation of the Democratic Party into the "liberal" party whose most important and most loyal support came from the working class of the northern industrial cities and whose policies championed their needs. To an extent never witnessed before in American history, voting and political loyalty became matters determined by social-economic class. In other words the Democratic Party became champion of blue-collar workers and of urban "ethnics," Americans who, by reason of their recent immigration, or because they were Catholics or Jews, had to a great extent been excluded from a voice and role in American national political life. This new Democratic Party still depended heavily on southern and western voters, especially the former, but it depended even more heavily upon the votes of workers and of the lower income masses in the great cities of the East and Midwest. To them, the Democratic Party had, reciprocally, given voice and status through its policies and political appointments. Social class and ethnic status thus became a major basis of voting behavior, and the Democratic Party became the acknowledged advocate of workers, the unemployed, and Americans of lower income and status generally.

This new configuration represented a sea change in the nature of party politics. In the period stretching from the 1890s through the 1920s, party conflict had arrayed regions of the country rather than social classes against one another. In this system the Republicans were normally politically dominant in the industrial states of the North, whereas the Democrats found their base in the agrarian regions, especially the South. The most important issues in national politics involved policy toward business and industry with the Republicans largely playing the role of promoter and protector of industrial progress.

The reconfiguration of the electorate that occurred during the Great Depression represented what political scientists call a "realignment" of the party system. American political parties normally are quite stable across elections. That is, the parties themselves continuously present the same political profiles. They maintain a familiar stand on issues, and the identity of the voting groups that support them changes little. Realignments occur rarely, only when political or economic circumstances generate stresses and create issues that invite political leaders to take up new policies and ideas. On these occasions parties shift their stances and voters rearrange their political loyalties. Realignment usually results in one party emerging as dominant. The most recent realignment prior to the 1930s had occurred in the 1890s, also a time of industrial and agricultural depression. In the re-aligning election of 1896, the Republicans emerged triumphant as the party representing the populous industrial states of the Northeast and upper Midwest. Republicans maintained a tight grip on a sizable majority of voters in this region during nearly all national elections from 1896 to 1932. Republican popularity in national elections was not limited to the upper and middle-income groups but extended down to much of the blue-collar working class. This political strength stemmed from the party's reputation as the party that protected and encouraged industrial growth and prosperity through the protective tariff, sound money, and a strong effort to protect and foster American commercial and industrial expansion overseas. The Democratic Party did have some reliable support in the North, largely through certain of the political organizations known as "machines" that ruled most of the major cities, but the Democrats hardly had a monopoly on machine power or the urban masses' votes. Some of the city machines were dominated by Republican bosses, though in many cases the boss and the machine were Democratic. The Democratic Party's main electoral strength, however, was limited through much of this period to the South and the Border States and to some extent the states of the Great Plains and the West. The Democrats won only two presidential elections between 1896 and 1932, those of 1912 and 1916, when divisions within the Republican Party, together with the emergence of a charismatic reformer, Woodrow Wilson, capable of attracting voters in the North, briefly gave the Democrats national leadership. Through most of the entire period however, the Republicans controlled the presidency and both houses of Congress.

This new Democratic Party consisted of what historians call the "New Deal Coalition," the political joining of southern and other agrarian voters from the old party with the working-class and lower class voters of the urban-industrial North. It first appeared as a dominating electoral coalition in the context of the presidential election of 1936, in which Franklin Roosevelt was reelected president by a popular majority representing over 60 percent of the electorate, one of the strongest landslide electoral victories in American history. The composition of the coalition starkly reflected the fact that it was precisely those Americans who had been hardest hit by the depression, and for that matter had held a lower place in the social and income ladder before the depression, who felt they had gained most from the New Deal programs and therefore were anxious to support the candidate who had presided over their creation.

ORIGINS OF THE NEW DEAL COALITION

The depression was not the only propellant that formed the New Deal Coalition. Many historians believe longer range forces that became operative in the decade before the depression also were at work. The immensely heavy immigration beginning in the 1890s from southern and eastern Europe had laid the basis, by the time of World War I, for social conflict between old and new stock Americans, a conflict that raged bitterly during the 1920s. Americans of older vintage tended to see the immigrants and their children, mostly Catholic and Jewish, from Italy, Poland, Russia, and other east European countries, who now formed the majority of the population of all the major cities of the East and industrial Midwest, as a threat to American political and social institutions. They saw them as clannish, as lacking independence, as too heavily influenced by priests and traditional religious folkways, as frequently criminal, and above all, as incapable of assimilation. These attitudes about the "ethnics" provided a major impetus for adoption of the Eighteenth Amendment in 1919, prohibiting the manufacture and sale of alcoholic beverages, and for the effort throughout the 1920s to enforce it. They accounted, too, for the congressional legislation in 1924, the National Origins Act, which severely and discriminatorily restricted immigration from the lands of southern and eastern Europe. These attitudes also fostered the birth of a reincarnated Ku Klux Klan, which focused on restricting the participation of Catholics and Jews in public life in the cities of the North, while trying to repress blacks in the South.

In the northern cities, the Democratic Party proved far more responsive to the growing resentment the newer Americans felt toward the refusal of some older Americans to recognize their worth and potential. In these cities Irish Americans typically led the party. The most powerful of these organizations was Tammany Hall, a political machine that had dominated New York City's government for over half a century. Led by a wise political boss, Charles F. Murphy, Tammany had in recent years governed more efficiently and responsively than in its earlier, more corrupt years in power, and even succeeded in having one of its sons, Al Smith, elected as governor.

In 1924 Smith sought the Democratic presidential nomination against William G. McAdoo. Smith, a Catholic and the son of an immigrant, a man who had risen from poverty to become the highly regarded governor of the nation's most populous state, represented the aspiration for recognition and acceptance felt by the new stock voters of the urban North. McAdoo represented the determination of the Democrats in the agrarian and less urban states to retain power and maintain Prohibition and other antiethnic measures. The result was a deadlocked convention that ended finally with the nomination of a weak candidate and a massive Democratic defeat at the polls. In 1928, the Democratic convention let Al Smith, the "hero of the cities," have his try at the presidency. Smith lost badly to Hoover in a contest marked heavily by subterranean anti-Catholic and anti-immigrant propaganda. Southern states that had never gone Republican now did so, so great was the feeling in that region, as well as in much of nonurban America, against what they deemed the threat of a president reeking of "fish oil" and urban corruption, who was also considered subservient to the orders of the Vatican.

Conversely, however, Smith's candidacy enjoyed an enormous upwelling of electoral support from the ethnic voters of the northern cities. Catholic voters mobilized with nearly one voice behind Smith. Many commentators see in the election of 1928 the beginning of what later would be called the New Deal Coalition, speculating that the Democratic Party, understanding now the prospects for uniting voters in the South and the northern cities, would have pursued that unity by adopting a more liberal course on social and perhaps also economic policy. In this interpretation, the Democrats might have overcome Republican ascendancy even had there been no depression.

FRANKLIN ROOSEVELT AND THE MAKING OF THE NEW DEAL COALITION, 1932–1935

Whatever the plausibility of this scenario, the elections held in 1928 indisputably played an important role in the Democratic Party's future success by bringing to the fore a leader capable of forging a new politics, Franklin D. Roosevelt. Believing that Roosevelt's running for governor of New York would strengthen support in that state for the national Democratic ticket, Smith urgently asked him to accept the nomination and make the race. In the upshot, Smith lost New York State but Roosevelt was elected governor. He thus would be well positioned to bid for his party's presidential nomination in 1932. During the next four years, displaying the political talents that served him so well later as president, Roosevelt strengthened his standing greatly both within his state and with the politicians and voters of the southern and western wings of the Democratic Party. He took a strong stand favoring development of New York's hydroelectric resources by the state government, pioneered programs to assist upstate farmers, and, as the depression intensified, created a state relief agency that served as a model for other states. In moderate but unmistakable terms, he let it be known that he favored federal assistance to agricultural and federal waterpower development.

In the fight for delegates to the 1932 Democratic convention, Roosevelt faced several opponents, the strongest of whom was Al Smith, who was aided by his friend, John J. Raskob, the chair of the Democratic National Committee and the leading contributor at this time to Democratic political coffers. The political bosses of most of the cities and states of the Northeast and industrial Midwest opposed Roosevelt bitterly and, backing Smith or a "favorite son," formed a coalition to prevent his nomination. They nearly succeeded. They blocked Roosevelt's nomination on the opening ballots of the convention, and his support was on the point of ebbing when John Nance Garner of Texas, the Democrats' leader in the House of Representatives for many years, fearing a replay of the deadlocked 1924 convention, abandoned his own candidacy and threw his support to the New Yorker.

Roosevelt's moderate and circumspect demeanor in the 1932 campaign contrasts sharply with the boldness of his early presidency a few months later. He took pains to reassure the business and financial community of his fiscal soundness, stressing the importance of a balanced budget. While endorsing the desirability of federal action in a number of areas, such as agriculture, waterpower, and railroad reorganization, he did so in general terms without committing to specific programs, except for his pledge to end prohibition by repealing the Eighteenth Amendment. Despite this, Roosevelt's manner and rhetoric were far more confident and reassuring than Hoover's and suggested a far greater disposition to take forceful and innovative action against the depression than his Republican counterpart. He pledged "a new deal for the American people" in his speech accepting the nomination, and in later speeches he underlined his activist disposition, asserting in one that "the country needs bold, persistent experimentation. It is common sense to take a method and try it. If it fails, admit it frankly and try another. But above all, try something." Believing such utterances meant that Roosevelt would lean in the direction of inflationary rather than his own sound money policies, Hoover tried to portray his opponent's economic tendencies as dangerous, predicting, in a passage the Democrats would ridicule for many years afterward, that "grass will grow in the streets of a hundred cities, a thousand towns," if FDR were elected.

The people disagreed, and, completely reversing the strong support they had given Hoover in 1928, endorsed the Democratic candidate in the November 1932 election by a heavy margin. Roosevelt carried over 58 percent of the popular vote, losing in only six states. The makeup of the vote behind this Democratic landslide, however, did not furnish much indication that a far-reaching shift in voter loyalties had occurred. The surge toward the Democrats in 1932 came from voters of all descriptions, from the middle as well as the working class, from those whose ethnic background was newer or older American. The task of creating a new Democratic Party that could consistently dominate American politics remained to be accomplished.

There are indications that FDR, from the beginning of his presidency, set out deliberately to build a Democratic Party that would supplant the Republican dominance of American politics. The goal was not merely a powerful, but also a reformist, or liberal, party that could fulfill his own inclination to use government actively, not only to cure the depression and prevent its return, but also to improve the lot of those who had fared poorly within the American economic system and give recognition and opportunity to a socially broader spectrum of Americans than was the custom of the Republicans.

Roosevelt's notions about the scope of liberal economic reform were relatively limited when he became president. We have seen already that FDR allowed much of the First New Deal, most notably the NRA and the AAA, to be shaped by the more powerful interest groups, and that it directly offered little to blue-collar labor and to farm workers or sharecroppers. The force of events and the changing temper and expectations of many voters gradually moved him toward a broader conception. For the most part, Roosevelt's performance as strategist for his party was an exercise in attunement to political reality, a response to the demands of and the limits imposed by the electorate and by political necessity. His quest for getting and maintaining political power in fact contained an element of amorality, for he was quite willing to grant favors to unsavory political forces in return for support. The generation of "progressive" reformers among whom Roosevelt had reached maturity and political office, before World War I, had attached paramount importance to political reform, to a war on corrupt bosses and the city machines. Roosevelt instead cooperated obligingly with Tom Pendergast of Kansas City and a number of notoriously corrupt bosses. It is also true that, when the opportunity arose, Roosevelt backed reformers. The most notable example of this was his strong support for Fiorello LaGuardia, who, through a third party, overthrew the Tammany machine in 1933 and as mayor initiated an era of political and social reform in New York City that lasted for over a decade.

Roosevelt's turn toward a more advanced economic liberalism took time, but he pursued a liberal social policy from the beginning. In the first place, after backing repeal of Prohibition in the 1932 campaign, he cheerfully requested, shortly after his inauguration, a revision of the Volstead Act that immediately legalized beer, anticipating ratification of the Twenty-First, or repeal, Amendment that had been enacted in the previous Congress. Most of America by this time probably supported repeal, but it was the Catholic and Jewish populations of the northern cities that had demanded it most vociferously. Roosevelt's appointments to government jobs similarly reflected a far greater recognition of the demands and aspirations of these groups than the Republicans had given during their long period of power since the turn of the century. Only a handful of the federal judges appointed by Harding, Coolidge, and Hoover were Catholics, for example, but nearly a quarter of those appointed during the New Deal years were. Many of Roosevelt's closest aides, including Jim Farley, the postmaster general who dispensed federal jobs, and Tommy Corcoran and Benjamin Cohen, who together played an influential role as the president's legislative advisors and speechwriters, were drawn from the ranks of Catholics or Jews.

Several factors emerged between 1933 and the election of 1936 that enabled Roosevelt then to go before the people openly and outspokenly as the head of a party dedicated to far-reaching economic and social reform. One factor was the sharp increase, resulting from the elections of 1932 and 1934, in the proportion of Democrats holding seats in the House and Senate who represented northern, urban-industrial constituencies. These senators and representatives were much more strongly inclined toward support for unions, large-scale work relief, and social welfare programs than the southern and western agrarians who had dominated the party's representation in Congress for so many years. These southern and western congressmen had, to be sure, staunchly supported the First New Deal legislation. Much of what proved enduring of the First New Deal—the AAA, the TVA, the banking and stock market reforms, the rural electrification program, increased spending on public works and relief—was in fact shaped in accordance with their agenda. Their capacity for reform ranged from moderate to radical, but for the most part their reform vision was limited to business regulation, taxation of high incomes, and aid for the agrarian regions of the country. Their reformism was in the tradition of the Democratic progressives of the Wilson era. They had little disposition to extend assistance to the industrial working class. The 74th Congress, however, elected in 1934, counted among its Democratic members a vastly higher percentage of representatives of urban-industrial constituencies than ever before.

A second factor, a drastic upward shift in the expectations of the people, interacted with this change in the nature of the Democratic Party in Congress. As we saw in the previous chapter, during 1934 and 1935 there appeared a more radical and demanding temper within the masses of Democratic voters. Labor militancy blossomed mightily during this period, and the voices of the three demagogues of the depression years, Fr. Coughlin, Huey Long, and Dr. Townsend, were listened to attentively by an impressively large and growing audience.

For a president as politically attuned as Roosevelt, as well as disposed toward a broader activist role for the government, these factors mandated a turn to the left. The legislation of the Second New Deal during the summer of 1935, secured with the president's blessing, and often at his prompting, directly appealed to the interests and welfare of blue-collar workers and other lower income Americans through the WPA, the Wagner Act, Social Security, and the wealth tax.

THE ELECTION OF 1936 AND THE EMERGENCE OF THE NEW DEAL COALITION

These new programs, whose impact workers, both those with jobs and the unemployed, felt immediately, thanks to ready enforcement of the new laws protecting unionization and unbelievably prompt creation of hundreds of thousands of WPA jobs by Harry Hopkins, laid the basis for the stunning Democratic electoral victory of November 1936. Roosevelt took 60.8 percent of the popular vote, the highest popular plurality in the history of presidential balloting except for the Johnson-Goldwater contest of 1964. The Democrats, moreover, carried both House and Senate by extraordinarily large margins, winning 75 of the 96 Senate seats and 333 of the 435 in the House of Representatives. Many Republicans now feared their party stood on the brink of expiring altogether. The great significance of the 1936 election rests, however, not in the sheer magnitude of the Democratic triumph. It lies rather in the makeup of the vote, in the extraordinarily high percentage of voters, 80 percent or more, in the large cities of the Northeast and Midwest that cast their ballots for Roosevelt. Detailed study of election returns and contemporary polls indicate that the Democrats attracted a very high proportion of Americans who occupied the lower rungs of the economic and social status ladder in American society. Blue-collar workers voted Democratic by huge percentages, and the same was true, regardless of the economic status (which often was that of a worker in any case) of Catholics and Jews, and of newer Americans from Italy, Poland, and other East European countries. A very high proportion of African-American voters also came into the Democratic Party fold, abandoning their long habit of loyalty to the Republicans.

The New Deal Coalition would prove durable over the next three presidential elections, though by lesser margins of the popular vote. The outsized Democratic victory of 1936 resulted in part from the particular circumstances of that election. Roosevelt campaigned with unusual aggressiveness, coming close to appealing to voters on the basis of class interest and class conflict, a tactic mainstream candidates had always eschewed as against the American grain. In his most famous speech of the campaign, he inveighed against "economic royalists," those in the financial and corporate world who held concentrated economic power and exercised "an almost complete control over other people's money, other people's labor—other people's lives." "The forces of selfishness and greed," he said in another speech, stood united in their hatred of him, "and I welcome their hatred."

These bitter words were prompted in part by expediency and in part by Roosevelt's anger at the intensity of the criticism many businessmen and conservative Republicans had leveled at him. A good part of this came from the American Liberty League, an organization formed in 1934 to fight the New Deal, especially by initiating a far-flung propaganda campaign proclaiming the unconstitutionality of the New Deal's legislation. Well financed by John J. Raskob, members of the DuPont family, and other big businessmen, the Liberty League succeeded in raising suspicions about Roosevelt's political intentions, suggesting he was taking the country toward fascism. Strong and strident criticism came from other quarters of the business community after the Second New Deal legislation of 1935 and as its implications became clear in 1936. The Wealth Tax of 1935 proved in application to have little bite, but it offended upper income receivers nevertheless. A grievous offense against the sensibilities of many big businessmen, especially those who controlled electrical and other public utilities, was the "death sentence" clause of the Public Utility Holding Company Act. The clause decreed the breakup of electrical power holding companies that had, by a certain date, failed in the government's estimate to reorganize satisfactorily to attain operating efficiency. Even more frightening, especially to the managers and shareholders that controlled the great industrial corporations, was the renewed wave of labor militancy that came in the wake of the Wagner Act. Supported now by the government, John L. Lewis and his Congress of Industrial Organizations during 1936 rapidly advanced toward the goal of organizing workers in the mass production industries, mobilizing workers to support Roosevelt politically at the same time through a new organization, Labor's Non-Partisan League (LNPL). The LNPL furnished the 1936 Democratic campaign with $770,000, a very large share of its financial resources that year.

Many other factors contributed to the magnitude of the New Deal's support in 1936. The threat earlier posed by the possible coalition of Coughlin, Long, and Townsend largely evaporated after Long was assassinated in 1935. Roosevelt had largely undercut their appeal through the measures of the Second New Deal. The third party, the Union Party, hastily organized by these forces, nominated William Lemke, an agrarian radical from North Dakota, who had only a narrow appeal. Another element was the weakness of the Republican candidate, a colorless Kansan, Alf Landon, who, until late in the campaign, when he adopted a more conservative stance, criticized the New Deal in mild tones, mainly asserting that Republicans could implement its programs more efficiently and at lower cost than the Democrats. Roosevelt was free to "run against Hoover," excoriating the Republicans as outmoded and dangerous to the economy's health.

Superior Democratic political organization also accounted for the party's remarkable showing in the balloting, for the New Deal helped reinvigorate Democratic machines in many of the nation's large cities. This was accomplished through strategic use of WPA funds, by using jobs to strengthen political machines or even, as in the case of Pittsburgh, to create strong Democratic organizations where none had existed before.

RISE OF THE CONSERVATIVE COALITION AND THE DECLINE OF THE NEW DEAL

November 1936, however, was flood tide for the New Deal coalition. Never again would voters back Roosevelt and his party in Congress as they did in 1936. Indeed disillusionment swiftly followed the election. Within a few months Roosevelt had to face both sharply diminishing popular support and a debilitating reduction in the loyalty of many Democratic congressmen as a series of events occurred in 1937 that led many erstwhile Roosevelt voters to wonder where the New Deal was taking them. These events began in the last days of 1936 with the United Auto Workers' (UAW) sit-down strike against General Motors, with the workers occupying factories and forcibly resisting efforts of the local police to dislodge them. The Democratic governor, Frank Murphy, a staunch New Dealer, refused to call out the National Guard, and the president, criticizing both sides, also declined to take any action. Many Americans who had thus far loyally supported Roosevelt perceived the union's methods as radical and antithetical to property rights and were given pause by the New Deal's toleration.

These troubling thoughts were reinforced when Roosevelt, in March 1937, unveiled a plan for reform of the federal court system. Though presented as a measure for general reform and expansion of the federal courts, everyone recognized that the measure was primarily designed to let the president pack the court with New Deal justices. Roosevelt's initiative proved a costly blunder. The very magnitude of his political victory in November 1936 apparently had left him overconfident, blind to the degree and intensity of the criticism his proposal would inspire. The "court-packing" plan was immediately and bitterly attacked by conservative critics who denounced it in extreme terms as the overthrow of one of the most cherished principles of the American constitutional order, the balance of powers. Some darkly hinted the plan was a step toward dictatorship.

Among the Democratic congressmen there had always been a few hard-core conservatives, such as Senators Carter Glass of Virginia and Josiah Bailey of North Carolina. With few sympathizers, they had bided their time. Now they found allies among the many Democratic senators and representatives from the southern and western states who had supported Roosevelt loyally and for the most part enthusiastically but who now feared the president was acquiring too much power and that he would use it to take the New Deal's direction too strongly toward an agenda favored by Democrats representing the needs of the workers and masses of the big cities of the North. Roosevelt's support for militant CIO unionism was evident and so was his sympathy for a federal wage and hour law and large appropriations for public housing in the cities. This agenda was opposed by many southern congressmen. The South, with its low wages and weak unions, was attractive to business investment. The creation of strong national unions and of a national wage and hour law would endanger the South's advantages and potential for rapid industrial growth. Southern congressmen feared too that their northern counterparts, supported by and representing the needs and wishes of big city voters, were beginning to listen to the demands of those who spoke for northern blacks, voters who had in 1936 cast aside their traditional loyalty to the Republicans and voted for Roosevelt. Leaders of the NAACP, the major national organization representing the interests of black people, had set enactment of a federal antilynching law as their primary goal. Now, early in 1937, northern liberal Democrats teamed up with Republicans to pass such a measure in the House. Though prospects for Senate passage of such a measure were low, fear that northern Democrats might try to interfere with subordination of black people in the South, and that the president might sympathize with this attempt, also bred a sense of unease among southern congressmen over the degree of power that he now seemed to wield.

In this setting Roosevelt's court-packing plan created a deep division within Democratic ranks in the House and Senate. Coalescing with Republicans, dissident Democrats defeated the measure. This coalition of conservative Democrats and Republicans proved enduring. During the remaining years of the 1930s, it blocked, or watered down, several major Roosevelt proposals that Democrats from the South and the agrarian West believed gave advantage to the northern cities, or concentrated power too greatly in the president's hands.

Roosevelt's popularity suffered another blow when the economy stumbled in the late months of 1937 and contracted sharply. Mounting unemployment and the president's indecision for several months into 1938 over what course to take gave Republicans an opening they used to good advantage. The congressional elections in November 1938 restored the Republican Party as a credible opposition. Equally significant was Roosevelt's failure in that election to rid his party of key conservatives who were thwarting his legislative leadership. In a virtually unprecedented move, Roosevelt attempted to purge a number of such figures, among them Senator Millard Tydings of Maryland and Representative John J. O'Connor of New York, by visiting their states and urging voters to reject them in the Democratic primaries. Nearly all these interventions failed, and the Conservative Coalition remained empowered.

THE ELECTION OF 1940

Though reduced, Roosevelt's power within his party still stood so high it enabled him to break with the two-term tradition established by George Washington. As the presidential election of 1940 approached, Roosevelt feared that, unless he sought it, the Democratic nomination would go to a candidate unable, or unwilling, to lead the country, and his party, in the right directions. Directing the party toward a more liberal future still was essential in his mind, but another challenge was now even more pressing: the war in Europe. By the time the Democrats met to nominate a candidate in July 1940, France had fallen to Hitler's army, and Britain, now facing devastating air and submarine attacks, survived alone. During the preceding decade, the United States had exercised little influence in European international affairs and done nothing to encourage its former allies in World War I, Britain and France, to resist German rearmament in defiance of the Versailles Treaty, or to intervene decisively when Hitler launched his expansionist plans in 1937–1938 with demands on Czechoslovakian territory. When Germany attacked Poland in September 1939 and Britain and France declared war, America continued to stand back, still in the grip of isolationism.

Based on the conviction that America's intervention in 1917 had accomplished little and benefited no one but the munitions makers, and that America should therefore take no responsibility for the solution of European problems lest she be dragged into another of its conflicts, Americans had fervently embraced an isolationist position throughout the depression years. Neutrality Laws enacted in 1935 and 1937 barred sale of munitions to any warring nation except on a "cash and carry basis." This was to ensure that no American shipping would be vulnerable to the submarine attacks that had been the tangible cause of America's 1917 declaration of war against Germany. Preoccupied with saving the nation from the depression and not wanting to risk support for his New Deal policies by supporting unpopular internationalist causes, such as greater American involvement in checking aggression, FDR deferred to the isolationists for a time.

But FDR chafed at the restrictions. He appears to have felt America had to be led toward active opposition to the threat of German domination of Europe and the equally dire threat of Japanese domination of China and East Asia. Japan had sent its armies into China from Manchuria in 1937 and by 1940 had subjugated much of it. The gravest immediate issue was whether to help Britain stave off surrender. During the presidential campaign Roosevelt received word from Winston Churchill, the British prime minister, that, without American help in slowing the success of German submarine destruction of British shipping, his country would soon be starved into submission. The president's response was dramatic and politically chancy, though also deft. He transferred fifty destroyers from the American to the British Navy, in return for the transfer of a number of British naval bases in the Caribbean to this country. In doing so he not only aided the beleagured British, whose survival FDR believed crucial to freedom and America's self-interest, but also he deflected the isolationists' wrath by having "removed" the British, and so the war, from the Western Hemisphere in a way that seemed to strengthen the revered Monroe Doctrine.

The Republican convention passed over the conservative Robert A. Taft of Ohio to nominate Wendell Wilkie, a utility magnate and Wall Street lawyer who, despite devoted opposition to the TVA, was a moderate who realized the futility of opposing the New Deal's fundamental reforms and also understood the danger in which America stood from abroad. Initially he endorsed the destroyers-for-bases deal, but, lagging behind Roosevelt, later in the campaign he appealed to isolationist sentiment, attacking the Democratic candidate for harboring policies that would lead the country into war. In the upshot, the New Deal electoral coalition held firm, though Roosevelt's percentage of the popular vote fell considerably below the previous two elections, to 55 percent. It would hold firm in 1944 and 1948 too, before failing in 1952 and 1956, though the Kennedy and Johnson victories in 1960 and 1964 represented in considerable measure its revival until major political realignments caused by the civil rights movement and the Vietnam War in the last 1960s and early 1970s redrew the electoral map in presidential politics and threatened the Democratic Party's hold on the South and among blue-collar workers.

5

Society and Culture in the Depression Decade

The depression wrought enormous changes in the nation's political structure and its economic policy system, and these changes in turn led to a genuine and extensive movement upward in the social-economic status of tens of millions of industrial workers and urban ethnics. In other social realms, the impact was less profound. Improvement in the social position and the roles of blacks and of women have been central concerns during recent decades, but the depression and the New Deal came and went without effecting much change in them. One might expect also that prolonged hard times for so many Americans would have bred profound disillusionment with traditional values and cultural habits and that the depression decade would have generated important alteration in them, perhaps disturbed faith in the tradition of individualism, or undermined confidence in American capitalism. Change there was but here too its scope was quite limited.

THE DEPRESSION AND NEW DEAL AND WOMEN

Women's place, as the decade of the 1930s began, still was principally the realm of domesticity. The societal expectation still presumed the sphere of women was the home, marriage, and children. The pre–World War I women's rights movement had registered important gains for women respecting legal quality and had climaxed in 1920 with the passage of the women's suffrage amendment. This triumph, however, betokened little change in the fundamental status of women. Rapid industrialization and urbanization since the 1880s had increased the number and proportion of women in the workplace decade by decade, until by 1930 over 10 million women worked outside the home, nearly a third of them married women. They worked primarily in "women's jobs," as nurses, teachers, secretaries and clerks, saleswomen, workers in clothing manufacture (the needle trades), and household servants. In these fields women predominated, in some cases holding a virtual monopoly on jobs, but these were lower paid and lower status fields. Women were virtually excluded from most occupations and from the opportunity to compete with men in most fields of work.

Paradoxically, the contribution women made to the economy actually increased during the depression by about 2 million workers, with the number of married women as a proportion of the total number of women employed rising steeply. The number rose overall because "women's jobs" were less affected by the depression than the industrial jobs where men predominated and even expanded as the need for clerical workers grew. The number of married women working rose disproportionately simply because they often could find work when their husbands could not.

Despite this growing role for women in the workplace, the New Deal did little or nothing to change their subordinate status. There was little or no political pressure pushing for the kind of equal rights reformism that characterizes the feminist movement of the late decades of the twentieth century. There was in fact no strong organization lobbying for women's rights in the 1930s. An equal rights constitutional amendment had its advocates in the National Women's Party, but its voice was weak. Most of the women who were recognized as leaders and exemplars by society had gained their status through their work and accomplishment in the field of social welfare and reform. They were the women, drawn often from the upper middle class, who had directed settlement houses, or, as leaders of private social work agencies, had lobbied state legislatures for measures that would protect the health and safety of women and children in the workplace, and for measures to protect families from unsafe food and housing. It was in these fields of endeavor, so closely connected in the public mind with the proper sphere of women, the home and the family, that women had seized the opportunity to assume the major leadership roles that they were otherwise denied.

Franklin Roosevelt had an intimate acquaintance with these women and their work through his experience as governor of New York State, a major seat of social reform organizations, and through his wife, for Eleanor Roosevelt during the 1920s had become thoroughly involved in social work. Prodded by his wife's insistence and himself wishing to reach out to women voters and bind them to him politically, from the first days of the New Deal Roosevelt appointed women in unparalleled numbers, nearly all of them drawn from social reform circles, to administrative positions in the government, beginning with Frances Perkins as secretary of labor. Most of the appointments were to positions that could be deemed by the public as suitable for women, to the Labor Department's Children's and Women's Bureaus, for example, though there were exceptions to this rule. Hallie Flanagan was named head of the WPA's Federal Theatre Project, and, in unprecedented appointments, Ruth B. Owen was named to a major diplomatic post (minister to Denmark) and Florence Allen was made a judge in a federal Court of Appeals.

Anetwork developed among these women in government in which Eleanor Roosevelt played a central role, conveying recommendations to the president and to the public through her speeches and writings, as did Molly Dewson, whom the president appointed to head the Women's Division of the Democratic Party, a function she fulfilled with vigor and administrative talent. The aim of the women's network was to improve the impact on women of the many New Deal programs that directly affected them. The NRA codes, for example, regulated wages and hours for many women workers, and unemployed women held a substantial number of WPA jobs. These benefits fell short in that they provided for gender differences in wage rates or job assignments, differences that favored men, and they proved impossible to amend in most cases.

Wedded to the concept that the women's reform agenda should principally be protection rather than equality for women in the workplace, the women's network failed to spur the New Deal toward fundamental reconsideration of the role of women in the workplace and in society. Though not feminists in the modern sense, they nevertheless did serve visibly to demonstrate the capacity of women to function effectively in significant administrative and leadership roles, an accomplishment that inevitably had some positive impact on the evolution of society's perception of the capacities of women and their right to equal opportunity.

THE NEW DEAL AND BLACKS

In 1944, Gunnar Myrdal, a noted Swedish economist, published *An American Dilemma*, a landmark study of the race question in the United States. It exposed in the harsh light of exhaustive research the virtual caste system that governed the role of black people in America and sounded an alarm for reform. Subsequent decades did bring profound change, beginning with President Harry S Truman's order to racially integrate the nation's armed forces, continuing with the landmark decision of the Supreme Court in 1954 overruling the "separate but equal" doctrine and later requiring desegregation of public facilities, and climaxing with the struggle for the civil and political rights of blacks of the 1960s.

Myrdal's study offered proof that the New Deal had left the social and legal policies that enforced racial discrimination largely intact. Not that the New Deal's programs always excluded African Americans entirely from their benefits. Sometimes they did, as in the case of the Civilian Conservation Corps (CCC), which simply shut out young black men almost completely. They did, however, receive relief payments under the FERA, and large numbers of them held WPA jobs. But even in these instances, the New Deal accommodated racial discrimination, giving blacks inferior relief payments and wages. Differential wage rates appeared in the NRA codes also, but, more importantly, types of work where blacks predominated simply were not covered, an omission that recurred in the 1938 Wage and Hour Law which did not extend to domestic servants or to farm laborers. Worse, some of the most significant New Deal programs actually had a severely negative impact on blacks, with the AAA providing the most notable case. Both the original AAA of 1933 and its replacement enacted in 1936 had curtailment of acreage under cultivation as a central aim. Payments flowed to landowners who agreed to acreage reductions. Three-quarters of American blacks still lived in the South during the 1930s, the majority of them living as tenant farmers or farm workers. Reduction of land under cultivation frequently meant the worst for black farmers and workers and their families. That many poor whites shared their fate was small consolation for the many blacks the AAA's policies forced off the land.

The entire picture however is not this bleak. The liberalism of a number of New Dealers extended to promotion of racial justice. Harold Ickes forbade racial discrimination in his Interior Department and in hiring for PWA projects, and the administrator of the Farm Security Administration (FSA), William Alexander, included blacks in his agency's effort to resettle landless farm families. Moreover, many New Dealers spoke out for racial fairness, not least among them Eleanor Roosevelt, who in 1938 publicly endorsed the antilynching law then before Congress. Lynching of black men by white mobs had served in the South for many years as a violent tool of intimidation and subordination. During the 1920s the incidence of lynching had dropped to historic lows, but the depression apparently generated tensions that led to a revival. The NAACP, the major organization representing African Americans nationally, early in the 1930s made enactment of a federal antilynching law its major priority. Northern liberals, such as Senator Robert Wagner, began promotion of such a measure early in the New Deal, but, as with all such efforts in the past, southern opposition and the threat of a filibuster prevented consideration of the bill Wagner introduced.

The same factors prevented the bill's enactment in 1938 also, but debate over it, and the first lady's endorsement of it, drew public attention to the horror of lynching and pricked the nation's conscience.

The president consistently refused to support the antilynching bill, telling those who urged him to endorse it that he could not risk alienating southern congressmen when he needed their support to pass more pressing measures. Roosevelt felt circumstances constrained him to give the question of racial justice a low priority, but he did not altogether ignore it. He did appoint over forty blacks to responsible positions in the departments and agencies. Many of these appointees came together for informal periodic meetings to discuss issues involving blacks and were dubbed "the Black Cabinet" by the press, even though their influence with the president and other prominent New Dealers was not great.

The New Deal for the most part accepted and worked within the confines of the prevailing system of racial discrimination, but still it can be said that some New Dealers challenged the system when they were able, both in the application of policy and by publicly raising their voices. By 1940 the system at least had been held up for national scrutiny and the long debate begun that would lead eventually to a greater measure of racial justice.

SOCIETY AND CULTURE IN THE DEPRESSION DECADE

How did the depression decade affect the ideas and behavior of Americans? The social, cultural, and intellectual trends of the 1930s are complex, but it appears that, despite significant detours, for the great majority of Americans the trajectory of social belief and behavior followed the trends established in the 1920s and earlier. Despite the traumatic experiences of the early 1930s and the relative economic stagnation of the later years of the decade, most Americans declined to reject their fundamental faith in the country's political and economic system or the dream of full participation in a consumerist society.

Many intellectuals, it is true, found radical rejection alluring. The Communist Party of America (CPA) attracted thousands to membership during the decade and many more into sympathy with its stated goal of replacing capitalism with an economic system controlled by and for the workers. The communists became all the more attractive after 1935 when they adopted the stance of the Popular Front, proclaiming that all segments of the left, including the New Deal liberals they had previously excoriated for cooperating with capitalism, should join forces to defeat fascism, especially the Nazi version that, under Adolf Hitler, had overtaken Germany. Disillusionment appeared in 1939, however, when Joseph Stalin, ruler of the Soviet Union and thus of the communist movement worldwide, signed a pact with Hitler that freed him to seize a chunk of Poland. Many members of the CPA now realized that they had been used as tools of Soviet Russia and left the party, often becoming its most vocal critics during the Cold War after 1945.

The "proletarian novels" that communist authors wrote to promote the downfall of capitalism went largely unread, but the many left-wing novels of the period that, while harshly criticizing middle-class social and economic values as hypocritical and destructive, avoided ideological preaching, were well received and widely read by educated Americans. One of the strongest of these novelists was James T. Farrell, whose *Studs Lonigan* trilogy bitterly depicted how capitalism defeated and dispossessed the urban working and lower middle class. Writers in this vein are sometimes referred to as the "hard-boiled school." Others who adopted this mode, in some cases less from a leftist than a harshly naturalistic viewpoint, included James M. Cain (*Mildred Pierce*, *Double Indemnity*, and *The Postman Always Rings Twice*), Erskine Caldwell (*God's Little Acre* and *Tobacco Road*), Richard Wright (*Native Son*), and John O'Hara (*Butterfield Eight* and *Appointment in Samarra*). The towering novel of this kind was John Steinbeck's *Grapes of Wrath*, which, with its sympathetic portrayal of the dispossessed dirt farmers of Oklahoma, found a wide reception.

These signs of ideological questioning among the educated were reflected to some extent during the worst years of the depression in the movie fare consumed by the masses. Widespread, if short-lived discontent with the system may have been reflected by the vogue during the early 1930s of gangster movies. Formally these highly popular films disapproved of lawlessness, but they probably were intended to be understood, and probably were understood by their huge audiences, as parables about how independent spirits who tried to challenge the system and move up the ladder of success were crushed by those in control.

By no means did all serious writers and intellectuals move to the left during the decade. The humanistic realists such as Ellen Glasgow, Willa Cather, and Edith Wharton, who had achieved secure fame during the previous decades, continued to write in much the same vein as before, and their ranks were strengthened by the addition of John P. Marquand (*The Late George Apley*). More importantly perhaps, a number of famed naturalistic writers from the 1920s now found positive values in American society. Sinclair Lewis had achieved towering fame in the 1920s for his novels *Babbitt* and *Main Street*, whose success rested on stinging and mocking depictions of the American bourgeoisie as narrow and sexually repressed. Surveying a suffering America in the 1930s, trying to work its way out of economic despondency, Lewis discovered democratic and social values worth reaffirming, as he did in *It Can't Happen Here* and *The Prodigal Parents*. Even more telling was the case of Ernest Hemingway, the message of whose 1920s writings had been that loyalty to self was the only value worth holding, but whose 1940 masterpiece, *For Whom the Bell Tolls*, portrays with compelling sympathy a young American who dies in the Spanish Civil War fighting, he believes, for the preservation of democratic values.

Affirmation of traditional American values also appears strongly in the other artistic forms during the 1930s. In painting, these years brought to the forefront the "American Scene" artists, the triumvirate composed of Thomas Hart Benton, Grant Wood, and John Steuart Curry, all three born and bred in the American heartland, in Missouri, Iowa, and Kansas, respectively; in music there were Aaron Copland, who turned during the 1930s to writing highly accessible music on traditional American themes, and Ferde Grofé, who musically painted American scenes.

Many popular vehicles, including books and films, reflected these reassuring themes that implied faith that the American people could surmount their problems through democracy and by loyalty to the traditions of self-reliance and individualism that had nourished America since its founding. The enormously popular *Gone With the Wind*, on which the even more popular movie was based, encoded this message to some extent, as did a number of famous movies from the later 1930s, such as filmmaker Frank Capra's *Mr. Smith Goes to Washington* and *Meet John Doe*, in which heroes, played by quintessentially American types such as Gary Cooper and James Stewart, worked for economic reform, along the way defeating the forces of moral and political corruption that blocked it.

If, however, the character of popular entertainment is a reliable index of popular attitudes, the American people preferred entertainment to discourse on questions of political and economic ideology. Motion picture technology rapidly improved. The "talkies" had replaced silent films in the 1930s, and attendance at the movies, helped by theater promotions such as ladies' night and giveaways of consumer goods, rose remarkably during the depression decade. Although Hollywood made a number of serious films capable of stimulating reflection on moral and social issues, movies were intended mainly as entertainment. Hollywood reverted to form, emphasizing stories of romance and adventure, but the depression-era films had their own style, which ranged from "screwball comedies" made by such stars as Katharine Hepburn and Cary Grant, to the extravagant musicals that began with the Ruby Keeler vehicle *42nd Street* early in the decade and were produced annually thereafter in great number. Hollywood also churned out westerns by the hundreds for Saturday matinee devotees, who weekly saw the "good guys" win over the "bad guys," and individual heroism triumph, though some westerns, such as those made by John Ford (*Stagecoach*, for example), were of solid dramatic quality. Still another genre was the costume movie, very imaginative and none too accurate historical dramas portraying everything from the life and loves of Catherine the Great to the travails of Louis XIV during the French Revolution.

Radio technology and the broadcast industry rapidly advanced also so that listeners, by the middle years of the decade, had a broad array of soap operas during the day and a wide selection of sports, comedy, drama, and variety shows in the evening. An interesting development was the melding by the radio networks of what had always been regarded as high-culture forms, previously available only to upper class consumers of entertainment, with the decidedly lower brow fare contained in the shows that purveyed folksy humor (a favorite was *Amos and Andy,* another *Fibber Magee and Molly*) or the heroic exploits of G-Men and other agents of law enforcement in shows such as *Gangbusters*. Thus the National Broadcasting Network supported and frequently presented over the airwaves its own major symphony orchestra under the direction of the era's greatest conductor, Arturo Toscanini, while Texaco began sponsorship of the Saturday afternoon presentations of Metropolitan Opera live performances that continue to this day.

The movies and the radio programming of the 1930s are often labeled as "escapist," as though the people ought to have been occupied with more serious cultural experiences, with more intensive political reflection and action perhaps, but this misses the meaning of what amounts to a quite remarkable flowering of the production and consumption of popular entertainment. The tremendously active absorption of the great mass of people of all classes with popular entertainment was perhaps an expression of their readiness, their longing, to take up again the consumerist mentality and habits that had flourished and become established in the 1920s. By the mid-1930s, American industry was again endeavoring to stimulate this mentality through its traditional methods of style change and technical improvement. Thus the products of a number of key consumer industries, notably electrical appliances, automobiles, radios, and clothing, exhibited significant evolution in design, style, and usability. The depression sharply reduced the ability of a high proportion of Americans to participate in a consumerist way of life but may actually have strengthened the propensity to pursue it. This propensity strengthened into preoccupation as the economy recovered in 1939–1941, soared during World War II, and settled into steady growth in the postwar years. An era of social and economic reform was closing, and an era of prosperity, of suburbs, television, and superhighways, was about to begin.

6

The New Deal: An Evaluation

The Great Depression wrought major alterations in America's governmental, political and social realms. Most of these changes were part of or closely associated with the New Deal. Were these changes for good or ill? What was their effect, in the short and the long run, on the fabric of American society?

Few would disagree that certain of the New Deal's fundamental reforms have helped to create, in the post–New Deal era, a political economy less vulnerable to major economic catastrophe, more fair in distribution of income, and more effectively considerate of those in need. The New Deal, for example, clearly left the banking system more secure and better regulated and the stock market less exposed to shoddy practices than before. Most successful political figures in both major parties, moreover, have acknowledged since the New Deal that the government should maintain, to some extent at least, a "safety net," of social insurance to assist the retired, those without jobs because of recessions, and those unable to work because of disability. Nor have they disputed the government's obligation to recognize and defend labor's right to organize freely and bargain collectively, although Democrats and Republicans might differ as to the particulars of that obligation.

The political and social changes of the depression years also would be judged by most Americans as positive. The New Deal coalition conferred upon the "ethnics," mainly Catholics and Jews, a new, more powerful position in American politics, and through that position a wider recognition in public life and soon in the private sphere as well. In 1938 Secretary of

Interior Harold Ickes, one of the New Deal's strongest liberals and advocates of civil liberties, could record without comment in his diary his conviction that the Catholicism of Jim Farley, Roosevelt's chief political strategist, at least in the realm of patronage dispensation, effectively barred him from trying for the Democratic nomination in 1940. "I do not believe that we have yet reached the stage where a Catholic could be elected," he wrote, matter-of-factly.[1] Over the next twenty years, the political facts changed radically. The Democratic Party that emerged from the New Deal had its center of gravity in the great cities of the North and soon came to represent the interests not only of the white working- and middle-class children, or grandchildren, of European immigrants, but also the flood of blacks who left the South and went north in large numbers during World War II and the postwar era.

Inevitably a Catholic was elected, in 1960. Of equal, or even more fundamental importance, was the gradual adoption by the party of Roosevelt of a civil rights agenda. As early as the Democratic national convention in 1948, northern urban liberals, led by Hubert Humphrey of Minnesota, were seeking to commit the party to a strong civil rights stance. In the next decade, this development was bolstered by the change the New Deal had made in the Supreme Court. Roosevelt lost the court-packing fight in 1937, but soon was able, simply by filling vacancies that occurred through deaths and retirements, to make enough appointments to bring the Court under the sway of justices more attuned to the New Deal and its implications. The Supreme Court's *Brown v. Board of Education* decision in 1954, overthrowing the "separate but equal" doctrine and requiring desegregation of public schools, strengthened the commitment of northern Democrats to the civil rights cause. This commitment, together with an upwelling of resistance by blacks in the South, led to the enactment of the great Civil Rights Act of 1964 and the Voting Rights Act of 1965, measures that helped free blacks, and others, from legal, political, and social subordination.

There is of course a more critical school of thought that berates the New Dealers for not accomplishing more—for not nationalizing the banks, for providing relief work for only a fraction of those who needed it, for not taxing wealth more heavily and redistributing income downward more extensively, for not creating a more generous social security system that included medical insurance, for not building public housing and directing public spending toward urban planning and renewal more liberally, for not directing more of the New Deal's energies toward aiding the sharecroppers and others among the poorest one-third of Americans, and so on.

How valid one judges this critique to be depends partly on one's own economic and moral philosophy, partly on one's estimate of its realism. But it is not necessary to assay the New Deal by using an impossible standard to find that it was seriously flawed. It was seriously flawed because it did not realize Franklin Roosevelt's own aim, which was the revival of the American capitalist economy in the context of significant but moderate reform, not a radical reorganization of it.

By that standard, the New Deal fell far short of success. Its failings are numerous and of major proportions, whether we examine its programs in the time frame of the depression-ridden 1930s or in terms of their long-term impacts in subsequent decades. Some of its most important initiatives, most notably the NRA, retarded rather than promoted recovery. What for many years was hailed as its most important and lasting contribution to American economic policy in the postwar era, the policy of using deficit spending deliberately as a tool to create and maintain prosperity, has fallen from grace in recent decades and been displaced by a reversion to faith in restricted spending and balanced budgets. One of its most significant social reforms, the jointly financed federal-state system of payments to people unable to work, turned out to have vast and utterly unintended consequences that led by the 1990s to its denunciation by leaders of both major political parties. During the 1990s, "welfare reform," replacing welfare with "workfare," supplied the basis for the favorable reputations of many mayors and governors and played no little part in the electorate's favorable view of President Bill Clinton, the standard-bearer of FDR's party.

This catalog of shortcomings could be greatly extended but even then would not impair the monumental achievements of Roosevelt and the New Deal. A number of examples have been given already of specific policies the New Deal pioneered or refashioned that usefully endure, to this very day, in many cases renewed and enhanced by a later generation. The New Deal's fundamental and greatest achievement, however, lies less in its policy legacies than in its impact within its own time. Misguided as some of its initiatives were, the New Deal from the beginning represented a reasonable and widely supported response to the dire need of the nation for a responsible, inventive, and democratically based offensive against economic prostration, for reassurance that palliative action together with structural reforms could bring recovery and prevent another such economic collapse. Gradual recovery did take place through the 1930s (except for the 1937–1938 downturn). Opinion remains divided over the question whether the New Deal's policies were responsible for this or whether they may have actually slowed recovery. What appears quite certain is that the New Deal's relief policies, its agricultural assistance programs, its support for labor unions, its enactment of a social insurance program, and more renewed the hope and confidence of the great majority of Americans in the nation's tra-

ditional political and economic system. That system, preserved and renewed, stood ready in 1940 to meet the great test America would face in
World War II and prepared to deliver sustained economic growth and prosperity for the remaining decades of the millenium.

NOTE

1. *The Secret Diary of Harold L. Ickes*, Volume II, *The Inside Struggle,
1936–1939* (New York: Simon and Schuster, 1954), 340.

A scene at the encampment of the Bonus Army in Washington, D.C., 1932. Here, a marcher's children are seen at a station for collection of tobacco money for penniless marchers. (Herbert Hoover Presidential Library-Museum)

Unemployed New Yorkers wait patiently in a 1932 breadline for a free meal. (FDR Library & Digital Archives)

Striking truckers in Minneapolis battle the police, 1934. (FDR Library & Digital Archives)

CWA workers building a boulevard in San Francisco, 1934. (FDR Library & Digital Archives)

Huey Long speaks to the Louisiana State Legislature, 1934. (Reproduced from the collections of the Library of Congress)

A waitress posts the Blue Eagle, the symbol of cooperation with the NRA, in a restaurant window, 1934. (FDR Library & Digital Archives)

FDR in a 1935 "fireside chat." (FDR Library & Digital Archives)

Landless farmers on a muddy road, en route to the West, 1935. (FDR Library & Digital Archives)

The mother of a migrant farm worker's family and four of her seven children, California, 1936. (Reproduced from the collections of the Library of Congress)

The New York World's Fair, by night, 1939. (Reproduced from the collections of the Library of Congress)

Hoover Dam in 1941. (Herbert Hoover Presidential Library-Museum)

Biographies: The Personalities Behind the Great Depression and the New Deal

Adolf Augustus Berle, Jr. (1895–1971)

Adolf Berle was one of the three key members of the Brain Trust, the circle of advisors who helped Franklin D. Roosevelt win the 1932 Democratic presidential nomination and then the general election, and who assisted him in developing the program that became the First New Deal in 1933. Afterward he continued to serve the president in a number of capacities.

Berle was born on January 29, 1895. Something of a prodigy, Berle graduated from Harvard College at eighteen and earned a degree from Harvard Law School three years later, in 1916. In 1927, he became a member of the faculty at Columbia University Law School. In 1932, he and economist Gardiner Means published *The Modern Corporation and Private Property,* a highly influential book which examined the very large concentration of economic power in America in the hands of the 200 largest corporations and argued the need for federal regulation.

Recruited by Raymond Moley to join the Brain Trust, Berle argued for a more even distribution of purchasing power, the restoration of wages, and the rescue of the nation's farmers. Berle remained in close contact with the president throughout the New Deal era. He continued to write speeches and to advise FDR on matters of foreign policy, and also served as a special counsel for the RFC. In 1938, Roosevelt named him assistant secretary of state for Latin American affairs. He served in that capacity until 1944, then becoming ambassador to Brazil from 1945 to 1946. Berle remained involved in foreign policy throughout the remainder of his career. He was active in Radio Free Europe, served on the Council on Foreign Relations, and headed the Twentieth Century Fund. In the early months of the administration of President John F. Kennedy, Berle served as coordinator of policy development for Latin American affairs. He died on February 17, 1971.

Louis Dembitz Brandeis (1856–1941)

In his early career, Louis Brandeis was one of the most important figures in the creation of the reform program of President Woodrow Wilson. Appointed by Wilson to the Supreme Court, he served on the bench for over twenty years, becoming one of the most influential jurists in American history.

Born in Kentucky on November 13, 1856, Brandeis graduated from Harvard Law School in 1877. He practiced law in Boston while teaching at both Harvard and the Massachusetts Institute of Technology. Aside from law, his real interest lay in politics. He became active in the political and economic reform movements developing at the turn of the century, with a special interest in life insurance reform. Brandeis early began to develop an aversion to big business and as a result became an advocate of workers' rights, industrial unions, and profit sharing, but continued to maintain a lucrative legal practice. In 1908, he submitted a revolutionary brief to the Supreme Court in the case of *Muller v. Oregon*. This ground-breaking document consisted of only two pages of legal argumentation and ninety-five pages of statistics to support his argument in favor of limiting the working hours of women. The brief represented an early example of the dedication to factual support for legal decisions that would characterize much of Brandeis's later writings for the Supreme Court. In 1910, he acted as counsel for *Collier's Weekly* during the congressional investigation of the accusations of corruption made by Gifford Pinchot against Richard K. Ballinger, President William Howard Taft's secretary of the interior. Later that year he helped to arbitrate the New York City garment workers' strike. In 1914, Brandeis became the leader of the American Zionist movement, a position he would maintain until 1921 and then resume in 1930 until the time of his death. Finally, after establishing himself as a leading progressive, he developed a close relationship with Woodrow Wilson and became a major contributor to the concepts that formed the president's New Freedom program. In 1916, Wilson rewarded his efforts with an appointment to the Supreme Court.

Brandeis became one of the most influential Supreme Court justices of the century. His jurisprudence centered around his antipathy toward giantism in the realms of both business and government. Brandeis bemoaned the "curse of bigness" in the American polity as a destructive force, believing that human fallibility made impossible appropriate management of large concentrations of money and power. This philosophical standpoint lay at the heart of the tension between Brandeis's support for the New Deal and his aversion to big government. He opposed both the National Industrial Recovery Act and the Agricultural Adjustment Act, fearing that both would result in large bureaucracies. As Brandeis declared, after the Court in *Schechter v. United States* (1935) ruled the NRA unconstitutional, "this is the end of this business of centralization"; the court was "not going to let this government centralize everything. It's come to an end." [1] Overall, however, Brandeis supported much of the New Deal legislation such as the Social Security Act, the Wagner Act, and the Fair Labor Standards Act. In addition to his beliefs regarding the evils of giantism, Brandeis was dedicated to the principle of judicial restraint. He advocated avoidance of constitutional questions whenever possible and strictly observed procedural and jurisdictional limitations upon the Court in an effort to restrict its power to the sphere carved out by the Constitution. Brandeis also strove to respect the federal principle by supporting state power, and he continually sought to promote the liberty of individuals, which he felt was tied to their economic independence and their ability to fulfill their own possibilities. His respect for the role of the individual within the democratic regime undergirded his dedication to protecting the civil liberties of all persons.

As a member of the Court, Brandeis was prevented from direct political activism, but he circumvented these constraints by asserting his influence through intermediaries. He developed a relationship with Roosevelt, and, with his close friend Felix Frankfurter, recommended key individuals who shared his liberal perspective for various government positions within the president's ever-expanding administration. This extrajudicial activity was the subject of much public scrutiny, despite the fact that such actions on the part of Supreme Court justices were not uncommon throughout American history. His relationship with FDR became strained during the latter's attempt to pack the Court in 1937, an action that Brandeis vehemently opposed. Eventually, he regained respect for the president, and the day before he died told Frankfurter that he considered Roosevelt not only to be a greater president than Jefferson but also to have approached Lincoln in stature. Brandeis retired from the Supreme Court on February 13, 1939, at the age of eighty-three; he died two years later, on October 5, 1941.

Benjamin Victor Cohen (1894–1983)

Benjamin Cohen, a young lawyer, came to Washington in 1933 during the One Hundred Days to serve in the new administration of Franklin Roosevelt. He quickly became one of the president's most trusted advisors and legislative draftsmen and acted in those capacities throughout the entire period of the New Deal.

Born on September 23, 1894, Cohen earned a Ph.D. in economics from the University of Chicago, in 1914 and one year later received his J.D. from the University of Chicago Law School. In 1916, he earned a. degree from Harvard Law School also, where he met Felix Frankfurter. After finishing school, Cohen worked in New York under Judge Julian Mack of the federal circuit court. During World War I, he served as an attorney for the U.S. Shipping Board and came into contact with Louis Brandeis. Beginning in 1919, Cohen spent two years working as counsel for the American Zionists, during which he participated in the negotiations concerning the Palestine Mandate at the Paris Peace Conference. He worked in private practice from 1921 until 1933, but remained active in public affairs. He voluntarily served as counsel for the National Consumers League.

Cohen was a soft-spoken, religious man, as well as a brilliant attorney whose area of expertise was property law, especially corporate reorganization. He became involved with the New Deal in 1933 when Frankfurter called on him to help draft the Securities Act. It was at this time that Cohen met Thomas G. Corcoran. The two men grew to be close friends, and they soon became known as the "Brain Twins" and the "Gold Dust Twins." Their personalities were nearly polar opposites, and they complemented each other well. Corcoran and Cohen shared an eagerness for reform, as well as a cynical attitude concerning the ability of corporations to regulate themselves. They worked together as FDR's speechwriters, as well as draftsmen for a host of New Deal measures, including the Securities and Exchange Act of 1934, the Rural Electrification Act of 1935, the Public Utility Holding Company Act of 1935, and the Fair Labor Standards Act of 1938.

Throughout the 1930s, Cohen served in various capacities in the Interior Department. In 1941, he left the Department of the Interior to work in England under Ambassador John Winant and thereafter became increasingly involved in foreign affairs.

Cohen continued in governmental service for several years after World War II before returning to private practice. In 1945, he became general counsel of the State Department, a post he held until 1947. From 1947 until 1952, he was a member of the U.S. delegation to the United Nations General Assembly and represented the United States on the United Nations Disarmament Commission in 1952. He died on August 15, 1983.

Thomas Gardiner Corcoran (1900–1981)

Thomas Corcoran was born on December 29, 1900. A former law student and star pupil of Felix Frankfurter at Harvard, "Tommy the Cork" was one of several young lawyers in Roosevelt's inner circle of advisors nicknamed "Frankfurter's happy hot dogs." Corcoran was a charming, witty, energetic Irishman who enjoyed singing and playing the accordion, but was also a brilliant legislative draftsman dedicated to serving the public good. Corcoran, like Brandeis, had a critical attitude toward corporate management and held firmly to a belief in free competition.

Together with his close friend, Benjamin V. Cohen, Corcoran helped to draft and defend before Congress the Securities and Exchange Act of 1934, the Public Utility Holding Company Act of 1935, and the Wealth Tax Act of 1935. From 1936 until 1940, he also contributed to a number of FDR's speeches, coining the phrase "rendezvous with destiny." Corcoran was often entangled in controversy, including the Passamaquoddy Dam incident in which Representative Ralph Owen Brewster of Maine accused Corcoran of threatening to cut off funding for the dam if he failed to vote in favor of the administration's holding-company bill. Corcoran supported Roosevelt in his efforts to pack the Supreme Court in 1937 and was also involved in the "purge" of 1938 in which Roosevelt attempted to unseat conservative Democrats who opposed the New Deal during the primary elections of that year. Corcoran helped to manage Roosevelt's third-term election campaign, but by 1940, he had become such a controversial figure that FDR phased him out of the White House. In 1941, he returned to private practice, although he did remain active in politics as an advisor until his death on December 6, 1981.

Fr. Charles Edward Coughlin (1891–1979)

Followers might have praised Fr. Coughlin, the "Radio Messiah," but he was increasingly denounced as a demagogue in his own time. Although his media career ended in disgrace amid accusations of anti-Semitism, in his early years he secured the loyalty of millions of Americans. His personal charisma and his appreciation for the power of mass media allowed him to disseminate his ideas over the airwaves to eager listeners from 1926 until 1942. Born in Hamilton, Ontario, on October 25, 1891, Charles Edward Coughlin studied for the priesthood in Toronto, settling in Royal Oak, Michigan, in 1926. His broadcasts began as an effort to attract support for his parish, the Shrine of the Little Flower, which was experiencing financial difficulty. His early radio sermons were mainly noncontroversial. Often they were simply catechism classes for children. However, as the economy began to take a downward turn, Fr. Coughlin began to preach increasingly contentiously on political subjects. His speeches wedded politics and religion, a powerful and persuasive combination that attracted the interest of a huge audience.

Coughlin considered himself to be a defender of tradition and the foe of radicalism. He adamantly denounced communism, yet he also rebuked capitalists and "international financiers," upon whom he laid blame for the stock market crash. Coughlin bitterly criticized Hoover and in 1932 indirectly supported Roosevelt and his platform in the election, later bragging that he had been instrumental in Herbert Hoover's removal from the White House. In terms of policy, he blamed the nation's troubles on the scarcity of money and claimed that this was an artificial condition that could be ameliorated by the nationalization of banks. He also advocated the revaluation of gold and a silver-backed currency.

After FDR took office, Fr. Coughlin endeavored to play a part in his administration, but he ended up making a nuisance of himself by frequently dropping in at the White House and offering unsolicited advice. By this time, Fr. Coughlin's media empire included his national weekly paper, *Social Justice*, and a network of over thirty radio stations that broadcast his weekly *Golden Hour of the Shrine of the Little Flower.* Gradually Coughlin's ambition to play an independent political role as well as, perhaps, his conviction that the New Deal's reformism would prove inadequate, led him to become more critical of Roosevelt and his policies. The president tried to avoid a break with Coughlin as long as possible, understanding the priest's popularity among voters, though he increasingly regarded him as arrogant and potentially dangerous. By 1935, Coughlin's criticisms of the New Deal became severe, and he created a grassroots interest group to mobilize support for the legislation that he favored.

Unfortunately for Coughlin, his Union for Social Justice lacked organization and began to flounder. In 1936, he chose to abandon it in favor of establishing a new third party, the Union Party. The party nominated William Lemke of North Dakota to run in the presidential election of 1936, and Coughlin pledged that he would raise 9 million votes in support of his candidate, or retire from political life. When Lemke failed to secure even one million votes, Fr. Coughlin tearfully kept his promise and left the air waves. His retirement was short-lived, however, and he returned to radio in 1937. After his return, Fr. Coughlin lacked the popularity that he had once enjoyed. His sermons became increasingly anti-Semitic, and his criticisms of the president grew more vitriolic. He condemned the New Deal as a communist conspiracy and began to express admiration for both Hitler and Mussolini. In 1940, his radio show was canceled, and in 1942, his newspaper was banned from the mail. Later that year, his bishop ordered Coughlin to cease his political activities. The priest submitted to this order and left the national spotlight. He performed the duties of a parish priest in Royal Oak until his retirement in 1966. He died on October 27, 1979.

Felix Frankfurter (1882–1965)

Born on November 15, 1892, Felix Frankfurter was an extraordinarily influential professor at Harvard Law School from 1914 until 1939, when President Roosevelt appointed him to the Supreme Court, where he remained for over two decades. A friend of FDR's from the time of their service together in Washington during World War I, Frankfurter was, during the years of Roosevelt's governorship of New York and presidency, one of his closest advisors.

Frankfurter joined the Harvard Law faculty in 1914 after substantial government service in the Justice and War Departments as an assistant to Henry Stimson. During World War I, he served as chairman of the War Labor Policies Board and as counsel to the Mediation Commission, a body charged with resolving labor disputes. During his service in the wartime Wilson administration, Frankfurter earned a reputation among conservatives as a dangerous liberal, even a radical, because of reports he made, at the president's request, into the circumstances surrounding two nationally known violent episodes in labor-capital relations, the copper strike at Bisbee, Arizona, and the San Francisco bombing for which labor organizers Tom Mooney and Warren Billings were tried for murder. Conservatives accused Frankfurter in both cases of taking the part of seditious radicals, as they did a few years later, during the 1920s, when he led the long struggle to overturn the conviction of two anarchists, Nicola Sacco and Bartolomeo Vanzetti, both of whom liberal opinion believed had been falsely charged of murder because of their political beliefs and activities.

Frankfurter and Roosevelt became friends in 1917 when the latter was assistant secretary of the Navy. When he became governor of New York in 1929, and president in 1933, Roosevelt turned to Frankfurter, a leader of liberal opinion on issues ranging from regulation of business to the organizational rights of labor, for advice on policy and for recommendations concerning appointments. In March 1933, FDR offered Frankfurter the position of solicitor general, which he turned down. However, at Roosevelt's request Frankfurter sent to Washington a steady stream of the brightest young lawyers recently graduated from Harvard to fill essential posts in the New Deal agencies and himself served continually as an unofficial but very influential advisor to the president. The young lawyers appointed through Frankfurter became known as the "happy hot dogs," and included New Deal luminaries such as Benjamin V. Cohen, Dean Acheson, Alger Hiss, David Lilienthal, Nathan Margold, and Thomas G. Corcoran. In addition to supplying Roosevelt with bright, young talent, Frankfurter also helped to shape several pieces of New Deal legislation, including the Securities Act of 1933 and the Public Utility Holding Company Act of 1935.

Although not publicly, Frankfurter supported Roosevelt during the president's struggle over his ill-fated plan to pack the Supreme Court in 1937. In 1939, Roosevelt appointed him to the Court, where he served until 1962. On the bench, he followed closely in the footsteps of his friend and fellow justice, Louis D. Brandeis. Like Brandeis, Frankfurter espoused the notion of judicial restraint. Many commentators have observed that Frankfurter's career as a Supreme Court justice was not as memorable as his earlier career, in the sense that, though his appointment finalized the movement of the Court toward a broad acceptance of the kind of economic regulation the New Deal had introduced, he did not usually support those on the Court working to advance its position in the area of civil liberties and rights and tended to defend the rights of the states against federal encroachment. He did, however, cooperate with Chief Justice Earl Warren in creating a majority in *Brown v. Board of Education*, the case that required desegregation of public schools. Frankfurter died three years after his retirement from the Court, on February 22, 1965.

John Nance Garner (1868–1967)

John Nance Garner was one of the most important leaders of the Democratic Party in Congress for over twenty years, becoming the party's minority leader in the House during the 1920s and achieving the speakership in 1930. In 1932 and 1936, he ran with Franklin D. Roosevelt as the party's vice-presidential candidate but in the New Deal's later years did not support many of the president's proposals.

Born in Blossom Prairie, Texas, on November 22, 1868, Garner, after admission to the bar, practiced law in Uvalde, Texas, while editing a local newspaper for several years and engaging in business dealings that gave him control of two local banks. In 1898, he was elected to the Texas House of Representatives, where he served two terms, and in 1902, was elected as a Democrat to the U.S. House of Representatives. As a congressman, Garner developed his skills in debate and parliamentary procedure and earned a reputation as a stubborn and persuasive adversary who was fiercely loyal to his home state of Texas, the South, and the Democratic Party. He preached economy in government spending, except where his own district was involved, in this case often successfully securing large appropriations.

Fond of playing poker and drinking whiskey, Garner was usually affable and had a talent for making friends among his fellow congressmen; he could also be contentious and prickly, which accounted in part for his nickname "Cactus Jack." During his early career in the House, he was, though a moderate and pragmatic legislator, attuned to the movement for progressive reform that was influencing elements within both the major political parties. During the Republican era of Theodore Roosevelt and William Howard Taft, he supported a graduated income tax, tariff reduction, and other measures progressives battled to enact, and was a leader during the presidency of Woodrow Wilson when newly elected Democratic majorities in both houses of Congress enacted a sweeping series of reforms under the banner of the New Freedom.

For over a decade following the elections of 1918, the Democrats were returned to minority status in Congress. Garner continued to serve as one of the major Democratic leaders in the House. In 1928, he was elected House minority leader and became the Speaker of the House when the Democrats became the majority after the elections of 1930. At the onset of the Great Depression, Garner supported most of Hoover's ideas for salvaging the American economy. In 1932, he at first backed Hoover's recovery plan that included creation of the Reconstruction Finance Corporation and enactment of a sales tax to balance the budget. However, hoping to secure the Democratic presidential nomination, Garner began to distance himself from Hoover and to press for more spending on relief and public works. At the Democratic convention, after realizing he was unlikely to win the nomination and fearing a deadlock, Garner withdrew and threw his support to Franklin Roosevelt, securing the latter's victory and receiving for himself the nomination for vice-president instead.

Although Garner played a considerable role in helping New Deal legislation to pass through Congress during his first term, he grew continually more critical of the New Deal's large expenditures and socially liberal principles. Though for the most part he supported the New Deal's proposals regarding regulation of big business, he was, by the standards of the late New Deal, a conservative who opposed the welfare state, administrative centralization, and deficit spending. As in the case of most previous vice-presidents, Garner proved to be rather inactive and once described his office as "not worth a pitcher of warm spit." After 1936, Roosevelt rarely consulted Garner, knowing that his vice-president opposed his court-packing plan and the renewal of heavy relief spending in 1938. In 1938, Garner also took issue with the president's attempt to purge a number of conservative Democrats from the party during the 1938 congressional elections. Finally, after he became aware that Garner disapproved of his attempt to gain a third term as president, FDR dropped him from his ticket and replaced him with Henry A. Wallace. Garner announced his own candidacy for the upcoming presidential election, but was unsuccessful.

In 1941, Garner left political life in order to return to Texas. Bitter over the unhappy end to his political career that resulted from his opposition to Roosevelt, Garner destroyed all of his personal papers from his many years as a Democratic leader, leaving behind only scrapbooks of newspaper clippings. He felt, as he later told a reporter from the *New York Times*, that his decision to leave his influential position as speaker of the house in 1932 in exchange for the less consequential vice-presidency had been the worst mistake of his life. Despite this sour end to his political life, he amassed a fortune through banking, real estate, and ranching before he died at the age of ninety-nine on November 7, 1867.

Herbert Clark Hoover (1874–1964)

Herbert Hoover's term as president began in March 1929, on the brink of the depression. Hoover had earned the people's confidence through his successes on the nation's behalf over the previous fifteen years, but, unable to reverse the economic downturn that engulfed America during his presidency, he left office in March 1933 regarded almost universally as a failure.

Born in West Branch, Iowa, of Quaker parents, on August 10, 1874, Hoover was orphaned at an early age and sent to be schooled by his uncle in Oregon. He made his own way in the world through brains and determination. He worked his way through Stanford University and graduated as a mining engineer. As a London-based mining consultant with interests around the world, Hoover had achieved wealth and status by the time World War I broke out in 1914. The war offered him the opportunity for the public service that his sense of obligation, instilled by his Quaker mother, and his desire for recognition disposed him to seek. In 1914, he answered the call of the Allied governments to direct the effort to get aid to the starving, German-occupied Belgians. In 1917, he accepted the challenge of America's wartime leader, the Democratic president, Woodrow Wilson, to come back to the United States to head the Food Administration, the wartime agency set up to maximize and control American agricultural output.

Hoover emerged from the war as one of the best known and most widely admired public figures of the day. His run for the Republican presidential nomination in 1920 failed, however, for the conservatives who dominated the party regarded Hoover as too independent, unpredictable, and unmanageable. Warren Harding, who won the Republican nomination and the election, however, recognized Hoover's usefulness and appointed him secretary of commerce. Hoover promptly turned that office into one of the most important Cabinet posts of the decade, endeavoring meanwhile to guide the policies of Harding and his successor, Calvin Coolidge, in many other areas as well.

Hoover was, in his own way, a progressive, not a conservative in the mold of Harding and Coolidge. Government's role, he believed, was to energize the people, to provide the scientific and economic knowledge and the stimulus that would enable them, through professional and other organizations, to solve social and economic problems themselves. The best known of Hoover's efforts to apply this method during the 1920s was his department's promotion of trade associations. Through such practices as standardization of product sizes and quality, trade associations could promote industrial efficiency and productivity and a rising standard of living for all, and by providing accurate information on an industry's prices and market conditions they could persuade businessmen to plan cooperatively to avoid economic booms and busts.

Elected president in 1928 on the basis of his reputation as the nation's leading trouble-shooter, Hoover soon faced the onset of the Great Depression. He pursued activist policies from the beginning of the depression, trying to prevent the market collapse from dampening business activity. His goal was to prevent erosion of spending, relying on the cooperation of businessmen to maintain wage rates and investment expenditures, and urging Congress and the states to maintain government spending.

Faced in the last months of 1931 with rapidly rising unemployment, a decline in agricultural prices that threatened farmers with ruin, and a banking system tottering on the brink of collapse, Hoover embarked on a new strategy, demanding from Congress a far-reaching recovery program. This program relied on balancing the budget, now severely out of balance because of falling government revenues, but at the same time initiating large-scale spending through a new agency, the Reconstruction Finance Corporation, to support the banking system. The aim was to arrest the trend toward collapse of the entire economic system, restore business confidence, and thus restart the economy. Hoover resisted strongly, however, adding another policy that now had wide support, that is, providing federal relief funds for the unemployed. Ultimately, however, he reached a compromise on relief with the now Democrat-controlled Congress.

Reviled by many, Hoover left the presidency discouraged and defeated. Deeply distrustful of Franklin Roosevelt, Hoover bitterly opposed much of the New Deal, asserting that the National Recovery Administration was tantamount to fascism. In the late 1930s, Hoover also opposed Roosevelt's foreign policy, playing a major role during 1940 in the America First movement that argued for a "Fortress America," and noninvolvement in the new European war. After World War II, Hoover's reputation was rehabilitated somewhat when President Harry Truman appointed him to head the commission whose work led to the Reorganization Act of 1949, a measure that greatly improved the federal bureaucracy's efficiency. He died on October 20, 1964.

John Edgar Hoover (1895–1972)

J. Edgar Hoover was director of the Federal Bureau of Investigation for forty-eight years, from 1924 until his death in 1972, an extraordinary achievement for a federal officeholder. His long tenure under so many successive presidents is attributable to the efficiency he imparted to his agency, his skillful use of publicity, and, as some commentators believe, his accumulation of information about the political figures he served.

John Edgar Hoover was born on January 1, 1895, in Washington, D.C. In 1924, when he was twenty-nine years old, J. Edgar Hoover replaced William J. Burns as director of the agency then known as the Bureau of Investigation. At that time the agency's role was under strict scrutiny by the American public. Hoover immediately set out to reform the Bureau's image, establishing strict rules for the personal behavior of his agents, prohibiting the consumption of alcohol, and establishing guidelines for dress and etiquette. Hoover earned a reputation for being highly idiosyncratic and authoritarian, but his administrative genius and talent for public relations allowed him to mold the Bureau into an efficient and conservative organization of which he was supreme ruler. When Roosevelt assumed office in 1933, Hoover feared that he would be replaced because he had been a Republican appointee.

Roosevelt's new attorney general, Homer Cummings, however, asked Hoover to remain at the helm of the Bureau. Together with Cummings, Hoover expanded the role of the FBI into areas of law enforcement that had previously been controlled by state and local governments. This increase in federal jurisdiction dovetailed quite well with the centralization that characterized the New Deal, and Roosevelt enthusiastically encouraged the federalization of the war against crime. He allowed Hoover to continue to shape the FBI into a powerful, hierarchical agency that enjoyed almost complete autonomy. In the 1930s, the Bureau concentrated on battling organized crime, and with the help of the media, it made legendary heroes out of Hoover and his G-men as they battled "Public Enemies" such as John Dillinger and Charles "Pretty Boy" Floyd.

Beginning in 1936, Hoover began to shift the focus of his energies to the surveillance and investigation of the activities of communists and Nazi-like groups within the United States, an expansion secretly authorized by the president. Hoover often utilized controversial methods of gathering information, such as wiretapping. Roosevelt sanctioned Hoover's efforts and often relied upon his resources for his own purposes, both official and private. During World War II, Hoover was responsible for the prevention of enemy espionage and sabotage, as well as the coordination of the domestic intelligence activities of all federal agencies. Although Hoover ruled supreme over domestic matters, his efforts to secure a role for the FBI in overseas intelligence were continually thwarted. By the end of the war, it was clear that this was one area that Hoover would never dominate.

Nevertheless, Hoover's bureaucratic genius and his ability, together with others who used the issue, to convince politicians and the public, during the 1940s and 1950s, that the FBI was America's bulwark against communist subversion and criminal syndicates, allowed him to achieve the longest reign of power of any official in American history. Many observers believe Hoover seriously overreached the boundaries of the FBI's appropriate role during the 1960s when he used the agency to investigate and engage in the surveillance, not only of radical organizations that might conceivably have approached illegality or posed a threat to security, but also of the most substantial civil rights leaders such as Martin Luther King. He died on May 2, 1972.

Harry Lloyd Hopkins (1890–1946)

Beginning his career as a social worker in New York, Harry Hopkins became Franklin Roosevelt's "Minister of Relief" at the outset of the New Deal and continued in that capacity during the 1930s until his appointment as secretary of commerce in 1938. During World War II, he was appointed as the lend-lease administrator, and he served the president on several crucial diplomatic missions.

Harry Hopkins was born in Iowa on August 17, 1890, and graduated from Grinnell College in 1912. Immediately afterward he went to New York and began a career in public service that would remain the focus of his energies until his death. He became a social worker for the Association for Improving the Condition of the Poor in New York, and in the early 1920s became director of the New York Tuberculosis Association. In 1931, Governor Roosevelt named him deputy chairman of the Temporary Emergency Relief Administration of New York. Shortly after FDR's inauguration as president in 1933, he appointed Hopkins as the chief administrator of the

Federal Emergency Relief Administration (FERA) created by Congress on May 12, which provided relief grants to be administered by the states. Passionately dedicated to serving the needs of the poor and the unemployed, Hopkins lobbied Roosevelt, as the winter of 1933–1934 approached, to establish the Civil Works Administration, a hastily created, federally administered, and very extensive work relief program. In 1935, after securing a large relief appropriation from Congress, Roosevelt appointed Hopkins to head the Works Progress Administration, the New Deal's agency for giving employment on a broad scale to those without jobs. The WPA proved to be one of the most popular of the New Deal's programs and employed millions of Americans during its existence.

In 1936, Hopkins began to suffer from a chronic digestive disorder that frequently interfered with his work and sapped his energy and had to undergo surgery in 1937. Though bedridden during much of the year, he was named secretary of commerce in 1938. By 1940, Hopkins had become one of FDR's most trusted advisors, and during that year he moved into the White House with his daughter, Diane (his second wife, Barbara Duncan, had died in 1937). During this time Hopkins shifted his focus from domestic to foreign affairs. In January 1941, Roosevelt sent him to London as his personal representative in order to assess more accurately the degree of assistance that Great Britain required from the United States. After Congress passed the Lend-Lease Act in March of that same year, Roosevelt appointed Hopkins to head the agency it created to furnish aid to Great Britain. Hopkins returned to London and then traveled on to Moscow to determine how the United States could be of help to the Soviet Union in its attempts to resist the German invasion that had begun in June, a visit that led to the furnishing of lend-lease aid to that nation as well.

During America's participation in World War II, Hopkins served in several capacities in Washington. He helped to mobilize industry, was a key Roosevelt advisor, and attended nearly all the major wartime conferences held between the American president and Churchill and Stalin. After Roosevelt's death, Hopkins served one more final mission under Truman, which entailed returning to Moscow to meet with Stalin in order to discuss questions concerning Poland, Germany, and Japan, as well as voting rights in the United Nations. He then left government service and returned to New York. In September 1945, Truman presented Hopkins with the Distinguished Service Medal. In poor health for many years, his strength now failed, and he died early the next year, on January 29, 1946.

Harold LeClair Ickes (1874–1952)

Harold Ickes, known as "honest Harold" to cynical reporters because of his attitude that there were few incorruptible men in Washington other than himself, was a progressive Republican with little background in national politics who, appointed by President Roosevelt in 1933 to head the Interior Department, was responsible for the spending of the Public Works Administration throughout the New Deal. Devoted to FDR and his reforms, Ickes became one of the most liberal and belligerent partisans of the New Deal and one of the president's most trusted lieutenants.

Born on March 15, 1874, Ickes received his B.A. from the University of Chicago in 1897, after which he worked as a journalist for the *Chicago Chronicle* and the *Chicago Tribune*. Eventually he returned to the University of Chicago to study law, receiving his J.D. in 1907. Ickes spent twenty-five years practicing law in private firms, but he continued to nurture his interest in politics by working for various campaigns, usually for independent candidates—most often progressives. In 1932, he organized the Progressive Republican League for Roosevelt, and, in February 1933, Roosevelt and Ickes met for the first time. FDR was impressed with him and, wishing to attract the support of independent Republicans such as Ickes, offered him the Interior Department.

As secretary of the interior, Ickes reorganized the department and dedicated it to the conservation of America's natural resources. Although Ickes's sharp tongue earned him many enemies, he was one of Roosevelt's most active and able Cabinet members. During his years at Interior, he wore a variety of hats. He headed the Public Works Administration, the New Deal's most important agency for providing work relief through construction projects. In this capacity he managed over $6 billion in construction projects, as well as the direction of the first federal housing program. He also acted as administrator of the "fair competition code" for the oil industry under the National Industrial Recovery Act.

Although Ickes was reputed to be one of the most vitriolic, ego-driven men in Washington, he was also unflaggingly energetic and vehemently opposed to corruption in government. He was an able administrator and was deeply loyal to both the president and to the causes that he held dear, such as conservation, the welfare of native Americans, civil liberties, and minority rights. Often Ickes was willing to act as a spokesman on these contentious issues when the president could not. He also had a particular interest in developing water-powered electricity and argued for the public ownership of facilities for generating electrical power. Ickes served as secretary of the interior until the very end of the Roosevelt period and continued under President Truman until he resigned after a dispute. In addition to his other responsibilities, Ickes also served on a variety of committees, including the National Resources Committee, during his years in the Cabinet. Upon his retirement, Ickes moved to a farm in Maryland, commuting frequently to a Washington office where he penned a column for the *New York Post* entitled "Man to Man" and wrote for a number of journals. He remained active in politics until his death on February 3, 1952, working for various campaigns and counseling public leaders.

Hugh Samuel Johnson (1882–1942)

Hugh Johnson played a starring, though relatively brief, role in the New Deal, serving as administrator of the National Recovery Administration during the critical period in 1933–1934 when the New Deal was desperately trying to ameliorate America's staggering unemployment problem. For a time he continued as a Roosevelt advisor, but then he gradually joined the New Deal's opposition.

Born in Kansas on August 5, 1882, Johnson spent his youth on the frontier in Alva, Oklahoma. At the age of sixteen, he attempted to run away and volunteer during the Spanish-American War. His attempt failed, but as a result his father sent him to West Point. He graduated in 1903 as a cavalry lieutenant and served in Texas, California, the Philippines, Arizona, and Mexico. During World War I, he helped to create the Draft Act and also served as the director of the Army's new Purchase and Supply Branch. In this capacity he developed links between the War Industries Board and military supply agencies and rose to the position of brigadier general. In 1919, Johnson left the military and became general counsel for the Moline Plow Company. Soon he was promoted to chairman of the board, but in 1927, he left the company to work for the fabled financier, Bernard Baruch. In 1932, Baruch offered Johnson's services to Franklin Roosevelt and Johnson became a peripheral member of the Brain Trust, the circle of advisors, with Raymond Moley, Rexford Tugwell, and Adolf A. Berle at its core, that advised the presidential candidate before and after he secured the Democratic nomination.

In 1933, Johnson assisted in the drafting of the National Industrial Recovery Act and was named administrator of the NRA by Roosevelt. Both Johnson and the NRA, however, proved to be disappointments for the president. Johnson espoused a vision of the NRA as an agency that could, through industry codes, raise prices sufficiently to establish decent wages for labor, but not so much as to raise prices unduly or to restrict production. Johnson was a talented writer and possessed a seemingly limitless amount of energy, yet his temperament was mercurial and explosive and he periodically drank excessively. He often conflicted with the Consumer's Advisory Board within the NRA, and his loud, aggressive personality eventually disintegrated into instability and rendered him incapable of developing a coherent policy for the recovery agency. In 1934, "Old Iron Pants" resigned from his position with the NRA, and Roosevelt quickly replaced him with an administrative board.

After leaving the agency, Johnson worked as head of the Works Progress Administration's operations in New York City, after which he chose to pursue a career as an author, penning his memoirs and writing a syndicated column called "Hugh Johnson Says." As the decade wore on, Johnson became increasingly critical of Roosevelt and his administration. He opposed the direction that the later New Deal had taken, as well as FDR's court-packing plan and American involvement in Europe. By 1940, Johnson was actively opposing Roosevelt and campaigned during the presidential election that year for Wendell Wilkie. He died shortly afterward, a victim of pneumonia on April 15, 1942.

John Llewellyn Lewis (1880–1969)

John L. Lewis was president of the United Mine Workers (UMW) for forty years, beginning in 1920. During the New Deal, Lewis was the single most important force behind the rise of industrial unions, the formation of the Congress of Industrial Organizations, and the vastly increased strength of organized labor that developed by the close of the 1930s.

Born in Iowa on February 12, 1880, at age seventeen Lewis began working as a coal miner with his father and gradually emerged as a leader of the coal miners' union, the UMW. By 1919, he was serving as the UMW's acting president. His election as president in 1920 came on the cusp of a trying period in mining history. After World War I, miners' wages fell and the unions suffered due to a postwar drop in coal consumption, as well as competition from nonunionized mines. The onset of the Great Depression exacerbated these problems, and Lewis turned to coal stabilization legislation as a remedy. In 1933, he became a member of the Labor Advisory Board of the National Recovery Administration. Although Lewis was a Republican, his relationship with Roosevelt during the president's first term was a congenial one.

In 1934, Lewis was elected to the American Federation of Labor (AFL) Executive Council, where he pushed for union expansion in the steel and automobile industries. Dissatisfied with the AFL's tendency to ignore unskilled workers through its preference for craft unionism, in 1935 Lewis formed the Committee for Industrial Organization. After the AFL leadership suspended the Committee, its name was changed in 1938 to the Congress of Industrial Organizations (CIO), and the constituent unions elected Lewis as president. As the CIO's leader, Lewis pioneered new organizational and bargaining tactics, such as the sit-down strikes that he used in labor's confrontation with General Motors and with the steel companies in 1936–1937. FDR attempted to remain neutral throughout the strikes, much to the dismay of Lewis, who believed the president had betrayed labor's interests. Their relationship grew acrimonious during FDR's second term, and in the 1940 presidential election Lewis spoke against him.

During America's participation in World War II, Lewis continued to press for higher wages and benefits for the coal miners and, despite the no-strike pledge that he, like all the major labor leaders, had taken earlier, led several wartime strikes that resulted, in 1943, in a government threat to draft strikers and enactment of the Smith-Connally Act, a measure that tightened government restrictions on unions. In 1946, while the government was operating the mines, he staged a walkout that resulted in charges of civil and criminal contempt and the levying of very heavy fines on the UMW.

During the 1950s and 1960s, the coal-mining industry, faced with mounting competition from oil, suffered a steep decline. Lewis, who now ruled the union with an authoritarian style, displayed little militancy during the 1950s, instead seeking to cooperate with the mine owners. He retired in 1960 in favor of W. A. Boyle. Lewis remained on the board that governed the union's investments but did nothing to interfere with Boyle's unwise handling of union funds that resulted in cuts in benefits for the members. Despite this decline in the quality of his leadership, Lewis retains his reputation as a towering figure in the history of the struggle of workers to secure the right of organization. He died on June 11, 1969.

Huey Pierce Long (1893–1935)

Huey Long entered the U.S. Senate in 1932 and, after initially backing Franklin Roosevelt, turned against him and the New Deal and created his own national following with his plan for radical redistribution of income and wealth. A buffoon to his enemies, a charismatic savior to his followers, Long was the most colorful and able of those who challenged FDR's popularity during the middle years of the 1930s.

Born on August 30, 1893, Long attended the University of Oklahoma briefly and for a few months studied law at Tulane University, but he never received a degree. He was nevertheless admitted to the Louisiana bar in 1915, practiced law for several years, and was elected to the Louisiana Public Service Commission in 1921. As a member, and then chairman, of the commission, Long championed the welfare of the people against the entrenched and heretofore well-protected interests of the state's oil companies and public utilities. In 1928, Long was elected governor of Louisiana and began one of the most controversial administrations in the state's history. Known as the "Kingfish," Long created a vast political machine that concentrated almost all state power in his hands. In 1929, an attempt was made to remove Long from power, but his supporters were able to defeat the impeachment resolution before a trial could be held. Despite the controversy surrounding his governorship, Long was responsible for vast public works projects, which included major additions to the state's paved roads, a new state capitol, and a new medical school. He also established adult night schools, a free textbook program for schoolchildren, increased funding for state schools, and reforms of the state's tax code.

In 1930, Long was elected to the U.S. Senate, but refused to resign as governor and surrender the office to Paul Cyr, the man who would have succeeded him. He retained the gubernatorial office until 1932, until he could secure the election of O. K. Allen, a puppet he could readily control. Entering the Senate in 1932, Long was an outspoken critic of the Hoover administration. That year he endorsed FDR's presidential candidacy and in 1933 initially supported many of the measures of the First New Deal. It was not long, however, before Long's ambition to sit in the White House himself, and his disgust with what he regarded as Roosevelt's timidity in dealing with the misery the depression was causing, led him into outspoken criticism of FDR and his legislative leaders in the Senate.

During 1934, Long rapidly emerged into nation prominence with his Share Our Wealth plan. The plan, and the organization of the same name he formed to promote it, offered radical redistribution of wealth as the panacea for America's depression ills. Share Our Wealth relied on confiscatory income taxes and inheritance taxes that took most of the estates of the wealthy. Families that possessed little would receive a "homestead"; a payment of $4,000 to $5,000 that would enable them to buy a home, a car, and a radio; and would also receive an annual income of $2,000 to $3,000. The Long Plan promised limited hours and a minimum wage to laborers, as well as pension benefits to the elderly, a moratorium on debts, free education through college for all children, and immediate payment of veterans' bonuses for those who had served in World War I.

Americans enthusiastically joined Share Our Wealth clubs, and the movement had gained so much momentum by 1935 that Democrats began to consider Long as a serious rival. Long did indicate that he might run himself or back another third party candidate in 1936 and showed signs of teaming up with the two other popular movements, those of Fr. Charles Coughlin and Dr. Francis Townsend, that were also popularizing economic nostrums and bitterly criticizing the New Deal. Roosevelt referred to Long as being dangerous and attempted, unsuccessfully, to bring him to trial for income tax evasion. Roosevelt publicly ignored Long, but the Second New Deal was influenced by his prescriptions.

Back in Louisiana, Long remained a controversial figure. In September 1935, after the close of the congressional session, Long returned to Baton Rouge to attend a special session of the state legislature. There, as he strode rapidly down the corridor of the state house, he was shot by Carl Austin Weiss, the son-in-law of one of Long's political enemies. Weiss was killed immediately by Long's bodyguards. Though it appears he could have been saved by more competent medical treatment, the Kingfish died of his wounds shortly afterward, on September 10, 1935.

Raymond Moley (1886–1975)

Raymond Moley was the central figure in the Brain Trust, the small group that helped Franklin D. Roosevelt develop ideas, speeches, and strategies during 1932 when he sought the presidency and during the early New Deal. Later, like many others who enthusiastically supported and assisted Roosevelt during the first phase of the New Deal, Moley became disenchanted and by the later years of the 1930s had become a severe critic.

As a young man in Ohio, where he was born on September 27, 1886, Moley was deeply impressed by the ideas of the reformers popular in the Midwest of his day. He greatly admired his party's leader and three-time presidential candidate, William Jennings Bryan, and the achievements and ideas of Tom Johnson, the reform mayor of Cleveland. Like Johnson, he felt Henry George, author of the widely studied *Progress and Poverty*, originator of the single-tax theory, and advocate of regulation of public utilities, was the great thinker of the age.

Moley earned a doctorate in political science from Columbia University in 1918, with the famous historian, Charles A. Beard, as his mentor. Moley rapidly developed a national reputation as an expert on the administration of justice and secured a position at Columbia. He met Roosevelt as a result of his work as research director for the New York State Crime Commission during the later 1920s. Early in 1932, Moley offered his talents to Roosevelt as advisor and speechwriter for the campaign FDR was about to initiate for the Democratic presidential nomination. Moley in turn recruited other academics who became the circle known as the Brain Trust. Moley pinned the cause of the depression on the decline of agricultural commodity prices that began in 1921 and was familiar with the range of reforms that economists and other commentators on current affairs were proposing to recover prosperity. He was a gifted writer and coiner of memorable phrases. He first coined the phrase "New Deal" in a memorandum early in 1932 in which he argued for a federal program that included banking reform, including the separation of commercial and investment banking; increased income as well as corporate taxes; and the restoration of wages and commodities prices.

After the election Moley helped Roosevelt select his Cabinet, and FDR appointed him assistant secretary of state. Moley's relationship with FDR, however, became strained later in 1933. Moley had consistently urged FDR to follow a nationalist policy, to abandon the gold standard, thus insulating the value of the American dollar from the effect of international monetary fluctuation, in order to seek inflation of commodity prices at home. In June 1933, however, at the London Economic Conference that had been called to discuss international financial and trade relations, Moley uncharacteristically entered discussions that appeared to be leading to an international monetary stabilization agreement. Learning of this Roosevelt sent his "bombshell" message to London, asserting that America would retain its freedom of action in monetary matters and undercutting Moley. Moley's ego was nearly as expansive as Roosevelt's, and he was left hurt and embarrassed by the episode. Partly for this reason, partly because a lucrative opportunity to start a new magazine with the aid of wealthy backers had arisen, Moley left the administration later in 1933. He continued to serve intermittently for several more years as speechwriter and advisor, but found himself increasingly uncomfortable with the direction the New Deal took in 1935 and afterward. Moley was deeply committed to the New Deal represented by the National Recovery Administration and suspicious of the social reformism and the antibusiness attitude of the Second New Deal. He also came to detect what he thought was Roosevelt's tendency to reach for excessive presidential power. He broke entirely with FDR and the New Deal in 1936.

In the later 1930s, Moley's writings, as editor of *Newsweek*, with which his new journal, *Today*, had merged, and in his brilliantly written *After Seven Years*, which appeared in 1939, became quite critical of Roosevelt and the New Deal, and he became a Republican partisan, supporting and advising a number of leading figures of that party over the next decades, including Robert A. Taft and Barry Goldwater. He received the Medal of Freedom from President Richard M. Nixon in 1970. He died on February 18, 1975.

Henry T. Morgenthau, Jr. (1891–1967)

Henry Morgenthau, Jr., was the trusted and devoted friend of Franklin Roosevelt, a relationship stemming from their acquaintance as neighbors in New York's Dutchess County dating from before World War I. From nearly the beginning of the New Deal until the end of World War II, Morgenthau served as Roosevelt's secretary of the treasury. He was, during the later years of the New Deal, probably the most conservative and business-minded of those within the close circle of advisors the president relied upon.

Morgenthau was born on May 11, 1891, into a family that was both financially secure and politically active. An indifferent student, Morgenthau never completed a college degree but did develop a passionate interest in agriculture and in 1913 purchased several hundred acres of land in Dutchess County, New York, spending many years as a successful gentleman farmer dedicated to agricultural improvement. He did, however, gain experience in the world of affairs by serving, during several trips abroad, as personal secretary to his father, who was the American ambassador to Turkey during World War I. Morgenthau first met FDR, his neighbor, in 1915 at a luncheon in Hyde Park. The two men quickly became friends. The friendship resulted in Morgenthau's appointment as head of the Agricultural Advisory Commission when Roosevelt was elected governor in 1928. With his sights set on Washington, Roosevelt appointed Morgenthau as New York's conservation commissioner in an effort to groom him for a future position in national government.

When Roosevelt was elected president, he failed to appoint Morgenthau to the position he had hoped for, secretary of agriculture, naming him instead chairman of the Federal Farm Board. In this position, Morgenthau contributed to the bill that created the Agricultural Adjustment Administration. As a result of the AAA, the Farm Board was soon replaced by the Farm Credit Administration, of which Morgenthau was appointed governor. In this position, Morgenthau supervised the granting of low-interest loans to farmers. During this time, he also took up and promoted with FDR the plan touted by the Cornell economist George F. Warren to devalue the dollar by raising the price of gold. Late in 1933, Roosevelt asked Morgenthau to become acting secretary of the treasury, and the following January he was given the official title when William Woodin resigned due to illness.

Morgenthau had earned a reputation as a humanitarian who favored efficiency and honest dealing, but he was often criticized as incapable of handling the intellectual rigors of his new position. His support for the gold-buying policy of 1934, as well as his belief that balancing the budget could solve the recession of 1937, were both vigorously criticized by other

New Dealers. During World War II, Morgenthau used his position at the treasury to oppose the incarceration of Japanese-Americans in internment camps, as well as to help create the War Refugee Board. In 1944, he presented a plan for dealing with postwar Germany that included provisions for disarming the entire country, distributing several of its territories to neighboring states, and dividing the remaining land into two separate nations, limited economically to agricultural production. Later the plan would be severely criticized because it would have created a power vacuum in central Europe that would have made it easier for Soviet Russia to dominate the region.

Shortly after FDR died on April 12, 1945, Morgenthau, unable to establish an effective relationship with the new president, Harry S Truman, retired from the world of politics. He spent the remaining years of his life on his beloved farm in Dutchess County but was active in philanthropical causes, such as the United Jewish Appeal, for several years. He died on February 6, 1967.

George William Norris (1861–1944)

George Norris was one of the most notable of the midwestern progressive Republicans of the generation of reformist political figures in both the major parties that rose in the early years of the twentieth century and served in Congress for decades afterward, advancing the proposals that came to fruition during the New Deal. Norris is especially associated with the expansion of governmental production of electrical power and effective regulation of private power companies.

Norris was born in Ohio on July 11, 1861. After spending his youth working on farms and attending public schools, he studied law at Baldwin University, and graduated with an LL.B. degree from what would later be known as Valparaiso University in 1883. He was elected judge of the 14th judicial district of Nebraska in 1895 and in 1902 was elected to the U.S. House of Representatives. His years as a Republican Representative for Nebraska were most noteworthy for the revolt he led against the speaker, Joseph G. Cannon. In 1912, he was elected on the Republican ticket to the Senate, where he first gained recognition for opposing the entrance of the United States into World War I.

Norris served as senator from Nebraska from 1913 until 1942. He was respected by his constituents and the president for his integrity and courage, as well as his dedication to the causes in which he believed, which included conservation of natural resources, public ownership of utilities, farm relief, labor rights, and election reforms. Some of Norris's most noteworthy legislative achievements include the Twentieth (or, Lame Duck) Amendment to the Constitution, which changed the date of presidential inaugurations, the Tennessee Valley Authority Act, and the act that established the Rural Electrification Administration. Norris and Roosevelt shared a congenial relationship that proved to be mutually beneficial, each man actively supporting the campaigns of the other. Norris chaired the National Progressive League for Roosevelt in the election of 1932 and organized the National Committee of Independent Voters for Roosevelt and Wallace in 1940.

While Norris remained loyal to Roosevelt, he did not show the same allegiance to his party, and in 1936, he ran successfully for reelection to the Senate as an independent candidate, with Roosevelt's endorsement. Though earlier in his career Norris tended toward isolationism in foreign affairs, he later softened his stand when Great Britain was threatened with defeat and supported the declaration of war against Japan after the bombing of Pearl Harbor. In 1942, Norris campaigned for reelection to the Senate, but was defeated. Roosevelt offered him numerous positions, all of which he declined in order to return to his home in McCook. From there he eventually served as a consultant to the State Department, as well as honorary chairman of the National Citizens Political Action Committee in support of Roosevelt's reelection campaign in 1944. In August of that year, Norris suffered a cerebral hemorrhage from which he never recovered. He died on September 2, 1944.

Frances Perkins (1880–1965)

During the 1920s, Frances Perkins served as chair of the New York State Industrial Commission under Governor Al Smith and, when Franklin Roosevelt became governor in 1929, as head of the state's labor department. When FDR won the presidency in 1932, he appointed Perkins to be secretary of labor, the first woman to hold that or any other Cabinet post. A staunch advocate of social legislation to protect and provide security for workers, Perkins wielded considerable influence within the New Deal and helped shape its reform agenda. She served as secretary of labor until the close of the Roosevelt era.

Born in Boston on April 10, 1880, Perkins graduated from Mount Holyoke College in 1905, and in 1910 received her A.M. degree from Columbia University where she studied sociology and economics. During 1910–1912, she served as executive secretary for the Consumers' League in New York and thus began her lifelong commitment to improving the lives of Americ's industrial laborers. After the infamous fire at the Triangle shirtwaist factory in 1911, Perkins accepted a position on the committee that investigated the incident and seized this opportunity to become involved in supporting legislation that limited working hours and established safety regulations in factories. In 1919 Governor Alfred E. Smith appointed her a member of the New York State Industrial Commission and its chair in 1926. When Franklin Roosevelt became New York's governor in 1929, he appointed Perkins to head the state's Department of Labor, where she focused on the issues of unemployment and workmen's compensation.

In 1933, Perkins became the first woman to serve in a presidential Cabinet when FDR appointed her secretary of labor. Despite this groundbreaking achievement, Perkins did not consider herself to be a feminist. Rather, her primary concern was the welfare of American workers, and she resolutely supported applying government remedies in order to improve their living and working conditions. As secretary of labor, she was instrumental in fashioning the Division of Labor Standards, expanding the Bureau of Labor Statistics, and purging the Immigration and Naturalization Service of corruption.

Perkins contributed to many steps taken by the New Deal. She strongly influenced the labor provisions in the National Recovery Administration's codes during 1933 and was a key advocate for the protections for working people that found expression in the Social Security Act of 1935 and the Fair Labor Standards Act of 1938. In 1939, Perkins received bitter criticism in the House of Representatives for refusing to deport a union leader accused of allegiance to the Communist Party, but she continued to serve in the Cabinet until resigning a few weeks after FDR's death.

President Harry Truman appointed Perkins to the Civil Service Commission later in 1945, a position she held until the end of his administration. Afterward she began teaching at Cornell University's School of Industrial and Labor Relations and continued in this role until shortly before her death on May 14, 1965.

Samuel Taliaferro Rayburn (1882–1961)

Samuel Rayburn was a key Democratic leader in the House of Representatives during the New Deal, elected majority leader in 1937 and Speaker of the House in 1940 after the death of William Bankhead. He remained speaker until his death in 1961, except for the brief interlude during the Truman years when the Republicans gained control of the House.

Rayburn was born on January 6, 1882, in Roane County, Tennessee. Five years later, his family moved to Fannin County, Texas. Young Rayburn developed a love for history from listening to his father's tales of the Civil War, and he attributed his love for books to his mother's influence. Educated at East Texas Normal College and the University of Texas, he was first elected to the Texas legislature in 1906 and in 1912 was elected to the U.S. House of Representatives. Throughout his career, "Mr. Sam," as he was known, held the regard of his constituents. He was particularly aware of the struggles of American farmers and, during the Wilson era and the 1920s, played a major role in advancing legislation connected with their interests. A protégé of John Nance Garner, Rayburn secured a seat on the Interstate and Foreign Commerce Committee during the 1920s and became its chairman when the Democrats took control of the House in 1930. He was highly critical of Hoover for his failure to take adequate steps to alleviate the suffering of Americans during the depression.

Rayburn was a loyal supporter of President Roosevelt and the New Deal and played a central role in much of the landmark legislation from the period. He helped draft a number of important New Deal measures and was instrumental in the enactment of many of them, including the Securities and Exchange Act of 1934, the Public Utility Holding Company Act of 1935, and the Rural Electrification Act of 1936. His involvement in regulating big business earned him a reputation as the friend of the small businessman. Like many other southern and western Democrats of his generation, Rayburn felt a certain hostility toward big business, finding, as he once said, little difference between state socialists and what he regarded as the power-hungry and tyrannical managers of the big corporations. Rayburn was regarded as a man of common sense, who espoused the cause of the underprivileged and earned the respect of FDR for his honesty and forthrightness.

As House speaker, Rayburn remained a key figure in Democratic affairs until his death in 1961. He was a close supporter of President Truman and of Lyndon Johnson, who became Senate majority leader in the 1950s. Though initially skeptical of John F. Kennedy, Rayburn faithfully supported him after his election to the presidency in 1960 and worked mightily to bring legislation Kennedy backed out of committee onto the floor of the House during the early months of 1961. By mid-1961 his health was rapidly failing and he returned to Texas, where he died on November 16, 1961.

Walter Philip Reuther (1907–1970)

The beginning of Walter Reuther's career as an influential labor leader coincided with the revolutionary expansion of unionism that began in 1935–1936 with the passage of the Wagner Act and the founding of the CIO. From his role in 1936 as an organizer for the United Auto Workers (UAW), Reuther swiftly rose to membership on the union's executive board and recognition as its most important spokesperson by reason of his leadership in the strikes that led to the union's recognition by General Motors and Ford in 1937. He soon became a UAW vice-president and then its president in 1946.

Born in West Virginia on September 1, 1907, Reuther began his career in manufacturing at a young age, dropping out of high school to become an apprentice in the tool room of the Wheeling Corrugating Company in his hometown. In 1927, he moved to Detroit where he found a job at the Briggs Manufacturing Company, but soon was hired by Ford Motor Company as a die maker. While continuing to work, Reuther enrolled at Fordson High School in 1928, after which he went on to study at Detroit City College. In 1930, Reuther's younger brother, Victor, also moved to Detroit, and the two organized a socialist student organization at their school. In 1932, Reuther campaigned for the Socialist candidate and early the next year left Ford. Soon afterward, the two brothers departed for a tour of Europe that included a two-year stay in the Soviet Union, where they took jobs at the Gorky Auto Works. Walter trained Russian workers in the art of the tool and die maker.

Upon his return to the United States, Reuther began lecturing about his experiences in the Soviet Union before various socialist groups, and in 1936, he established a rather close connection with the Communist Party, including a possible membership. During this time, he also began working for the newly chartered United Automobile Workers Union and was instrumental in organizing Detroit's West Side Local 174. From 1936 to 1942, he served on the UAW executive board and, in 1942, was elected its vice-president. Reuther played a central role in planning and leading the great UAW strikes of 1937 against General Motors and Ford. In 1939, Reuther became director of the General Motors department of the UAW, where he successfully negotiated for vacation pay for GM workers, in addition to establishing an umpire system for grievance arbitration which set a precedent for the rest of the auto industry.

In contrast to CIO leader John L. Lewis, Reuther strongly supported the Roosevelt administration and the New Deal. In fact, when Lewis threatened to resign if Roosevelt were reelected in 1940, Reuther responded with a ringing declaration, in a UAW radio address, that FDR was a champion for social justice and that Lewis was acting out of hatred and spite.

Reuther broke his links with socialsts and communists in the late 1930s and was by now an avowed anticommunist. He was, nevertheless, thought to be dangerously radical by high managerial circles during World War II and the immediate postwar years because of the proposal he made as the war approached for "500 planes a day." This entailed a plan for joint operation of the auto industry by government, labor, and management. Reuther's intention, as management feared, was in fact to bring about a profound reorganization of capitalism. This he never achieved, but after the war, now the UAW's president, he secured the path-breaking 1948 agreement with GM for annual pay adjustments based on changes in the cost-of-living plus increases in productivity, a model that contributed greatly to the postwar rise in the income and status of the members of the powerful labor unions.

Despite coming under fire from J. Edgar Hoover during the war for alleged communist associations, Reuther in fact then and after the war pursued an anticommunist policy. His union, moreover, was never plagued by the corruption and slackness that appeared in some organizations as the labor movement matured during the 1950s and 1960s. He became president of the CIO in 1952 and helped bring about the merger of the American Federation of Labor (AFL) and CIO in 1956 but withdrew his union from the combination in 1968. Reuther continued as UAW president until his tragic death in an airplane crash on May 9, 1970.

Anna Eleanor Roosevelt (1884–1962)

By pursuing, during the New Deal, an active career as writer and lecturer and by supporting liberal causes, Eleanor Roosevelt, the niece of President Theodore Roosevelt and wife of Franklin Roosevelt, became the most active and noted of all First Ladies. After her husband's death, she continued to offer leadership in the causes of international peace and social reform.

Eleanor Roosevelt was born on October 11, 1884, into one of New York's privileged families, yet her childhood was often unhappy. Her mother, who was a beautiful woman, found Eleanor homely and lacking in vivacity and called her "granny." Eleanor's only comfort was the love of her father, though his alcoholism seriously detracted from his reliability. Both parents died when she was young, her mother when she was eight, her father two years later, in 1894. Eleanor and her brothers were sent to live with their grandmother, a stern woman who was excessively strict in the rearing of her grandchildren. As an adolescent, Eleanor was sent to Allenswood, a finishing school in London, where she began her intellectual awakening and developed an awareness of social problems and the need for reform. Upon her return to New York, she entered into the social life of her class but also became active in social reform, working in a settlement house and as a member of the National Consumers League, an organization devoted to the improvement of working conditions. She developed a friendship with her cousin, Franklin Delano Roosevelt, that became a courtship, and they were wed on March 17, 1905. For the next fifteen years, her life was devoted to childbearing and raising a family. Her mother-in-law, Sara Delano Roosevelt, dominated Eleanor's home and interfered with her relationship with her family so that, despite her devotion to her young, handsome, and dashing husband, these years were not entirely happy.

Unfortunately, her marital relationship with FDR soured after she discovered his affair with Lucy Mercer, her social secretary, in 1918. Yet she remained dedicated to aiding his political career and using her position to further the cause of reform. She had, in fact, resumed her active participation in social causes during the war and during the 1920s became increasingly involved in social reform movements. Through her involvement with groups such as the Women's City Club of New York, the League of Women Voters, and the National Consumers League, she emerged a devoted activist.

When FDR became president, Eleanor rejected the role previously played by First Ladies. She fulfilled the normal social responsibilities of the mistress of the White House, but also took an active part in the administration's affairs by traveling and talking with the people and reporting to her husband on social conditions in depression-era America. She acted as an advocate for the social groups whose special needs society generally, and the New Deal too, tended to ignore: blacks, marginal workers such as migratory farm laborers, and women. Soon she also launched a career as a lecturer, traveling thousands of miles annually, and began writing a syndicated daily column, titled *My Day*, which attracted a devoted and broad readership.

One area that concerned her especially was gaining civil rights for blacks. Though FDR avoided the issue for fear of losing the support of southern Democrats, Eleanor actively worked for the broadening of civil rights and employment opportunities for blacks. Beginning in 1934, she assisted NAACP Executive Secretary Walter White in promoting a national antilynching bill, and, during World War II, she played a role in persuading her husband to create the Fair Employment Practices Commission (FEPC), which banned racial discrimination in industries with government contracts. In 1945, she was named to the Board of Directors of the NAACP.

Eleanor Roosevelt vigorously supported several of the New Deal's efforts that provided for relief and reform, such as the National Youth Organization (NYA), the Works Progress Administration (WPA), and the Civilian Conservation Corps (CCC). Eventually Mrs. Roosevelt's vision of reform extended to the international community, and after her husband's death, she was appointed as a U.S. delegate to the United Nations by President Truman. Throughout the remainder of her life, Mrs. Roosevelt continued to advocate reforms; she earned a place in history as a champion of human rights and democracy. She died on November 7, 1962.

Franklin Delano Roosevelt (1882-1945)

Most historians rank Franklin Delano Roosevelt among the handful of truly great presidents, in the same category as George Washington, Thomas Jefferson, and Abraham Lincoln. Elected in 1932 at the worst point in one of America's worst crises, the Great Depression, Roosevelt is credited with bringing recovery and reform to a prostrate nation and then, during World War II, leading Americans in a great crusade to defeat fascism and aggression and secure international stability and peace.

Franklin Delano Roosevelt was born on January 30, 1882, to privilege, the offspring of a wealthy Hudson River landowner, the only child of a doting young mother, Sarah Delano. Educated at elite schools, Groton and Harvard, Roosevelt had attempted legal practice in New York City after receiving a degree from Columbia Law School, but soon found it too dull and forsook it for a plunge into politics. Elected to the New York State Assembly from Dutchess, his home county, in 1910, he stood apart from the Tammany Democrats from New York City and earned a modest reputation as a reformer.

An early supporter of Woodrow Wilson for president in 1912, Roosevelt was well positioned to receive an appointment in the new administration. Named assistant secretary of the Navy, he was thrust into national prominence when the United States entered World War I in 1917. In 1920, the Democratic convention named him running mate for the party's presidential nominee, James Cox. Roosevelt campaigned gamely and effectively in a year when the Democrats faced an uphill battle because of popular disillusionment with Wilson and his policies. Roosevelt's performance attracted much favorable attention within his party despite its smashing loss in 1920 to Harding and Coolidge. Disaster struck him in 1921, however, when, while vacationing at his summer home at Campobello, Maine, he contracted polio and lost nearly all use of his legs.

Roosevelt intermittently pursued a business career during the 1920s but was mainly absorbed by the task of keeping up his leadership role in the Democratic Party and by his valiant but fruitless attempts to regain use of his legs. The Democrats suffered badly during the 1920s from a split that divided the party into a northern wing, drawing its support from an urban population that was largely Catholic, Jewish, and wet (opposed to Prohibition), and a wing based upon the agrarian and small town voters of the South and West, who were Protestant, suspicious of the immigrant cities of the North, and, to a great extent, devotedly dry (supportive of Prohibition). Though he was a New Yorker and even nominated Al Smith in 1924 as the Democratic "Happy Warrior," Roosevelt's attractive personality, and his frequent efforts to lead the party's factions to common ground, made it possible for him to avoid alienating leaders of the party's agrarian wing.

In 1928, Al Smith, nominated at the Democratic convention to run against Herbert Hoover for president, persuaded Roosevelt to run for governor of New York State in the hope this would bolster Democratic chances of carrying the state in the presidential election. Smith, the first Catholic to be nominated for president by a major party, was soundly beaten in an election marked by religious antagonism on the part of much of the electorate. But Roosevelt won his gubernatorial race and thus gained a very favorable position for winning his party's presidential nomination in 1932. By that time, the Great Depression, then nearing its worst point, had discredited Hoover and the Republicans and made election of the Democratic candidate almost certain. Roosevelt did secure the nomination after a strenuous fight with the party leaders who controlled the eastern, conservative wing of the Democratic Party; they believed he was too closely allied with the southern and western wings of the party, which they regarded as too progressive and unorthodox on economic issues.

Gathering around him an advisory group of Columbia University professors that newspapers soon dubbed the "Brain Trust," Roosevelt won the election by a wide margin and pushed a far-reaching program, known as the "First New Deal," through Congress during the first three months of his presidency, the period known as the "One Hundred Days." The program failed to produce recovery sufficiently to prevent rising popular discord, and in 1935, Roosevelt pressed Congress to enact another reform program, the "Second New Deal," which included a large-scale federal work relief program, the Works Progress Administration.

In 1940, Roosevelt decided to break with tradition and seek a third term, believing no other Democrat would be able to guide the nation toward further reform and toward the proper course of action regarding the war that now raged in Europe. Isolationism, the belief that America should stay out of Europe's wars, remained strong, but Roosevelt believed the country's interest lay in supporting England against Germany and in defending its interests in the Far East, where Japan threatened to subjugate China and exclude the Western nations from the region altogether.

After the December 1941 Japanese attack on Pearl Harbor, the American naval base in Hawaii, Roosevelt led the nation in a great mobilization of human and material resources to fight a far-flung war in Europe and the Pacific. Roosevelt not only presided during these years over the normal governmental offices but also over the array of wartime agencies that tightly regulated production and consumption so as to maximize America's military potential. Wartime diplomacy required frequent dealings, often in person, with the leaders of the countries allied with the United States: England's Winston Churchill and the Soviet Union's Joseph Stalin. Through agreements made at these wartime conferences, at Cairo, Teheran, and Yalta, Roosevelt attempted to shape understandings that would create a stable, peaceful, and prosperous postwar world order, with a new international organization, the United Nations, playing a major role. Roosevelt died on April 12, 1945, of a cerebral hemorrhage, shortly before Germany's surrender on May 8 ended the war in Europe, and two months before Japan's surrender brought the war's end, without successfully completing the task of establishing the basis for peace. Divergence between American goals and those of the Soviet Union would soon lead to bitter confrontations, first over Soviet control of eastern Europe and then over conflicting aims worldwide.

Rexford Guy Tugwell (1891–1979)

Of the three main members of the Brain Trust, Rexford Tugwell had the most innovative ideas. He continued, in various capacities, with Roosevelt through most of the New Deal, though his ideas and proposals increasingly drew charges of radicalism.

Rexford Tugwell was born on July 10, 1891, in upstate New York. In 1932, as a young professor of economics at Columbia University, he was deeply involved in thinking and writing about the problems of the American agricultural and industrial systems. In March 1932, Raymond Moley, a colleague from Columbia, invited him to join a group, to become known as the Brain Trust, that Roosevelt, then New York's governor, was gathering to advise him. Tugwell was an institutional economist who advocated national economic planning, and he hoped to persuade FDR, if he won the Democratic nomination and the presidency, to incorporate his ideas into the new administration's program. Tugwell's thought was greatly influenced by M. L. Wilson, John Dewey, and Thorstein Veblen, and by a trip he took to the Soviet Union in 1927. In an article he published in the *American Economic Review* in 1932, Tugwell had outlined the elements involved in his vision of a planned economy for the United States. He explained that his plan would call for the abandonment of laissez-faire and the abolition of private business as it was traditionally understood. In place of competitive industries motivated by profit and self-interest, he envisioned a group of integrated enterprises supervised by a central body of experts who would implement a scheme for planned production and consumption. His vision also entailed an enlarged national police power for enforcement, and the revision of American constitutional and legal practice to enhance the power of the national government at the expense of the states. He also supported creating import and export boards to plan for international trade, as well as strengthening the graduated income tax to promote the redistribution of wealth. His ideas for concentration and control also extended to the realm of agriculture, for which he advocated crop control and domestic allotment.

In 1933, Roosevelt appointed Tugwell assistant secretary of agriculture. Tugwell's position in that office became untenable, however, after he took the side of tenant farmers and sharecroppers in a dispute over the policies of the Agricultural Adjustment Administration (AAA). In 1935, Roosevelt appointed Tugwell head of the Resettlement Administration, a position that allowed him to experiment with rather advanced ideas for dealing with the plight of landless farmers. Still devoted to the ideal of national economic planning, Tugwell was, however, deeply disappointed by the direction taken by the Second New Deal, and he left the administration in 1936.

Tugwell remained close to FDR, however, and in 1941 was appointed governor of Puerto Rico, a position he held until 1946. Afterward he resumed an academic career, teaching at a number of universities and writing prolifically about his experiences with Roosevelt and the New Deal. He died on July 21, 1979.

Henry Agard Wallace (1888–1965)

As secretary of agriculture, Henry Wallace introduced and carried out the New Deal's policy for alleviating the farm problem, the restriction of production. Increasingly liberal and somewhat visionary, Roosevelt selected him as his running mate in 1940.

Born in Iowa on October 7, 1888, Henry A. Wallace represented the third generation of men in his family to be actively involved in agriculture and politics. His grandfather, a former United Presbyterian clergyman, was appointed to the Country Life Commission in 1908 by Theodore Roosevelt. His father, Henry Cantwell Wallace, was a professor at Iowa State University and also served as editor of the family's journal, *Wallaces' Farmer*. However, in 1921, his father was appointed secretary of agriculture by President Harding, and he relinquished the editorship in favor of his son, who had worked for the journal since graduating from Iowa State College in 1910. In 1933, Wallace left his journal, and the state of Iowa, and broke entirely with the Republican Party to accept the position of secretary of agriculture in the Roosevelt Cabinet.

During his years at Iowa State College, Wallace had first begun to question laissez-faire capitalism and the effects of unrestricted competition upon farmers. He was greatly influenced by the thought of Thorstein

Veblen, although his overall philosophy of social justice encompassed science, religion, and politics, as well as economic theory. He emphatically opposed isolationism and protectionism, and eventually split with the Republican Party over the issue of tariffs. He was actively promoting the domestic allotment plan, a scheme envisioning control of agricultural production by limiting the amount of land under cultivation, when Henry Morgenthau, Jr., in 1932 arranged for Wallace to meet FDR. By this time, he was an adamant supporter of federal assistance for the rural poor and the redistribution of national wealth. After meeting with Wallace and listening to his ideas on agricultural reform, Roosevelt appointed him secretary of agriculture in February 1933. Soon after assuming his appointment, Wallace and other leading promoters of federal assistance for farmers, such as Rexford Tugwell, Mordecai Ezekiel, and George Peek, made plans for a program that led to the Agricultural Adjustment Act. Eventually Wallace expanded his sphere of interest beyond agriculture to include the broader concerns of the general public, including industrial labor and foreign policy. In 1940, Roosevelt, wishing to secure a liberal as his running mate, endorsed Wallace for the vice-presidency, a step resented and resisted by many leaders of the Democratic Party.

As vice-president, Wallace became increasingly preoccupied by international affairs. He was morally opposed to violence and war, and he favored American neutrality in Europe. When the United States became involved in World War II, Wallace envisioned a postwar world characterized by perpetual peace and economic abundance. He became a leading spokesman for postwar international cooperation, supported a future international organization that would exercise authority over all nations and prevent worldwide unemployment, and became a strong advocate of Soviet-American friendship. In 1944, Wallace, even a more controversial figure than before among his fellow Democrats, lost the battle for renomination as vice-president after receiving a lukewarm endorsement from the president. In 1945, Wallace was appointed secretary of commerce, replacing his former foe, Jesse Jones. After Roosevelt's death later that year, Wallace became highly critical of the Cold War with Russia that was developing under Truman, and he was dismissed by the president for a speech he made in 1946. In 1948 he joined with a broad array of leftist and liberal political forces, which included the influence of the Communist Party of America, to form a third party, the Progressive Citizens of America. He ran as its presidential candidate but received very little support in the election. Wallace gradually retreated from the world of politics and spent most of the last seventeen years of his life pursuing his interest in scientific farming on a farm he had purchased in New York State. He died on November 18, 1965.

NOTE

1. Quoted in Arthur M. Schlesinger, Jr., *The Politics of Upheaval* (Boston: Houghton Mifflin, 1960), 280.

Primary Documents of the Great Depression and the New Deal

Document 1
THE DEBATE OVER RELIEF

On February 2, 1932, a debate began in the U.S. Senate over a federal un-employment relief bill sponsored by Robert M. La Follette, Jr., of Wisconsin, and Edward P. Costigan, of Colorado, both counted among the progressives of their parties. This was the first time during the depression that a bill to provide federal relief had reached the floor of either house of Congress. La Follette and Costigan had held extensive hearings during the preceding two months and collected an enormous body of testimony showing that the funds available both to private charitable organizations and to city and state relief agencies were now overwhelmed by the sheer magnitude of the unemployment problem. Staunchly opposed by Republican regulars and the president, providing federal money to the states for relief now had substantial support among Democrats and progressive Republicans. Too much disagreement over the method of furnishing federal relief still remained at this point in the session to permit the La Follette-Costigan Bill to pass. The February debate, however, focused national attention on the issue. Later in the session the Democratic leadership succeeded in passing a bill that, after compromise, the president agreed to sign. La Follette had opened the process that led to the massive relief effort of the New Deal.

La Follette opened the debate with a three-hour speech, excerpted here, in which he summarized the evidence his hearings had accumulated and passionately exposed the fallacies of those who still opposed federal relief. Note that the custom of the Senate is for its members to address the chair when speaking, rather than to address one another directly. The chair, the presiding officer (the vice-president of the United States, if he is present), is addressed as "Mr. President." La Follette is not addressing the president of the United States.

Mr. President, we are in the third winter of the most serious economic crisis which has ever confronted this country.

Mr. President, the wage earner is not primarily concerned with the fall in prices of securities; he is not forced merely to postpone the purchase of a new automobile; he cannot reduce his living standard by abandoning his country house in Florida during the winter season; he loses his economic all in a period of protracted depression.

During the period since this depression began, this is the first time that Congress has turned seriously to the consideration of the rank and file of the people of the United States.

We met in regular session on the first Monday of last December. Immediately there was ready for the consideration of Congress the major portion of the President's so-called reconstruction program, namely, the bill creating the Reconstruction Finance Corporation. After hearings which lasted four days, the Banking and Currency Committee hurriedly reported the bill to the floor of the Senate. It was taken up and jammed through under whip and spur.

Two billion one hundred and sixty million dollars has already been provided by the Congress and the administration during this depression for the relief of those who own property and securities in the United States. Now, when it is proposed that the Congress shall give consideration to a measure providing for the relief of those in the United States who, through no fault of their own, find themselves destitute, cold, hungry, and homeless, the contention is raised that there is not sufficient evidence to demonstrate the necessity for Federal action on this crisis.

It is contended by the opponents of this measure that the responsibility rests upon the local government, that it rests upon the cities, counties, and States, and that the Federal Government has no obligation to relieve the suffering which is now prevalent in this country. It is said that there is no evidence to support the necessity for Federal action to assist the cities, counties, and States in meeting unemployment relief.

Practically every witness testified to the Herculean efforts that have been made on the part of private agencies and the efforts which have been made on the part of local governments to meet the problem. I think that not one witness would want his testimony to be construed as a criticism of the great efforts which have been made by private charity and by the local governments in trying to meet the situation.

But [we] . . . must realize . . . that the burden which has fallen upon these communities is so tremendous and is increasing at such a rate that they are all becoming embarrassed in their efforts to keep financially sound.

The attempt has been made on the part of opponents of Federal relief to brand it as a dole and to carry conviction to the country that the inauguration of this policy would undermine our institutions. There is not only the factor of local pride but there is also the factor of the position which the present Republican administration has taken concerning Federal aid for relief, which of course would make it a matter of embarrassment for Republican governors generally to take a position in direct opposition to the policy of the administration.

I think the evidence shows that both public and private agencies within these communities have manfully endeavored to meet the problem which has been thrown upon them. I think, furthermore, it shows that the burden has become so great that they can not adequately meet it.

The municipalities have reached the end of their rope. The suggestion is made that the Federal Government should not do anything because the local communities should do it. Those who make such a contention are making a football of relief. . . . The municipalities are now being forced to curtail their normal public-works programs because of two things: First, the increasing tax delinquencies, and the resultant diminishing revenues; and, second, they are unable to float perfectly sound securities because of the attitude of the bankers and the condition of the money market.

Mr. President, I do not know what will be required to convince the Members of this august body that there is need for action by the Federal Government. Evidence has been presented here to show the absolute breakdown of family life, the overcrowded conditions. I have demonstrated that those in distress are upstanding, independent, industrious citizens of the country. They have been driven only by sheer force of necessity to seek relief. Six families are crowded into a 6-room house in hundreds and hundreds of instances in [for example,] the city of Philadelphia.

Mr. President, no one can examine this evidence without being convinced that the need for action by the Federal Government in assisting the cities, counties, and States in meeting the problem of unemployment relief is one of the greatest emergencies that has ever confronted this Government. . . . Failure to step in and to provide more adequate relief will result in breaking up hundreds of thousands of families. It will break down health standards. We shall be paying the toll in malnutrition and its effect upon adults and children for 50 years to come if action is not taken to meet this emergency and to raise the standards of relief. The non-epidemic type of diseases will become prevalent. The public-health director of the State of

Pennsylvania has already publicly stated that an increase in tuberculosis, due to malnutrition, was evident in that State. The social progress which we have made in this country during the last 50 years will be wiped out, so far as millions of our population are concerned, if the relief burden is not adequately met. Our institutions themselves may be endangered by a prolongation of this depression, and a failure of Congress to meet its responsibility and to come to the assistance of citizens who are suffering as a result of economic disaster over which they had no control.

I ask Senators also to consider the situation which will confront this Government if no action is taken. True, there have been enormous losses on the part of individuals owning property and securities; but for the most part they have had their standards of living reduced—not wiped out. So far as the wage earners are concerned, they have been catapulted by the effects of this prolonged depression into a bottomless pit of poverty and despair.

Proceed, if you will; make the record that you will extend relief to organized wealth in this situation to the tune of $2,160,000,000, and that you will turn your backs upon the millions of upstanding American citizens who are suffering want, privation, and misery. But I say that if you fail to meet this issue now, you will meet it later. You cannot duck it; you cannot dodge it; you cannot meet it by offering substitutes that fail to meet the emergency character of the situation.

Senators say that this is a problem for local government; that it is no concern of the Federal Government.

Mr. President, the Federal Government is just as much concerned in the future citizenship of this Republic as the local communities, if not more so. If we permit this situation to go on, millions of children will be maimed in body, if not warped in mind, by the effects of malnutrition. They will form the citizenship upon which the future of this country must depend. They are the hope of America.

Source: *Congressional Record*, 72nd Congress, 1st Session (1931–1932), 3068–3070, 3080–3082, 3092, 3095.

Document 2
THE NEW DEAL BEGINS

One of FDR's great strengths was his almost unparalleled ability to speak to the people dramatically and persuasively, on both formal occasions and informally, as in the "fireside chats." The content and language of the speeches depended in great part on the abilities of his speechwriters, who included men of great talent. During the 1932 campaign Raymond Moley was the key speechwriter, but the other members of the Brain Trust, notably Rexford Tugwell and Adolf Berle, also were major contributors and assisted with speechwriting through much of the New Deal era. Moley remained the central figure throughout the One Hundred Days, but his role diminished after 1933 as he began to part ways with Roosevelt. Thomas Corcoran and Benjamin Cohen, young attorneys sent to Washington by Felix Frankfurter early in the New Deal, swiftly became key drafters of the administration's legislative proposals and influential presidential advisors, and by 1935 were heavily relied on as speechwriters also.

FDR participated very directly in writing many of the speeches. The language of FDR's speeches and addresses is authentic, thanks to this participation and the skill of his writers, who knew him and his manner of speaking at firsthand and endeavored to employ Roosevelt's own modes of expression as much as possible.

What were those modes? Contemporary readers, unless their experience extends well back in time, will immediately recognize a tone quite different from presidential speeches they have themselves heard. The language managed to be at once dignified yet very direct, and almost conversational and was readily understood both by Americans of little or of much education. The speeches often evoked the manner of biblical expression, for this was an idiom to which Americans of that period, including Roosevelt himself, were well accustomed.

The speech excerpted here is the first inaugural address, March 4, 1933, an appeal for support to the entire people, and a pledge to take whatever action was necessary to restore the economy. In the speech FDR blames the depression for the most part on economic imbalances rather than sinister forces in the business and financial communities, and he appeals to all Americans to join him in a great cooperative effort. He invokes the image of a nation at war and asks for the same degree of support and, if necessary, the same broad powers that the president was given to mobilize the economy during World War I, a circumstance still fresh in the minds of most of his auditors.

I am certain that my fellow Americans expect that on my induction into the Presidency I will address them with a candor and a decision which the present situation of our Nation impels. This is preeminently the time to speak the truth, the whole truth, frankly and boldly. Nor need we shrink from honestly facing conditions in our country today. This great Nation will endure as it has endured, will revive and will prosper. So, first of all, let me assert my firm belief that the only thing we have to fear is fear itself—nameless, unreasoning, unjustified terror which paralyzes needed efforts to convert retreat into advance. In every dark hour of our national life a leadership of frankness and vigor has met with that understanding and support of the people themselves which is essential to victory. I am convinced that you will again give that support to leadership in these critical days.

This Nation asks for action, and action now. Our greatest primary task is to put people to work. This is no unsolvable problem if we face it wisely and courageously. It can be accomplished in part by direct recruiting by the Government itself, treating the task as we would treat the emergency of a war, but at the same time, through this employment, accomplishing greatly needed projects to stimulate and reorganize the use of our natural resources.

Hand in hand with this we must frankly recognize the overbalance of population in our industrial centers and, by engaging on a national scale in a redistribution, endeavor to provide a better use of the land for those best fitted for the land. The task can be helped by definite efforts to raise the values of agricultural products and with this the power to purchase the output of our cities. It can be helped by preventing realistically the tragedy of the growing loss through foreclosure of our small homes and our farms. It can be helped by insistence that the Federal, State, and local governments act forthwith on the demand that their cost be drastically reduced.

Finally, in our progress toward a resumption of work we require two safeguards against a return of the evils of the old order: there must be a strict supervision of all banking and credits and investments, so that there will be an end to speculation with other people's money; and there must be provision for an adequate but sound currency.

Through this program of action we address ourselves to putting our own national house in order and making income balance outgo. Our international trade relations, though vastly important, are in point of time and necessity secondary to the establishment of a sound national economy. I favor as a practical policy the putting of first things first. I shall spare no effort to restore world trade by international economic readjustment, but the emergency at home cannot wait on that accomplishment.

It is to be hoped that the normal balance of Executive and Legislative authority may be wholly adequate to meet the unprecedented task before us. But it may be that an unprecedented demand and need for undelayed action may call for temporary departure from that normal balance of public procedure.

I am prepared under my constitutional duty to recommend the measures that a stricken Nation in the midst of a stricken world may require. These measures, or such other measures as the Congress may build out of its experience and wisdom, I shall seek, within my constitutional authority, to bring to speedy adoption.

But in the event that the Congress shall fail to take one of these two courses, and in the event that the national emergency is still critical, I shall not evade the clear course of duty that will then confront me. I shall ask the Congress for the one remaining instrument to meet the crisis—broad Executive power to wage a war against the emergency, as great as the power that would be given to me if we were in fact invaded by a foreign foe.

For the trust reposed in me I will return the courage and the devotion that befit the time. I can do no less.

We do not distrust the future of essential democracy. The people of the United States have not failed. In their need they have registered a mandate that they want direct, vigorous action. They have asked for discipline and direction under leadership. They have made me the present instrument of their wishes. In the spirit of the gift I take it.

In this dedication of a Nation we humbly ask the blessing of God. May He protect each and every one of us. May He guide me in the days to come.

Source: See Samuel I. Rosenman, ed., *The Public Papers and Addresses of Franklin D. Roosevelt,* Vol. II (New York: Random House, 1938), 11–16.

Document 3
FDR'S THIRD FIRESIDE CHAT

This document was the third of the memorable informal radio addresses, known as the "fireside chats," that FDR made frequently during his presidency. They represented an innovation, the president addressing the people informally by radio, explaining actions he had taken, and, as is so clearly evident in this chat, rallying listeners to his side. FDR used informal and colloquial language to reach the "whole nation" in terms the people collectively could understand. (Note the use of expressions such as "in a flash," and "half boom and half broke.") FDR used the fireside chat to speak to Americans as he would have spoken to neighbors, and one can judge from the texts (though not nearly so well as from actually hearing his voice) how successful he was. This was no mean feat considering that Roosevelt belonged by birth and upbringing to a branch of American aristocracy, the landed gentry of the Hudson Valley, and as a young man had been rather arrogant in many ways. His biographers believe the suffering he underwent when attacked by polio, and his fruitless battle during the 1920s to regain use of his legs, had given him a deep capacity for compassion and empathy with the sufferings with others. However that may be, FDR did have, by the time he became president, the ability to talk to the people, high and low, in language that seemed to them unaffected and convincing. His ability to communicate so effectively with the people, both in his speeches and in the "fireside chats," contributed immeasurably to his vast success as a political leader, in peace and war.

In this fireside chat of July 24, 1933, Roosevelt explained the recovery program, enacted during the One Hundred Days, to the people. A major purpose was to generate a broad and strong national support for the industrial recovery program that the NRA was then launching to lift wages and shorten hours, so strong that employers who failed to cooperate would be subjected to unbearable public pressure to join the NRA effort. This talk began with comments on the steps he and the Congress had taken to balance the budget, increase relief spending and public works, and resurrect the banks. Then he came to the programs for increasing farm income and the wages of industrial workers, which he depended on to restore prosperity.

No w I come to the links which will build us a more lasting prosperity. I have said that we cannot attain that in a nation half boom and half broke.

For many years the two great barriers to a normal prosperity have been low farm prices and the creeping paralysis of unemployment. These factors have cut the purchasing power of the country in half. I promised action.

First, the Farm Act: It is based on the fact that the purchasing power of nearly half our population depends on adequate prices for farm products. We have been producing more of some crops than we consume or can sell in a depressed world market. The cure is not to produce so much. Without our help the farmers cannot get together and cut production, and the Farm Bill gives them a method of bringing their production down to a reasonable level and of obtaining reasonable prices for their crops.

It is obvious that if we can greatly increase the purchasing power of the tens of millions of our people who make a living from farming and the distribution of farm crops, we shall greatly increase the consumption of those goods which are turned out by industry.

That brings me to the final step—bringing back industry along sound lines.

We can make possible by democratic self-discipline in industry general increases in wages and shortening of hours sufficient to enable industry to pay its own workers enough to let those workers buy and use the things that their labor produces. This can be done only if we permit and encourage cooperative action in industry, because it is obvious that without united action a few selfish men in each competitive group will pay starvation wages and insist on long hours of work. Others in that group must either follow suit or close up shop. We have seen the result of action of that kind in the continuing descent into the economic hell of the past four years.

There is a clear way to reverse that process: If all employers in each competitive group agree to pay their workers the same wages—reasonable wages—and require the same hours—reasonable hours—then higher wages and shorter hours will hurt no employer. Moreover, such action is better for the employer than unemployment and low wages, because it makes more buyers for his product. That is the simple idea which is the very heart of the Industrial Recovery Act.

On the basis of this simple principle of everybody doing things together, we are starting out on this nationwide attack on unemployment. It will succeed if our people understand it—in the big industries, in the little shops, in the great cities and in the small villages. There is nothing complicated about it and there is nothing particularly new in the principle. It goes back to the basic idea of society and of the Nation itself that people acting in a group can accomplish things which no individual acting alone could even hope to bring about.

Here is an example. In the Cotton Textile Code and in other agreements already signed, child labor has been abolished. That makes me personally happier than any other one thing with which I have been connected since I came to Washington. In the textile industry—an industry which came to me spontaneously and with a splendid cooperation as soon as the Recovery Act was signed—child labor was an old evil. But no employer acting alone was able to wipe it out. If one employer tried it, or if one State tried it, the costs of operation rose so high that it was impossible to compete with the employers or States which had failed to act. The moment the Recovery Act was passed, this monstrous thing which neither opinion nor law could reach through years of effort went out in a flash. As a British editorial put it, we did more under a Code in one day than they in England had been able to do under the common law in eighty-five years of effort. I use this incident, my friends, not to boast of what has already been done but to point the way to you for even greater cooperative efforts this summer and autumn.

We are not going through another winter like the last. I doubt if ever any people so bravely and cheerfully endured a season half so bitter. We cannot ask America to continue to face such needless hardships. It is time for courageous action, and the Recovery Bill gives us the means to conquer unemployment with exactly the same weapon that we have used to strike down child labor.

The proposition is simply this: if all employers will act together to shorten hours and raise wages we can put people back to work. No employer will suffer because the relative level of competitive cost will advance by the same amount for all. But if any considerable group should lag or shirk, this great opportunity will pass us by and we shall go into another desperate winter. This must not happen.

We have sent out to all employers an agreement which is the result of weeks of consultation. This agreement checks against the voluntary codes of nearly all the large industries which have already been submitted. This blanket agreement carries the unanimous approval of the three boards which I have appointed to advise in this, boards representing the great leaders in labor, in industry, and in social service. The agreement has already brought a flood of approval from every State, and from so wide a cross-section of the common calling of industry that I know it is fair for all. It is a plan—deliberate, reasonable and just—intended to put into effect at once the most important of the broad principles which are being established, industry by industry, through codes. Naturally, it takes a good deal of organizing and a great many hearings and many months, to get these codes perfected and signed, and we cannot wait for all of them to go through. The blanket agreements, however, which I am sending to every employer will start the wheels turning now, and not six months from now.

There are, of course, men, a few men, who might thwart this great common purpose by seeking selfish advantage. There are adequate penalties in the law, but I am now asking the cooperation that comes from opinion and from conscience. These are the only instruments we shall use in this great summer offensive against unemployment. But we shall use them to the limit to protect the willing from the laggard and to make the plan succeed.

In war, in the gloom of night attack, soldiers wear a bright badge on their shoulders to be sure that comrades do not fire on comrades. On that principle, those who cooperate in this program must know each other at a glance. This is why we have provided a badge of honor for this purpose, a simple design with a legend, "We do our part," and I ask that all those who join with me shall display that badge prominently. It is essential to our purpose. Already all the great, basic industries have come forward willingly with proposed codes, and in these codes they accept the principles leading to mass reemployment. But, important as is this heartening demonstration, the richest field for results is among the small employers, those whose contribution will be to give new work for from one to ten people. These smaller employers are indeed a vital part of the backbone of our country, and the success of our plan lies largely in their hands.

When Andrew Jackson, "Old Hickory," died, someone asked, "Will he go to Heaven?" and the answer was, "He will go if he wants to." The essence of the plan is a universal limitation of hours of work per week for any individual by common consent, and a universal payment of wages above a minimum, also by common consent. I cannot guarantee the success of this nationwide plan, but the people of this country can guarantee its success. I have no faith in "cure-alls" but I believe that we can greatly influence economic forces. I have no sympathy with the professional economists who insist that things must run their course and that human agencies can have no influence on economic ills. One reason is that I happen to know that professional economists have changed their definition of economic laws every five or ten years for a very long time, but I do have faith, and retain faith, . . . in the strength of unified action taken by the American people.

Source: See Samuel I. Rosenman, ed., *The Public Papers and Addresses of Franklin D. Roosevelt,* Vol. II (New York: Random House, 1938), 295–303.

Document 4
HUEY LONG AND SHARE OUR WEALTH

Appealing to the dirt farmers of Louisiana, in the late 1920s Huey Long built an unbeatable political machine in Louisiana and, as governor, launched a number of popular programs that won favor among the state's lower classes. In 1932, he entered the realm of national politics, strongly supporting FDR at the Democratic convention, while getting himself elected U.S. Senator. At first supportive of the New Deal, his own ambitions, as well as his disposition to pursue more radical remedies for unemployment and poverty than FDR would countenance, soon turned him into a severe critic.

By 1934, Long had formed and enlisted a broad membership for Share Our Wealth, an organization devoted to securing a radical redistribution of income and wealth. He had become also a mocking foe of the president and the Democratic leadership in the Senate. In the following excerpt from his Senate speech of May 15, 1935, Long exhibits fully the rhetorical strategies that rural and small town Americans appreciated throughout the Mississippi Valley states, where his following was strongest. He treats Roosevelt himself and his Senate leaders, Joseph Robinson of Arkansas, the Senate majority leader, and Alben Barkley of Kentucky, with venomous sarcasm, interjects folksy humor, and ends, after explaining his fantastic plan for radical redistribution of wealth and income, with an appeal to biblical authority. Long's performance may appear comical to a modern reader, but his message earned him a following that made him a political force the New Dealers genuinely feared and were forced to take steps to preempt.

Note that when speaking, Senators address the chair as the "President" of that assembly. Note too the several points at which the text, drawn from the *Congressional Record,* indicates outbursts of laughter and applause following one of Long's sarcasms at the expense of his party's leadership.

Mr. LONG. Mr. President, about 4 weeks ago . . . the Senator from Arkansas [Mr. Robinson] and the Senator from Kentucky [Mr. Barkley] made speeches over the radio in which they . . . rather sneeringly referred to the phrase "share-our-wealth."

I desire to give them to understand where the "share-our-wealth" phrase was first used. I want them to understand that that "share-our-wealth" phrase did not come from the senior Senator from Louisiana, but was the phrase and promise of the present President of the United States in his acceptance speech delivered at the Chicago . . . Democratic National Convention of 1932. . . . I am quoting Mr. Roosevelt:

Throughout the Nation, men and women, forgotten in the political philosophy of the Government of the last years look to us here for guidance and for more equitable opportunity to share-

S-H-A-R-E-

In the distribution of national wealth. [Applause and Cheering]

My friend from Kentucky was the keynoter of that convention. He forgot all about it and went on the radio to denounce "share-our-wealth" the other night. He has become disloyal to the party. [Laughter.] "Share our wealth," "share our national wealth," "share in the distribution of wealth," were the phrases of Franklin D. Roosevelt when he accepted the nomination in Chicago. I want my friend from Kentucky [Mr. Barkley] . . . and my friend from Arkansas [Mr. Robinson] . . . to realize when I first adopted that phrase for our organization. It is a pretty big organization in this country, Mr. President. It is in every State in the Union. It has thousands of members in every State. It has probably millions in some States, not counting, of course, that they may not all be voters. There may be many below the voting age. But the "share our wealth" phrase was the promise—yes; I said the "promise"—the "share our wealth" phrase was the promise of Franklin D. Roosevelt in the Chicago convention when he accepted the nomination.

What did Roosevelt say? . . . He said we have got to give a purchasing power to the masses. Then is when Franklin Delano Roosevelt announced that he was in favor of the share-our-wealth platform. Then is when he got up in the Chicago convention, when a man was supposed to be a man, and stood on his hind legs and said that "the crying need of the country is for more and equitable opportunity to share in the distribution of wealth," and our report says "applause and cheers" when he made that statement on the floor of the convention.

What did we do through the leadership of the Senator from Arkansas . . . What did we do? Did we come into the United States Senate and provide that we would give the people more money so they could buy the things which the United States Government said they had to have in order to live?

Did we come here and provide that they could buy more and provide that instead of the farmer continuing underproduction he might produce what was expected to be consumed by the people?

No. . . . We allowed the rich to become richer and the poor to become poorer. . . . We gave the masses less with which to buy.

Why, Gentlemen of the Senate, someone has said I am at war with the President. With which President am I at war? Am I at war with the President who took the nomination of the Democratic convention in Chicago in 1932? No. That man is my brother. Is he demised? . . . Is that man to whom we gave the nomination and who uttered those words at the Chicago convention in 1932 still alive? If he is alive, he is a boon companion of mine because I am standing where he stood in 1932. Yea, more, I am standing where I stood before he took that stand.

We have reduced the purchasing power of the masses in the last 3 years; and the figures here show it. We have 22,000,000 on the relief dole and 10,000,000 to 15,000,000 more people trying to get on it. The United States Relief Department says that $8 is enough for one family to eat on, and, therefore, with that starvation diet we have prescribed under the dole they have forgotten the diet the health authorities of the Department of Agriculture, in 1929, and up to now, said was necessary for the human family, and have decided to reduce the people to where it is a bread-line proposition of getting a cup of soup for supper and some little hand-out for breakfast in the morning.

It makes me think of a man who seized the 140-acre farm of a man for a debt he owed to the store. The old man went off, and a few years later he came back, and meanwhile the other man has discovered oil on the land. The old man went in and said, "Mr. So-and-so, you seized that 140 acres of land for a $100 debt, and you have got $1,000,000 of oil off it. Don't you think you ought to help me out and give me a little something?" The man said, "Why, certainly my friend. I think I owe you something." He called his clerk and he said, "Come here, Jim. Go back of that counter and get this man a bottle of Sloan's liniment. He may have rheumatism for all I know." [Laughter.]

Mr. President, the Senators from Arkansas and Kentucky want me to tell them how I would draw the legislation [to share the wealth].

First, I would guarantee that there would be no such thing in the United States as a man possessing more than somewhere around 100 to 200 times the average family wealth. What would that mean in the United States today? It would mean that there would be nobody in the United States who could own more than between a million and a half and three million dollars as a fortune. I might get it down a little below that. . . . No person shall own or possess wealth or property in the United States of America beyond an amount in excess of 200 times the average family fortune. This means that we would limit fortunes tomorrow to somewhere around $3,000,000.

[Second, I would guarantee] a homestead to every family in the United States of America.

No one should have a homestead worth less than one-third the average family fortune. How much would that have been, according to the United States estimates, in the prosperous days, and if my plan were adopted you would not find a record of a time in the past when our people were as prosperous as they would then be.

There was national wealth amounting to around $421,000,000,000 at one time, according to the estimates. Take that $421,000,000,000 and divide it into 24,000,000 families in the United States, and you have an average wealth of $17,000 to the family.

Guarantee to every family a homestead of one-third that amount, somewhere between five and six thousand dollars, and that will mean that every family of an average of four and a half to five people, according to the figures—the number varies depending on whether times are good or bad—would have a shelter under which to live, and would have those things necessary to enable them to live in respectable comfort and happiness. They would be able to have a home in which to live, land to till if they were farmers, and the furniture and the accoutrements of a house up to the value of $5,000, free of debt, and there would be no trouble about it. Each family might have some kind of automobile and radio. All free of debt.

[Third], the income of every family of America shall not be less than from one-third to one-half the average family income of the particular year. The income of no one person shall be more than 100 times the income of the average family for that year.

Without the least trouble at all there can be at least an average family income of around $5,000 a year in America if wealth and income are reasonably distributed, so that people can purchase, and mechanical appliances can be used, rather than prohibited because of a lack of distribution of income and capital.

Therefore if it can be guaranteed that a family will never be below the poverty line of somewhere around $2,000 in annual income, it would still leave somewhere around one-half of the income of the head of such a family, if not more—perhaps two-thirds of it—to be used and to be garnered by the man with better intellect and by the financial masters who weave not, but who nevertheless are arrayed in such manner that not even Solomon in all his glory appears as one of them.

Mr. President, how are we going to get this money? We are going to take into the ownership of the United States of America every dollar, every bit of property that anybody owns above a few million dollars, and we are going to distribute that property, either by selling it and distributing it or otherwise, to those who have less than a homestead of around $5,000. That is how we are going to get it.

It is said that cannot be done. It has been done. The Bible says it has been done.... The Bible says that every man will rest under his own vine and under his own tree, and that they who have houses, goods, and things of which they have no need, will bring them in to those who rule, and those who rule will distribute them out to those who have need of them. That is what is said in the Bible. You do not have to go very far to find out how it is all going to be done, or how it must be done.

Now, Mr. President, I have no objection to the Senate recessing.

Mr. BARKLEY. Mr. President, I do not know of anything, which the Senate would rather do at this moment.

Source: Congressional Record, 74th Congress, 1st Session (1935), 7585–7586, 7589–7594.

Document 5
THE SECOND NEW DEAL—THE FIGHT AGAINST ECONOMIC ROYALISTS AND FOR REFORM

The two speeches excerpted here well illustrate the vast change in the fundamental tone of FDR's appeal to the people that occurred between the early years of New Deal and the election of 1936. Documents 2 and 3 illustrate the "concert of interests" approach Roosevelt intoned during the First New Deal, appealing to Americans of all classes to cooperate. The two speeches excerpted here—the first his speech accepting the Democratic presidential nomination on June 27, 1936, and the second FDR's inaugural address of January 20, 1937—illustrate a major theme that developed during the enactment of the Second New Deal during 1935 and more openly during the 1936 campaign. Now FDR blames vicious elements within the business and financial communities for the depression and the difficulty the nation has in achieving recovery. A second thematic difference emerges too from a comparison of Roosevelt's message in documents 2 and 3 and the one in the speeches excerpted here, a pronounced shift in emphasis from the goal of economic restoration in 1933 to the goal of social reform and welfare in the 1936–1937 speeches.

These speeches contain images, expressions, and ideals that have entered America's language and its consciousness. Reading the texts of FDR's speeches cannot, however, adequately convey their impact, and the reader who has not done so should seize the first opportunity to hear them electronically.

[Speech accepting the presidential nomination, June 27, 1936]

It was to win freedom from the tyranny of political autocracy that the American Revolution was fought. That victory gave the business of governing into the hands of the average man, who won the right with his neighbors to make and order his own destiny through his own Government. Political tyranny was wiped out at Philadelphia on July 4, 1776.

Since that struggle, however, man's inventive genius released new forces in our land which reordered the lives of our people. The age of machinery, of railroads; of steam and electricity; the telegraph and the radio; mass production, mass distribution—all of these combined to bring forward a new civilization and with it a new problem for those who sought to remain free.

For out of this modern civilization economic royalists carved new dynasties. New kingdoms were built upon concentration of control over material things. Through new uses of corporations, banks and securities, new machinery of industry and agriculture, of labor and capital—all undreamed of by the fathers—the whole structure of modern life was impressed into this royal service.

There was no place among this royalty for our many thousands of small business men and merchants who sought to make a worthy use of the American system of initiative and profit. They were no more free than the worker or the farmer. Even honest and progressive-minded men of wealth, aware of their obligation to their generation, could never know just where they fitted into this dynastic scheme of things.

It was natural and perhaps human that the privileged princes of these new economic dynasties, thirsting for power, reached out for control over Government itself. They created a new despotism and wrapped it in the robes of legal sanction. In its service new mercenaries sought to regiment the people, their labor, and their property. And as a result the average man once more confronts the problem that faced the Minute Man.

The hours men and women worked, the wages they received, to the conditions of their labor—these had passed beyond the control of the people, and were imposed by this new industrial dictatorship. The savings of the average family, the capital of the small business man, the investments set aside for old age—other people's money—these were tools which the new economic royalty used to dig itself in.

Those who tilled the soil no longer reaped the rewards which were their right. The small measure of their gains was decreed by men in distant cities.

Throughout the Nation, opportunity was limited by monopoly. Individual initiative was crushed in the cogs of a great machine. The field open for free business was more and more restricted. Private enterprise, indeed, became too private. It became privileged enterprise, not free enterprise.

A small group had concentrated into their own hands an almost complete control over other people's property, other people's money, other people's labor—other people's lives. For too many of us life was no longer free; liberty no longer real; men could no longer follow the pursuit of happiness.

Against economic tyranny such as this, the American citizen could appeal only to the organized power of Government. The collapse of 1929 showed up the despotism for what it was. The election of 1932 was the people's mandate to end it. Under that mandate it is being ended.

The royalists of the economic order have considered political freedom was the business of the Government, but they have maintained that economic slavery was nobody's business. They granted that the Government could protect the citizen in his right to vote, but they denied that the Government could do anything to protect the citizen in his right to work and his right to live.

Governments can err, Presidents do make mistakes, but the immortal Dante tells us that divine justice weighs the sins of the cold-blooded and the sins of the warm-hearted in different scales.

Better the occasional faults of a Government that lives in a spirit of charity than the consistent omissions of a Government frozen in the ice of its own indifference.

There is a mysterious cycle in human events. To some generations much is given. Of other generations much is expected. This generation of Americans has a rendezvous with destiny.

In this world of ours in other lands, there are some people, who, in times past, have lived and fought for freedom, and seem to have grown too weary to carry on the fight. They have sold their heritage of freedom for the illusion of a living. They have yielded their democracy.

I believe in my heart that only our success can stir their ancient hope. They begin to know that here in America we are waging a great and successful war. It is not alone a war against want and destitution and economic demoralization. It is more than that; it is a war for the survival of democracy. We are fighting to save a great and precious form of government for ourselves and for the world.

[Second Inaugural Address, January 20, 1937]

Let us ask again: Have we reached the goal of our vision of that fourth day of March, 1933? Have we found our happy valley?

I see a great nation, upon a great continent, blessed with a great wealth of natural resources. Its hundred and thirty million people are at peace among themselves; they are making their country a good neighbor among the nations. I see a United States which can demonstrate that, under democratic methods of government, national wealth can be translated into a spreading volume of human comforts hitherto unknown, and the lowest standard of living can be raised far above the level of mere subsistence.

But here is the challenge to our democracy: In this nation I see tens of millions of its citizens—a substantial part of its whole population—who at this very moment are denied the greater part of what the lowest standards of today call the necessities of life.

I see millions of families trying to live on incomes so meager that the pall of family disaster hangs over them day by day.

I see millions whose daily lives in city and on farm continue under conditions labeled indecent by so-called polite society half a century ago.

I see millions denied education, recreation, and the opportunity to better their lot and the lot of their children.

I see millions lacking the means to buy the products of farm and factory and by their poverty denying work and productiveness to many other millions.

I see one-third of a nation ill-housed, ill-clad, ill-nourished.

It is not in despair that I paint you that picture. I paint it for you in hope—because the Nation, seeing and understanding the injustice in it, proposes to paint it out. We are determined to make every American citizen the subject of his country's interest and concern; and we will never regard any faithful, law-abiding group within our borders as superfluous. The test of our progress is not whether we add more to the abundance of those who have much; it is whether we provide enough for those who have too little.

Source: See Samuel I. Rosenman, ed., *The Public Papers and Addresses of Franklin D. Roosevelt,* Vol. V (New York: Random House, 1938), 230–236; Vol. VI (New York: Macmillan, 1941), 1–5.

Document 6
THE SUPREME COURT'S SWITCH

One of the most memorable events of the 1930s was FDR's clash with the Supreme Court in 1937, occasioned by what he deemed the threat the Court posed to key measures of the New Deal. In May 1935, the Court had found the N.I.R.A. unconstitutional in the Schechter case. Abandoning the NRA approach to recovery and reform, the New Deal turned during the summer of 1935 to a new approach, producing the National Labor Relations Act, the Social Security Act, and a number of other monumentally important measures. Much that FDR hoped to achieve remained undone, however, such as a national minimum wage and maximum hour law. Two Supreme Court decisions the next year, however, threatened what the New Deal had done and might still accomplish. The first, *Carter v. Carter Coal Co.*, overturned the Guffey Act, a 1935 law designed to allow the coal industry collectively to fix prices and wages. The second, the *Tipaldo* decision, declared unconstitutional a New York state minimum wage for women. The constitutional doctrines asserted in *Carter* clearly threatened the viability of the National Labor Relations Act, for the Court clung to a narrow interpretation of the Constitution's commerce clause, to the concept that "manufacture is not commerce," and that the federal government, therefore, cannot regulate the conditions of manufacture. *Tipaldo* was equally bad, from the New Deal's viewpoint, because, by reaffirming the reasoning of the 1923 *Adkins* decision, the Court appeared to say that the "liberty of contract" doctrine implied by the due process clause of the Fifth and Fourteenth Amendments outlawed both state and federal laws fixing minimum wages.

These 1936 decisions persuaded FDR, following his electoral triumph in November of that year, early in 1937 to challenge the Court openly with what would be called the "court packing plan." This proposed law would have let the president, in effect, enlarge the number of justices on the Court from nine by several more, under certain circumstances, and thus gain control of it. The Court's response was a dramatic shift, the "switch in time that saved nine." In two key decisions delivered early in that year, one involving a Washington state minimum wage law and a hotel worker named Parrish, the other a dispute between the NLRB and the Jones & Laughlin Steel Corporation, the Court reversed the reasoning it had employed less than a year before. In the *Parrish* decision the court now acknowledged a broad power of the government to regulate working conditions, and in the NLRB case the Court abandoned the narrow interpretation of the commerce clause it had enforced for over fifty years.

Perusal of the following excerpts from these four cases, presented chronologically, will repay a careful reader with a good deal of understanding of the constitutional issues at stake in 1936–1937.

[*Carter v. Carter Coal Co.*, May 18, 1936]

Mr. Justice Sutherland delivered the opinion of the Court.

The purposes of the "Bituminous Coal Conservation Act of 1935," involved in these suits, as declared by the title, are to stabilize the bituminous coal-mining industry and promote its interstate commerce; to provide for cooperative marketing of bituminous coal; to levy a tax on such coal and provide for a drawback under certain conditions; to declare the production, distribution, and use of such coal to be affected with a national public interest; to conserve the national resources of such coal; to provide for the general welfare, and for other purposes. . . . The constitutional validity of the act is challenged in each of the suits.

The questions involved will be considered under the following heads.

The purposes of the act as set forth in § 1, and the authority vested in Congress by the Constitution to effectuate them.

Whether the labor provisions of the act can be held as an exercise of the power to regulate interstate commerce.

[The Court finds, under each of these points, as follows, that:]

Certain recitals contained in the act plainly suggest that its makers were of opinion that its constitutionality could be sustained under some general federal power, thought to exist, apart from the specific grants of the Constitution.

The ruling and firmly established principle is that the powers which the general government may exercise are only those specifically enumerated in the Constitution, and such implied powers as are necessary and proper to carry into effect the enumerated powers. Whether the end sought to be attained by an act of Congress is legitimate is wholly a matter of constitutional power and not at all of legislative discretion. Legislative congressional discretion begins with the choice of means and ends with the adoption of methods and details to carry the delegated powers into effect. The distinction between these two things—power and discretion—is not only very plain but very important. For while the powers are rigidly limited to the enumerations of the Constitution, the means which may be employed to carry the powers into effect are not restricted, save that they must be appropriate, plainly adapted to the end, and not prohibited by, but consistent with, the letter and spirit of the Constitution. *McCulloch* v. *Maryland.*

Since the validity of the act depends upon whether it is a regulation of interstate commerce, the nature and extent of the power conferred upon Congress by the commerce clause becomes the determinative question in this branch of the case. The commerce clause vests in Congress the power—"To regulate Commerce with foreign Nations, and among the several States, and with the Indian Tribes." The function to be exercised is that of regulation. The thing to be regulated is the commerce described. In exercising the authority conferred by this clause of the Constitution, Congress is powerless to regulate anything which is not commerce, as it is powerless to do anything about commerce which is not regulation. We first inquire, then—What is commerce?

As used in the Constitution, the word "commerce" is the equivalent of the phrase "intercourse for the purposes of trade," and includes transportation, purchase, sale, and exchange of commodities between the citizens of the different states. And the power to regulate commerce embraces the instruments by which commerce is carried on.

The distinction between manufacture and commerce [is a vital distinction].

That commodities produced or manufactured within a state are intended to be sold or transported outside the state does not render their production or manufacture subject to federal regulation under the commerce clause.

Much stress is put upon the evils which come from the struggle between employers and employees over the matter of wages, working conditions, the right of collective bargaining, etc., and the resulting strikes, curtailment and irregularity of production and effect on prices; and it is insisted that interstate commerce is *greatly* affected thereby. But, in addition to what has just been said, the conclusive answer is that the evils are all local evils over which the federal government has no legislative control.

[*Morehead, Warden, v. New York ex rel. Tipaldo*, June 1, 1936]

Mr. Justice Butler delivered the opinion of the Court.

This is a habeas corpus case originating in the supreme Court of New York. Relator was indicted in the county court of Kings county and sent to jail to await trial upon the charge that as manager of a laundry he failed to obey the mandatory order of the state industrial commissioner prescribing minimum wages for women employees.

The state court rightly held that the *Adkins* case controls this one and requires that relator be discharged upon the ground that the legislation under which he was indicted and imprisoned is repugnant to the due process clause of the Fourteenth Amendment.

Upon the face of the act the question arises whether the State may impose upon the employers state-made minimum wage rates for all competent experienced women workers whom they may have in their service. That question involves another one. It is: Whether the State has power similarly to subject to state-made wages all adult women employed in trade, industry or business, other than house and farm work. These were the questions decided in the *Adkins* case. So far at least as concerns the validity of the enactment under consideration, the restraint imposed by the due process clause of the Fourteenth Amendment upon legislative power of the State is the same as that imposed by corresponding provision of the Fifth Amendment upon the legislative power of the United States.

The right to make contracts about one's affairs is a part of the liberty protected by the due process clause. Within this liberty are provisions of contracts between employer and employee fixing the wages to be paid. In making contracts of employment, generally speaking, the parties have equal right to obtain from each other the best terms they can by private bargaining. Legislative abridgement of that freedom can only be justified by the existence of exceptional circumstances. Freedom of contract is the general rule and restraint the exception. . . . [and, according to Adkins,] "we cannot accept the doctrine that women of mature age . . . require or may be subjected to restrictions upon their liberty of contract which could not lawfully be imposed in the case of men under similar circumstances. To do so would be to ignore all the implications to be drawn from the present day trend of legislation, as well as that of common thought and usage, by which woman is accorded emancipation from the old doctrine that she must be given special protection or be subjected to special restraint in her contractual and civil relationships."

The decision and the reasoning upon which it rests clearly show that the State is without power by any form of legislation to prohibit, change or nullify contracts between employers and adult women workers as to the amount of wages to be paid.

[*West Coast Hotel Co. v. Parrish et al.*, March 29, 1937]

Mr. Chief Justice Hughes delivered the opinion of the Court.

This case presents the question of the constitutional validity of the minimum wage law of the State of Washington.

We think that the question which was not deemed to be open in the *Morehead* case is open and is necessarily presented here. The Supreme Court of Washington has upheld the minimum wage statute of that State. It has decided that the statute is a reasonable exercise of the police power of the State. In reaching that conclusion the state court has invoked principles long established by this Court in the application of the Fourteenth Amendment. The state court has refused to regard the decision in the *Adkins* case as determinative and has pointed to our decisions both before and since that case as justifying its position. We are of the opinion that this ruling of the state court demands on our part a reëxamination of the *Adkins* case. The importance of the question, in which many States having similar laws are concerned, the close division by which the decision in the *Adkins* case was reached, and the economic conditions which have supervened, and in the light of which the reasonableness of the exercise of the protective power of the State must be considered, make it not only appropriate, but we think imperative, that in deciding the present case the subject should receive fresh consideration.

The principle which must control our decision is not in doubt. The constitutional provision invoked is the due process clause of the Fourteenth

Amendment governing the States, as the due process clause invoked in the Adkins case governed Congress. In each case the violation alleged by those attacking minimum wage regulation for women is deprivation of freedom of contract. What is this freedom? The Constitution does not speak of freedom of contract. It speaks of liberty and prohibits the deprivation of liberty without due process of law. In prohibiting that deprivation the Constitution does not recognize an absolute and uncontrollable liberty. Liberty in each of its phases has its history and connotation. But the liberty safeguarded is liberty in a social organization which requires the protection of law against the evils which menace health, safety, morals and welfare of the people. Liberty under the Constitution is thus necessarily subject to the restraints of due process, and regulation which is reasonable in relation to its subject and is adopted in the interests of the community is due process.

In dealing with the relation of employer and employed, the legislature has necessarily a wide field of discretion in order that there may be suitable protection of health and safety, and that peace and good order may be promoted through regulations designed to insure wholesome conditions of work and freedom from oppression.

What can be closer to the public interest than the health of women and their protection from unscrupulous and overreaching employers? And if the protection of women is a legitimate end of the exercise of state power, how can it be said that the requirement of the payment of a minimum wage fairly fixed in order to meet the very necessities of existence is not an admissible means to that end?

Our conclusion is that the case of *Adkins v. Children's Hospital, supra,* should be, and it is, overruled. The judgment of the Supreme Court of the State of Washington is Affirmed.

[*National Labor Relations Board v. Jones & Laughlin Steel Corp.,*
April 12, 1937]

Mr. Chief Justice Hughes delivered the opinion of the Court.

In a proceeding under the National Labor Relations Act of 1935, the National Labor Relations Board found that the respondent, Jones & Laughlin Steel Corporation, had violated the Act by engaging in unfair labor practices affecting commerce. . . . The unfair labor practices charged were that the corporation was discriminating against members of the union with regard to hire and tenure of employment, and was coercing and intimidating its employees in order to interfere with their self-organization. The discriminatory and coercive action alleged was the discharge of certain employees.

The National Labor Relations Board, sustaining the charge, ordered the corporation to cease and desist from such discrimination and coercion, to offer reinstatement to ten of the employees named, to make good their losses in pay, and to post for thirty days notices that the corporation would not discharge or discriminate against members, or those desiring to become members, of the labor union. As the corporation failed to comply, the Board petitioned the Circuit Court of Appeals to enforce the order. The court denied the petition, holding that the order lay beyond the range of federal power. [We agreed to review the Circuit Court's decision.]

We think it clear that the National Labor Relations Act may be construed so as to operate within the sphere of constitutional authority.

It is a familiar principle that acts which directly burden or obstruct interstate or foreign commerce, or its free flow, are within the reach of the congressional power. Acts having that effect are not rendered immune because they grow out of labor disputes.

In its present application, the statute goes no further than to safeguard the right of employees to self-organization and to select representatives of their own choosing for collective bargaining or other mutual protection without restraint or coercion by their employer.

That is a fundamental right.

Respondent [i.e., the corporation] says that whatever may be said of employees engaged in interstate commerce, the industrial relations and activities in the manufacturing department of respondent's enterprise are not subject to federal regulation. The argument rests upon the proposition that manufacturing in itself is not commerce.

The congressional authority to protect interstate commerce from burdens and obstructions is not limited to transactions which can be deemed to be an essential part of a "flow" of interstate or foreign commerce. Burdens and obstructions may be due to injurious action springing from other sources. The fundamental principle is that the power to regulate commerce is the power to enact "all appropriate legislation" for "its protection and advancement."

Although activities may be intrastate in character when separately considered, if they have such a close and substantial relation to interstate commerce that their control is essential or appropriate to protect that commerce from burdens and obstructions, Congress cannot be denied the power to exercise that control.

When industries organize themselves on a national scale, making their relation to interstate commerce the dominant factor in their activities, how can it be maintained that their industrial labor relations constitute a forbidden field into which Congress may not enter when it is necessary to protect interstate commerce from the paralyzing consequences of industrial war?

Experience has abundantly demonstrated that the recognition of the right of employees to self-organization and to have representatives of their own choosing for the purpose of collective bargaining is often an essential condition of industrial peace.

Our conclusion is that . . . the Act is valid as here applied.

Sources: *Carter v. Carter Coal Co.,* 298 U.S. 238 (1936) at 278, 286, 289–291, 297–299, 301, 308; *Morehead, Warden, v. New York ex rel. Tipaldo,* 298 U.S. 602 (1936) at 609–611; *West Coast Hotel Co. v. Parrish et al.,* 300 U.S. 379, at 386, 389–393, 398, 400; *National Labor Relations Board v. Jones & Laughlin Steel Corp.,* 301 U.S. 2 at 22, 30–34, 36–37, 40–42, 49.

Document 7
THE NEW DEAL AND RESTORING FREE ENTERPRISE

When a sharp economic recession began in mid-1937, arresting the trend of the previous four years toward recovery, Roosevelt and his advisors were thrown into a quandary. Some advised a return to policies similar to those of the NRA years, whereas others, almost in the manner of Hoover, urged reliance on budget balancing to restore business confidence. The voices that won out were those that urged a revival of heavy spending for work relief and other purposes, even though it would mean large budget deficits. Many of these same advisors also urged FDR to couple this spending with a revival of enforcement of the antitrust laws on the theory that prices throughout the economy were kept too high by industrial concentration and monopolistic behavior, thus robbing the people of purchasing power and stifling a full-blooded recovery of consumption and employment. By the spring of 1938, Roosevelt had been converted to these views. He appointed Thurman Arnold to head a revitalized antitrust enforcement and, in April, asked Congress to launch an investigation of the concentration of economic power. By joint resolution, in June of the same year Congress created the Temporary National Economic Committee (TNEC) to study and report on the issues the president had raised. Under the leadership of Senator Joseph C. O'Mahoney of Wyoming, the TNEC made one of the most useful investigations in congressional history. Extensive hearings were held, and many of the nation's most noted economists were enlisted to write extensive analyses of the many ways in which noncompetitive behavior, stemming from economic concentration or from illegal price-fixing agreements, endangered the nation's economic health.

The following document, excerpted from the committee's final report, summarizes the TNEC's conclusions and reveals the extent to which mainstream New Deal thought had, at the close of the 1930s, swung to the thesis that the creation of genuine prosperity and the preservation of democracy, depended on the restoration of a more freely competitive and open enterprise capitalism.

If the [American] political structure is designed to preserve the freedom of the individual, the economic structure must not be permitted to destroy it.

The Temporary National Economic Committee, therefore, avows its faith in free enterprise. Every recommendation which it makes is intended to keep enterprise free. It condemns the regimentation of men by government because that is the antithesis of individual liberty. It also condemns the regimentation of men by concentrated economic power because that likewise is the antithesis of liberty.

The records of this Committee prove beyond possibility of successful contradiction that restrictive practices are used by some business organizations not only to destroy competition but to regiment men.

We must find the way to foster and encourage private enterprise. Private enterprise must be protected from destruction by concentrated group activity. The concentration of economic power and wealth by means of practices, devices, and organizations which decency and common sense condemn must be stopped, if enterprise is to be kept free from government control.

The committee therefore recommends the vigorous and vigilant enforcement of the antitrust laws, confident that an awakening business conscience will realize the necessity of complete cooperation in the elimination of monopolistic practice.

We must, however, not only stop the processes of concentration by the action of government and business under the antitrust laws, but the Government should actively encourage the development of new private enterprise by positive programs designed to foster and protect it. We cannot continue to rely upon government expenditures, whether by way of contribution or loan, to sustain enterprise and private employment unless we are willing to invite eventually some form of the authoritarian state. If the opportunity for the employment of idle men and idle money is to be found in a free, private enterprise system then, obviously, we must find the way to stimulate that enterprise by encouraging the investment of private savings in new private enterprise.

The work of the . . . Committee has not culminated in a set of recommendations designed to turn the economic clock back. . . . [Nor are our recommendations] intended to expand the power of Government over business or over the individual. The purpose . . . is to suggest such policies as seem calculated to restrain the continued progress of concentration which so obviously is undermining the foundations of both free enterprise and free government.

Evidence presented to the . . . Committee for many of our basic industries showed definite curtailment of production by monopoly concerns or dominant industrial groups in order to maintain prices and insure profits. The interests of other segments of the economy and the welfare of consumers were often disregarded. The present emergency brought these unhealthy conditions into national prominence and remedies are sought to cope with them.

The voluminous testimony before the . . . Committee conclusively demonstrated the potential capacity of the American economy to produce an abundance of goods and services. We are committed to the purpose of making that potential capacity the actual quantity of goods and services available to the people of this Nation. We reject as un-American and unrealistic the belief that the limits of economic achievement have been reached in the United States.

[Our] hearings and studies . . . have disclosed the restraints placed on the competitive system by the concentration of economic power with respect to the disadvantages under which small independent business labors in attempting to operate successfully. Important avenues of credit for small business have either disappeared or so altered in their conditions as no longer to be readily available. Yet small business is the seed-bed of a growing system of free enterprise upon which a healthy industrial economy depends. Its encouragement is essential to a dynamic economy.

This does not blind us to the facts developed concerning the lack of private investment sufficient to absorb in economic production the savings of our citizens during the past decade or more. Vast hoarding of unused capital has resulted. It cannot be denied that the present system of production and distribution permits the amount set aside in savings to increase at a much faster rate than the national income itself increases, causing an imbalance of serious proportions. Nor is the answer found in continued Government spending to counterbalance the accumulation of unused savings in a relatively few hands. The ultimate answer must be in such a stimulus to private enterprise that an expanding economic endeavor will immediately put all savings to work in providing the capital required for a more adequate standard of living for all our people.

No single remedy will achieve this result. Many of the recommendations offered in this report will go far, in combination, to effect it. An equitable tax system will do much. A wise program of aid to the underprivileged to increase their purchasing power will do a great deal. Strict enforcement of existing antitrust laws and more adequate antitrust legislation to prevent monopoly and insure a system of free competition in a free market will accomplish great things.

Source: U.S. Senate, *Investigation of Concentration of Economic Power: Final Report and Recommendations of the Temporary National Economic Committee*, Document No. 35, 77th Congress, 1st Session (1941), 5–10, 23, 30–31.

Document 8
A REPUBLICAN ASSESSMENT OF THE NEW DEAL

Robert A. Taft, son of President William Howard Taft, was the most influential Republican of his generation. Born in 1889, he was elected to the U.S. Senate from Ohio in 1938 and quickly became recognized as a major spokesperson for his party and as a prospective presidential candidate. His years of greatest influence would come after World War II, when he led the Republican resurgence in Congress during much of the Truman period. He failed, however, to secure the presidential nomination in either 1948 or 1952. He died in 1953.

In the radio speech of March 18, 1939, excerpted here, Taft forcefully articulated the line of thought to which all but the most right-wing Republicans of this period would subscribe. He acknowledged the necessity of federal relief and of other measures intended to relieve acute insecurity and distress but excoriated the New Dealers for preventing genuine recovery by stifling business initiative. Remember that Taft was speaking in the aftermath of the economic downturn of 1938, the "Roosevelt Recession," as the Republicans called it, which had deflated the New Deal's promise of steady recovery. For this and other reasons, Taft was speaking to a nation much more receptive to his moderately phrased but strongly anti–New Deal message than would have been true in the earlier years of the depression decade.

The New Deal tide is rapidly receding, and . . . the people are again looking to the Republican Party for leadership. It is most important that the Republicans, even though they are still in the opposition, formulate their program on which to appeal to the people for a change of administration.

After 6 years of New Deal rule, after every kind of experiment, and the addition of $20,000,000,000 to the national debt the fundamental problems are still unresolved. More than 10,000,000 people are unemployed in the United States today, about 3,000,000 of them receiving a bare subsistence from the W.P.A. Twenty million people are looking to the Government for food. Millions more are receiving inadequate wages and fall in that underprivileged class for whom the New Dealers have shed tears in every speech, and to whom they have repeatedly promised prosperity and security. And yet there are more people underprivileged today, more people who have barely enough to live on, than there have been at any time except at the very bottom of the depression.

[The New Deal has] relied on three types of Government activity. The first type consists of direct relief, in different forms, to the lower-income groups. The attempt to administer from Washington a great work-relief program throughout the entire United States has resulted in inefficiency, politics, and a vast expense which threatens a complete bankruptcy of the Federal Government.

The second type of New Deal activity included the Government regulatory measures, which attempt to raise the income of this group or that group by controlling prices, wages, hours, and practices throughout the United States. Such were the N.R.A. and the A.A.A. Such are the laws regulating agriculture today, the Guffey Coal Act, the wage-hour law. This type of law has completely failed in its purpose.

This type of law is one of the most discouraging to private enterprise. No man can tell when the Government may step into his business and nullify all of the effort and energy and ingenuity he may have shown in developing that business. He is hounded by inspectors, excessive regulation, reports, and red tape. Many have gone out of business and many have stayed out of business because they could not feel certain that with all this Government regulation they might be utterly wasting their time and their money.

The other type of New Deal experiment is direct Government-business activity in fields where the Government thinks that private enterprise has fallen down on its job. Of this character are the T.V.A., the Rural Electrification Administration, the lending agencies extending Government credit to home owners, the building of canals and other self-liquidating public works. Unquestionably some of this activity is justified, though usually the reason that private capital has failed the entire field is because the enterprise is unprofitable in spite of the glowing prospectus of some Government departments.

But there are some unprofitable things which a government should start, and governments always have done something of this kind. It is a question of degree. It is very doubtful in my mind whether the T.V.A. ever was justified in view of the development of public utilities in the Tennessee Valley, but now we have it and have to operate it to the best advantage.

I have pointed out that the New Deal seemed to be inspired with a hostility to the entire preexisting American economic system. The result is that these three types of measures which I have described have not been administered with any special care to preserve the best features of private industry and encourage it to bring about recovery. The relief measures have been inefficient and expensive. They have resulted in a tremendous burden of taxation which beats down on the man who is trying to make his own living. There has been no effort to preserve conditions under which a man, striving for a private job and doing his job well, shall be encouraged and preferred to the man on W.P.A. The other two types of measures, Government regulation and Government competition, have directly discouraged private activity of every kind. More men have gone out of business in the last five years than have gone into business because of the complete uncertainty whether they can survive a constant Government interference.

What then should be the Republican program? It must combine a policy of encouragement to private industry, which can put millions of men to work, with sincere and effective administration of relief measures to assist directly the lower-income groups. It must recognize the absolute necessity of relief measures in this country for many years to come. . . . We must assist the lower-income groups by direct relief, by work relief, by old age pensions, by unemployment insurance and by some form of housing subsidy.

But the administration of this relief must be carried on with the greatest care that it may not destroy our entire American system and put the whole population on relief. It must be carried on with economy because the cost of supporting those who do not work is undoubtedly borne by those who are working.

[And] we must take every possible measure to cure the unemployment problem. It can only be cured by more jobs in private industry. We must, therefore, take every possible measure to encourage people to put their time and money again into the development of private industry. . . . The people must feel again that the making of a deserved profit is not a crime, but a merit. They must feel again that the Government is interested in the prosperity of the businessman. They must feel again that the Government does not regard every businessman as a potential crook.

But there must be more than mental reassurance. There must be an abandonment as far as possible of Government fixing of prices, wages, and business practices. Americans must be assured that they will not be met by Government competition in their field of business activity. They must feel that Government activity will be confined to keeping their markets open, free, and competitive, so that they will have an equal chance with their little neighbor or their big neighbor. They must feel that Government expenses will be held down as far as possible, so that the tax burdens may not deprive them of the fruits of their most successful efforts. They would like to know that the currency is stable, the Government's fiscal policy sound, and all danger of inflation of the currency removed.

Prosperity can only be brought about by increased production. This country was built up by millions of men, starting new enterprises. . . . Employment increased steadily for 150 years, not by arbitrary building up of consumers' purchasing power, but by encouraging production and putting men to work. The theory that relief payments stimulate production is disproved by our own experience.

If we can stop spending money now, if we can stop the tremendous expansion of Government activity, regulation and taxation, it is not too late to resume the progress which made this country the envy of the world; but if we continue for 6 years more, the course which we have pursued, he is a bold man who will say that we can then restore prosperity under a democratic form of government.

Source: "New Deal and the Republican Program," Radio Address by Senator Robert A. Taft, March 18, 1939, reproduced in *Congressional Record*, 76th Congress, 1st Session (1939), Appendix, 1355–1357.

Document 9
THE NEW DEAL AND THE REMAKING OF THE WEST

Construction of public works during the New Deal years changed the face of America. Thousands of schools, courthouses, and other public buildings rose through the contracts awarded by Harold Ickes's PWA. The most ambitious construction projects were awesome in scope and impact, and for many Americans served to renew faith in the country's capacity to recover from the depression and renew prosperous growth. The highest profile projects were in the West, all connected to harnessing the region's rivers to supply water and power for extensive agricultural and urban growth. The projects required great technical skill and inventiveness and tended to confer something akin to heroic status on the engineers who planned and carried them out, and to restore confidence in the power of technological progress as the way to a better future.

There were many western projects, but the damming and harnessing of the Columbia and Colorado Rivers had pivotal significance. Both projects included massive primary dams that would form gigantic man-made lakes, a system of subsidiary dams and irrigation systems to make an extensive region of arid but fertile land bloom. The origins of both these projects antedated the depression. The Boulder Dam Project Act became law in 1928, and initial construction began under Hoover, though most of the construction of the great dam itself, as well as the subsidiary dams, canals, and aqueducts, was done during the Roosevelt years. The Columbia project, though proposed and argued about for many years previously, was entirely the product of the 1930s in planning and execution.

This document is an excerpt from a story appearing in 1939 in *The Saturday Evening Post*, a very high-circulation family magazine that reached many middle-class homes. It featured both fiction and stories about the current American scene and often reflected the mood and spirit of its middle-class readership. To the writer of this article, these federal projects clearly signified the nation's capacity for renewal and expansion, and it is likely that his readers resonated with his message. The author's descriptions in themselves are interesting, but more important is what his tone suggests about America's attitude, in 1939, to these "Great Works" in the West.

Fed by ice and snow, the Columbia River rises in British Columbia, enters the United States by the northeastern corner of the state of Washington and cuts its way through the mountains to the Pacific Ocean. Of the fast rivers it is the largest on the continent; it is second in point of flow only to the slow Mississippi.

[The] earth material gouged out and ground up by the river was deposited in the form of silt over a large, fairly flat area, and that area now is fertile, or would be if it had any water. We found it there and named it the Big Bend country, at a time, unfortunately, when the rainfall was more than normal. The railroads made a land boom on it. Thousands of settlers rushed in to plant bonanza wheat. After one or two good crops, it all dried up again. Many of the forsaken farmhouses are still there, falling down. . . . [The] cost of . . . water [brought by canal] would be more than irrigated agriculture could afford to pay . . . [but] the Government got the idea of the multiple-purpose dam, which is a dam to control . . . floods, to aid navigation, to provide water for irrigation, and to produce cheap hydroelectric power for the people, all at one time, within the argument that profits from the power business will make it possible to provide water for irrigation at a price that agriculture can afford to pay; besides, . . . by the same stroke the wicked power trust will be cut off at the pocket.

But after it has done all this, . . . [the water] left to go over the top of the dam will . . . come to Bonneville dam. It is intended that there shall be ten dams between Grand Coulee and the Pacific Ocean.

Bonneville dam, now finished, is in the lower Columbia River, 140 miles from its mouth at tidewater. Ocean-going vessels are expected to navigate the river beyond this point. How shall an ocean-going vessel get over a seventy-foot dam? For this purpose the highest lock in the world is provided.

The Colorado was a ferocious river. . . . Gathering up the . . . waters of Wyoming, Colorado and Utah, it came to Northwestern Arizona and made there the Grand Canyon, 200 miles long, fifteen miles across and more than a mile deep. . . . From there it went on south looking for the Gulf of California and taking with it the materials it had gouged out of Grand Canyon. When it came to the low desert land, it used those materials to build itself a bed higher than the surrounding country. In fits of tumescence it would break its own banks and go marauding at large with a destructive mania. Once when it did that it made a new river, flowing north in the Imperial Valley, where the first peas and lettuce and cantaloupes come from; and this was disastrous, because Imperial Valley is below sea level and there is no way for flood water ever to get out.

For many miles both ways from the river the land was arid and thirsty. The future of Los Angeles' civilization was limited for want of water. In this one river was water enough for all purposes, enough to irrigate millions of acres of desert land, enough to supply Los Angeles to the end of its imagination—if only it could be controlled. Many years ago a dam was built where it was easy to build one, for the Yuma reclamation project in the extreme southwestern corner of Arizona, just where the river enters Mexico and turns west for the Gulf: also, a canal was built through the top of Mexico into the Imperial Valley of California for irrigation. [But this was insufficient.] There was only one way to control [the river]. That was . . . at a narrow place in . . . [the] Grand Canyon ravine . . . behind a concrete dam. It was done. That is what Boulder Dam was for.

Boulder Dam—first called Hoover Dam—is one of the great engineering feats of all time. . . . The height of it is 727 feet, which makes it by far the highest dam in the world, and if you wish something to scale it by, it is a third as high again as Washington Monument, or as high as a sixty-story skyscraper.

[When] water began to rise behind the dam . . . it rose until there stood behind Boulder Dam the biggest lake man ever made. The amount of water in it is equal to 4,500 gallons for each man, woman and child of the whole human race.

Never again shall there be such a thing as a Colorado River flood, nor any waste; and in place of a river running as it will down to the sea, you have a scientific water system.

Downstream 155 miles from Boulder Dam is solitary Parker Dam.

This is the most beautiful dam structure in the world. . . . Yet it is merely a diversion dam, lifting the river only seventy feet in order that Los Angeles may take here a billion gallons of water a day and conduct it 242 miles, across deserts by steps and pump lifts, through mountain ranges by tunnel, under one natural river bed by inverted siphon, to a perpetual fountain for the dippers of Los Angeles and the twelve satellite cities of the Metropolitan Water District of Southern California. Never in the world was there an aqueduct like this one, never one so long, nor one with anywhere near its capacity. It will be opened this year.

For all that Los Angeles takes out of it . . . a large body of . . . water goes on from here.

Downstream 100 miles from Parker Dam is new Imperial Dam . . . to herd most of the river into the new All-American canal. . . . By means of this dam three quarters of the river will be turned into All-American canal, which will be opened this year.

The All-American Canal is a ditch 200 feet across and 80 miles long, and the water in it will be 21 feet deep. . . . The use of it will be to take to the Imperial Valley, of California, so much more water than it got before out of the old international canal that 1,000,000 more acres of desert land can be made to produce the succulent vegetable and melon crops for which this sunken garden, 250 feet below sea level, with a salt sea in the middle, has long been famous.

Thus, the ferocious Colorado River comes to a sad end. You will be having it at breakfast in flavored juices from the Imperial Valley and never think of it. The little of it that ever gets to the sea will be very weary water with no spirit at all. You had better not be a spirit of waters in these times. It is a bad business. If you are a little creek eroding a farmer's back pasture lot, the AAA will get you. If you are a bad and powerful river, the PWA will get you.

Source: Garet Garrett, "Great Works," *Saturday Evening Post* 211 (April 8, 1939), 5–7, 86–88.

Document 10
THE NEW DEAL AND THE FIRST LADY

Written in 1939, the article from *Life* magazine excerpted here portrayed Eleanor Roosevelt in much the same way as she is pictured by historians today. Throughout the 1930s she acted on occasion as the president's representative, visiting and reporting back on the New Deal's projects. She very successfully pursued a career as newspaper columnist and lecturer, but refrained, except on rare occasions, from outspoken political commentary or advocacy of particular social reforms. Yet her strong support of social and economic reform, and of improvement in the position blacks and women held in American society, were well known. After FDR's death, Mrs. Roosevelt continued to serve her country. She was a member of the U.S. delegation to the United Nations from 1946 to 1953, and, under President John F. Kennedy, she served as honorary head of his Commission on the Status of Women.

Not everyone during the 1930s admired her. The author alludes to the mocking imitations of Eleanor performed by Alice Longworth, her cousin, which guests at some Washington dinner parties appear to have enjoyed, and to the scorn publicly directed at her by some members of her class. The well-to-do, the social sophisticates, and Republicans generally did not always appreciate Eleanor Roosevelt.

Today's reader may be somewhat puzzled by aspects of the author's tone and some of his references. There is a hint of gentle mockery, of coyness at least, in his description of the women reporters. As for Mrs. Roosevelt, though he evidently agrees with her political orientation and ideas and admires her abilities greatly, he attributes her success in considerable part to her possession of the hallmarks of her social class—good manners, a sense of *noblesse oblige*, and restraint.

A good many of the Washington newspaperwomen who meet Mrs. Roosevelt for press conferences every Monday that she is in the White House are not sure that they want to see the President re-elected, but they do feel that in any case Eleanor Roosevelt should not be demoted. . . . The assumption that Mrs. Roosevelt's historical importance has reached a point where it should not be affected by the vicissitudes of her husband's job is increasingly shared by the country at large.

During the last seven years, Mrs. Roosevelt has . . . traveled 280,000 miles, written one million words, earned and given away over half a million dollars, shaken half a million hands, delivered several hundred lectures, radio speeches and interviews to the press knitted several dozen tiny garments for Roosevelt babies, cooked hot dogs and poured a second cup of coffee at several dozen picnics and probably not wasted as much time as the average person does in a week. . . . She has talked, intimately with more people, and covered, attentively, more American territory than the most garrulous and peripatetic Fuller Brush man. Her prodigious activities and the general impression she gives of being in a mine shaft one minute and presiding at the White House tea the next, have given rise to the legend that Mrs. Roosevelt is leading some sort of triple life.

She used to make two lecture trips a year, but she has been gathering momentum and now she makes three. She offers five talks—"The Individual and the Community," "Problems of Youth," "A Typical Day at the White House," "The Mail of a President's Wife," "Peace"—the proceeds of which she gives to charity, notably the Quakers. She has besought her lecture manager, W. Colston Leigh, to let her add some more political topics to her repertoire, but Mr. Leigh has thus far said no.

Eleanor Roosevelt is a *grande dame* in the larger sense of the phrase. Her invitations of Negroes to the White House, her visits to slums and blighted areas, her efforts to help unfortunate people who write her, are the natural results of warm heartedness in a woman of special position and surplus energy. She feels that she should take advantage of her own circumstances to help others. Her sense of social responsibility made her the main spirit behind Arthurdale, a pioneer subsistence project for the benefit of stranded West Virginia coal miners, and a disinclination to capitalize on the distress of others has caused her to discourage photographers from following her to wretched deserted mining towns from which people who go to places like Arthurdale are recruited. She is so co-operative with newspaper people most of the time that when she wants to pay an off-the-record visit she is seldom bothered by the press.

Mrs. Roosevelt's pet Government agency is the National Youth Administration, and on her trips she functions as a kind of inspector-general of NYA projects. This serves the double purpose of enabling her to keep NYA on its toes and of furnishing a good excuse to get out of tiresome local receptions in the towns she visits.

It is significant that Mrs. Roosevelt has resigned from the Colony Club, New York's swankest women's club, while retaining membership in the Cosmopolitan whose members, equally well born, are not quite so conventional. Typical of Mrs. Roosevelt's own disregard for convention is her friendly attitude toward Negroes. Instances of her sympathy with this group include her sharply critical comment at the exclusion of Marian Anderson, the singer, from Constitution Hall in Washington, and the giving of a White House tea party a few years ago for a number of delinquent girls, most of whom where colored. Once, arriving a few minutes late for a welfare conference at a church in Birmingham, Ala., where white and colored people were segregated, she sat down in a seat on the Negro side. When it was pointed out to her she tactfully asked to have a special chair placed for her at the front of the church.

The position of women is a favorite topic with Mrs. Roosevelt.

She insists that her regular press conferences be attended exclusively by female reporters, thus creating jobs for a number of newspaperwomen. Monday mornings 40 or 50 of them gather in a second floor sitting room at the White House and fire questions at Mrs. Roosevelt. . . . Some of the reporters used to sit on the floor at her feet in the early days, in order to hear better, but this was so widely ridiculed by cartoonists that they now all sit on chairs. Mrs. Roosevelt always shakes hands with the girls, saying "Good morning" in a variety of inflections. . . . Most of the girls regard Mrs. Roosevelt in the affectionate light of a slightly older and rather busy sorority sister. There have been instances, however, in which reactionary reporters have sought to protect what they considered the traditional dignity of the First

Lady's position by asking, after a particularly frank remark on Mrs. Roosevelt's part, "Do you *really* want to be quoted on that?"

My Day [Mrs. Roosevelt's syndicated newspaper column] has been an eminently successful feature ever since it started in December, 1935.

In the five years of *My Day*, Mrs. Roosevelt has only once given real comfort to the President's enemies. That was when she wrote that his projected cottage at Hyde Park would naturally cost more than the sum he had set aside for it, as he always underestimated costs. She made an attempt to cover this up later by saying the he had been right after all, and that the building had been erected within his estimate.

Intentionally or not, *My Day* is getting to be more political than it used to be. It commended the appointment of Justice Douglas to the Supreme Court, and last summer it plugged for revision of the Neutrality Act. . . . Her remarks on Fascism once inspired Mussolini's paper, *Il Popolo d'Italia*, to call for an embargo on Mrs. Roosevelt, a demand which she received with equanimity.

Mrs. Roosevelt's enormous personal charm is her own conscious handiwork. . . . She has told in her autobiography what an ugly duckling she was in her youth and as late as her husband's first campaign, some of the Roosevelt advisers were honestly worried about the impression of awkwardness which she made on people. But several years of earnest self-improvement . . . have worked wonders. She can now accept with amusement the imitations with which her cousin, Alice Longworth, whose column has fallen by the wayside while Mrs. Roosevelt's has flourished, occasionally brightens up Washington parties.

There used to be widespread criticism, especially in quarters politically opposed to her husband, of Mrs. Roosevelt's way of life. Just before the last Presidential election, at the Velvet Ball in the Waldorf in New York, as Mrs. Roosevelt walked down the ballroom, she was hissed by a group of people whose names are extremely well known in Newport and Tuxedo Park. She merely held her head a little higher as she walked on.

Source: Geoffrey T. Hellman, "Mrs. Roosevelt: Her Admirers Have Their Own 1940 Platform: A New President But the Same First Lady," *Life* 8 (February 15, 1940), 70–72, 78–80.

Glossary of Selected Terms

Antitrust laws: The Sherman Act of 1890 is the fundamental antitrust law. It prohibited "every restraint of trade." Under the Supreme Court's decisions, this meant that businessmen were prohibited from collusive behavior regarding prices or how much to produce, and that firms could not use unfair means to attain great size. The Federal Trade Commission Act and Clayton Act, both Democratic measures enacted under Woodrow Wilson, strengthened these prohibitions somewhat, as well as the government's means for enforcing them. The New Dealers, acting on the theory that too much competition had made the depression worse by lowering prices and wages, in 1933 exempted the industry codes drawn up under the aegis of the NRA from the reach of the antitrust laws, thus in effect legalizing anticompetitive agreements. After the Supreme Court nullified the NRA, the administration did little to revivify the traditional policy. In 1938, however, FDR, seeking a new policy to deal with the downturn in the economy that year, was persuaded to renew deficit spending and to blame the recession on the prevalence of monopolistic behavior in the economy. Thurman Arnold, appointed an assistant attorney general, is credited with modernizing antitrust enforcement by creating an efficient Antitrust Division within the Department of Justice and initiating hundreds of suits over the next few years. At the same time, at Roosevelt's request Congress set up the Temporary National Economic Committee (TNEC) to make a study, ably conducted and exceptionally useful when completed in 1940, into the extent of monopoly power in the economy. Between them, Arnold and the TNEC laid the basis for an active and effective renewal of antitrust enforcement after World War II.

Associationism: In his career as secretary of commerce during the 1920s, and as president, Herbert Hoover put forward the concept that, in the solution of social and economic problems, the federal government's role should be to facilitate, not supercede, the responsibilities of those groups or organizations in the private sphere that were best positioned to take effective action. The federal government's role, he argued, should be energetic and extensive but should be limited to providing information for and assisting the work of such groups. In the 1920s, for example, Hoover hoped the problem of low farm prices could be solved largely through cooperative marketing agencies owned and directed by farmers. As president, Hoover attempted to use the associationist method to turn the depression around by persuading business leaders to work together cooperatively to maintain wages and spending. His attempt failed, but the concept of associationism, of trade and professional groups taking responsibility for problems stemming from the workings of their fields, was deeply embedded in American tradition. It was so deeply embedded that his successor, Franklin Roosevelt, employed it also, appealing to businessmen, in 1933, to comply voluntarily with the program of the National Recovery Administration to abolish child labor, raise wages, and initiate a movement toward recovery from the depression.

Conservative Coalition: The Democratic Party, after the election of 1932, held a strong majority in both houses of Congress, a majority enhanced by the elections of 1934 and 1936. The Democratic increase came in large part from the big-city states of the Northeast and the industrialized Midwest. These urban Democrats pushed the party and the New Deal toward a greater emphasis on social welfare and workers' rights legislation, a movement resented by many congressmen from the more agrarian parts of the country. The loyalty of many Democratic congressmen who had entirely supported Roosevelt's legislative requests had therefore weakened somewhat by 1937. An episode in 1937, Roosevelt's presentation of his plan to pack the Supreme Court, offered Democratic congressmen a golden opportunity to oppose him, as the plan was unpopular with much of the public. Moderates now joined conservative Democratic congressmen in opposing a Roosevelt proposal, and they coalesced with the Republicans to defeat it. This coalition between Republicans and a considerable proportion of Democratic congressmen was strengthened by the 1938 elections, which enlarged the number of Republicans, often at the expense of liberal Democrats. The conservative coalition would block, or moderate, administration proposals frequently in the following years.

Court Packing Plan: Fearing the Supreme Court would continue to find key measures of the New Deal unconstitutional, early in 1937 FDR proposed a law to Congress that would enable the president to appoint an additional justice to the court for every justice over the age of seventy who failed to resign. This would have enabled him to gain control of the court, as a majority of the sitting justices were over that age. Both within and without Congress the plan was bitterly opposed as a violation of the separation of powers. The opposition arose in part from conservatives who needed a pretext to attack Roosevelt, but also in part, from a genuine concern shared by many Americans who otherwise supported the president but feared presidential overreaching in an age when dictators ruled in much of Europe. Roosevelt's plan was rejected, and, as a result of the bitter fight over it, his influence with Congress was permanently damaged. In the midst of the controversy, the Supreme Court quietly shifted away from its previously narrow interpretation of the power of Congress to regulate economic behavior. Roosevelt had in a sense won his battle, but the political cost was high.

Deficit spending: Government spending in excess of tax receipts is deficit spending. According to the ideas of John Maynard Keynes, proposed during the 1930s but not widely accepted at that time, deficit spending is a sound remedy for depressions. Traditionally, it was an article of faith that a balanced budget was the sound policy. The New Deal experienced deficits in 1933 through 1937, not because FDR believed they would promote recovery, but because the New Deal's relief programs could not otherwise be maintained. Fearing inflation as the economy strengthened, in 1937 the New Deal actually reduced planned spending for 1938 at a time when tax receipts were rising, which helped to bring on the recession of 1938. Contemporary economists regard the deficit spending of the New Deal years as very modest in relation to the need.

Domestic allotment: During the 1920s farm leaders proposed to remedy the problem of low commodity prices by having the government make sufficient purchases to drive the price up, dumping the "surplus" on the foreign market. This was the solution posed by the much-supported McNary-Haugen Bill. By 1932, opinion was shifting to support of domestic allotment, a plan pioneered by, among others, M. L. Wilson, an agricultural economist. The plan entailed limiting production of basic farm commodities by paying farmers to limit acreage under production. Both approaches were incorporated into the New Deal's Agricultural Adjustment Act of 1933, but domestic allotment was selected as the preferred method and put into effect, serving as the basis of government policy in this area for decades.

Gold standard: Throughout most of the nineteenth century and up to the time of the Great Depression, the United States and the nations of Europe observed the gold standard, the practice of fixing the value of a nation's currency in terms of a specified weight of gold. The virtues of the system are that the value of every nation's unit of money does not fluctuate and that exchange rates between the money of different countries are stable. A money system that is resistant to unpredictable change obviously is superior to the alternative. Nearly every country suspended the gold standard during World War I. The United States returned to it soon after the war, but the European nations found this difficult. England returned to it in the late 1920s. President Hoover believed it was of crucial importance for the United States to maintain and defend the gold standard, even after England abandoned it in 1931 and even though this made it more difficult to prevent further deflation of American price levels. Franklin Roosevelt, however, took the United States off the gold standard almost immediately after taking office, believing that this would make it easier to reverse the deflationary trend of the past several years.

Great Crash: Values on the New York Stock Exchange rose to unprecedented heights during the 1920s with the rate of increase especially rapid during and after 1927. Values nearly doubled between mid-1927 and September 3, 1929, the day the highest point was reached. A break occurred on September 5 and thereafter the market's course was uneven. On October 19 a series of bad trading days began, culminating in Black Tuesday, October 29. That day the index of stock prices fell 43 points, a loss that balanced all the gain of the previous year. Declines continued so that by year's end the average value of stocks was down by one-third compared with September 3. The impact was heavy because so many individuals, and investment trusts, had borrowed heavily to buy stocks. The banks that had extended these loans lost heavily, weakening many of them. Contemporary economists tend to discount the crash as the main cause of the Great Depression, though unquestionably it reduced the willingness and ability of many people to spend and had a severe dampening effect on the expectations of businessmen and investors.

Isolationism: Americans felt disillusioned by the treaty settlements made after World War I, as they appeared to be predicated on the selfish goals of England and France rather than on the principles of international justice President Woodrow Wilson had enunciated in his Fourteen Points. It was feared that the Versailles Treaty, by treating Germany badly, simply sowed the seeds of a new war. Promoted by a congressional investigation into the armaments industry conducted by Senator Gerald Nye, the conviction took hold that the United States had sacrificed without purpose in declaring war on Germany; that the only real gainers had been the munitions makers, the "merchants of death"; and that the United States should stay out of any future European conflict. The result was passage of the Neutrality Act by Congress in 1935, banning all arms sales to nations at war. President Roosevelt felt this was misguided and that self-interest demanded that America support those who opposed Germany, which was now controlled by a Nazi dictatorship. Isolationist feeling ran high, however, especially in parts of the Midwest, and Roosevelt had to proceed cautiously. In 1937, the administration secured a revision of the Neutrality Act permitting "cash and carry" sales of arms, and in 1940 and 1941, after World War II began, the United States moved toward support of Hitler's enemies.

Keynesian economics: For over a generation, John Maynard Keynes had been a leading British economist when he published, in 1936, his *General Theory of Employment, Interest and Money*. Presaged by earlier writings, the *General*

Theory revolutionized thinking about the determinants of the overall level of economic activity. The traditional wisdom of economists, embodied in Say's law, was that an economy's production of goods necessarily entailed the generation of income sufficient to buy all that was produced. Keynes showed this was not true because a great deal of a nation's income went to those who spent on investment in new plants and equipment, not just on consumption. If this class felt opportunities to invest in new means of production were insufficiently profitable, they might prefer to keep their money in a liquid (near to cash) form. A "liquidity trap" could develop, in which too much income was saved rather than invested. This would cause an economic downturn. The solution was for government to make up the shortfall in spending by running deficits, by borrowing and spending well in excess of tax receipts.

New Deal Coalition: The policies FDR pursued as president created a remodeled Democratic Party. The major change was the solidification of the Democratic grip on the allegiance of the voters of the big-city industrial states of the Northeast and Midwest. Since the turn of the century, the Democratic Party's reliable strength had been in the South and the agrarian West. The industrial region of the nation had been reliably Republican. This realignment of the electorate may have begun during the 1920s. Much of the working class of the industrial region was composed of the millions of immigrants from southern and eastern Europe, and their children, who had entered the United States in the decades before World War I. The Al Smith candidacy in 1928 gave these voters, mostly Catholic and Jewish, reason to vote Democratic. Roosevelt's attention to them in appointing public officials reinforced this precedent, but, more importantly, his relief, welfare, and prounion policies anchored an overwhelming majority of working-class voters firmly in the Democratic column. The New Deal coalition joined the workers of the North with the traditionally Democratic voters of the South and part of the West.

Progressives: The term "progressive" dates from the period from the turn of the century until World War I when reform of political and economic institutions was on the agenda of both the major parties. The reformers called progressives varied a good deal in terms of objectives. In national politics the progressive presidents, Theodore Roosevelt and Woodrow Wilson, were above all concerned with taming the lawless power of the new corporate capitalism, with regulating railroads and dealing with the power of the giant industrial companies, the "trusts." Progressives at the state and local level often had the same concerns, but for many of them, a major objective was political reform that would break the power of corrupt political bosses. Some progressives, finally, were in addition concerned with social reform and strove to ameliorate the working and living conditions of the working class. Franklin Roosevelt himself was rooted in the progressivism of prewar America, as were a number of important figures he relied on, such as Felix Frankfurter. Many Democratic congressmen of the New Deal period were veterans of Wilsonian reform, including John Nance Garner and Sam Rayburn. Often, however, surviving progressives from the prewar era, most of them from the trans-Mississippi West or the South, whether Democrat or Republican, found much of the New Deal hard to accept. Many could not abide the NRA, for example, because it flouted the policy many progressives revered of making the business system more, not less competitive, and often they could not accept the redirection of the New Deal that directed its energies less to the agrarian and more to the urban regions.

Annotated Bibliography

GENERAL WORKS ON THE ERA OF THE DEPRESSION AND THE NEW DEAL

Badger, Anthony J. *The New Deal: The Depression Years, 1933–1940.* New York: Hill and Wang, 1989. A very thoughtful and useful synthesis of the literature on the depression, Hoover, and the New Deal. Includes the most extensive and helpful bibliographical essay available in print.

Bernstein, Barton J. "The New Deal: The Conservative Achievements of Liberal Reform." In *Towards a New Past: Dissenting Essays in American History.* Edited by B. J. Bernstein. New York: Pantheon, 1967. One of the key essays that launched the "new left" critique of the New Deal popular in the 1970s and still influential today.

Biles, Roger. *A New Deal for the American People.* De Kalb: Northern Illinois University Press, 1991. A recent survey of the period, based on a thorough review of the literature, with a good bibliography.

Braeman, John. "The New Deal and the 'Broker State': A Review of the Recent Scholarly Literature." *Business History Review* 46 (1972): 409–420. A very useful review of writing on the New Deal through the 1960s.

Burns, James MacGregor. *Roosevelt: The Lion and the Fox.* New York: Harcourt, Brace, 1956. Another classic work and still useful, though old. Good on Roosevelt as a politician.

Conkin, Paul K. *The New Deal.* London: Routledge & Kegan Paul, 1968. A brief but challenging book, severely critical of the New Deal's shortcomings as a reform movement.

Edsforth, Ronald W. *The New Deal: America's Response to the Great Depression*. Malden, MA: Blackwell, 2000. A new synthesis, stressing the thesis that the depression led to a widespread breakdown of law and order and underscoring the importance and achievement of the New Deal.

Finegold, Kenneth, and Theda Skocpol. *State, Party and Policy: Industry and Agriculture in America's New Deal*. Madison: University of Wisconsin Press, 1995. Introduces the author's conception of "state capacity" into the debate about what theoretical conceptions best explain the workings of the New Deal.

Goldman, Eric. *Rendezvous with Destiny: A History of Modern American Reform*. New York: Knopf, 1952. Though outdated now in many ways, this classic work still offers useful insights regarding the motivations and ideals of the New Dealers.

Gordon, Colin. *New Deals: Business, Labor, and Politics in America, 1920–1935*. New York: Cambridge University Press, 1994. Finds that the origins of New Deal labor policy derive largely from the needs of certain industries to control production.

Hawley, Ellis W. *The New Deal and the Problem of Monopoly: A Study in Economic Ambivalence*. Rev. ed. New York: Fordham University Press, 1995. First published in 1966, this is a classic and still the best book on the New Deal's changing and contradictory policies toward business.

Kennedy, David M. *Freedom from Fear: The United States, 1929–1945*. New York: Oxford University Press, 1999. An extensive narrative of the entire period, ably synthesizing the literature. May become the standard survey.

Kyvig, David E., and Mary Ann Blasio. *New Day/New Deal: A Bibliography of the Great American Depression, 1929–1941*. Westport, CT: Greenwood Press, 1988. A very extensive but not annotated bibliography, with forty-one topics.

Leuchtenburg, William E. *Franklin D. Roosevelt and the New Deal, 1932–1940*. New York: Harper & Row, 1963. Though dated in some respects, this was for many years and to a degree still is the best one-volume work on the New Deal. Though sympathetic, the book was one of the first efforts made by those of liberal persuasion to illuminate the New Deal's shortcomings.

McElvaine, Robert S. *The Great Depression: America 1929–41*. New York: New York Times Books, 1984. An entertaining and in many ways original survey of the entire period. Argues that the depression experience caused profound shifts in popular culture and values, away from competitive individualism.

Olson, James S. *Historical Dictionary of the New Deal*. Westport, CT: Greenwood Publishing, 1985. A very useful reference tool.

Romasco, Albert U. *The Politics of Recovery: Roosevelt's New Deal*. New York: Oxford University Press, 1983. Stresses the thesis that in fashioning the New Deal Roosevelt was guided above all by political considerations. A useful book, especially concerning monetary policy in the early New Deal.

Rosenof, Theodore. *Dogma, Depression, and the New Deal: The Debate of Political Leaders over Economic Recovery*. Port Washington, NY: Kennikat, 1975. An extended commentary on the economic ideas of New Dealers, which argues that they, in almost all cases, accepted the prevailing economic and political system and that their differences with conservatives were more of degree than kind.

Schlesinger, Arthur M., Jr. *The Age of Roosevelt*. Boston: Houghton Mifflin. In three volumes, *The Crisis of the Old Order* (1956), *The Coming of the New Deal* (1958), *The Politics of Upheaval* (1960). This is a classic work, written with verve by a brilliant historian who is at the same time a highly committed New Deal liberal. It takes the story from the 1920s through 1936.

Schwarz, Jordan A. *The New Dealers: Power Politics in the Age of Roosevelt*. New York: Knopf, 1993. This book contains useful essays on many of the era's figures, some from a fresh point of view, and argues that "state capitalism" (the attempt by the government to supply and direct investment capital) was an important and overlooked aspect of the New Deal.

Watkins, Tom H. *The Hungry Years: A Narrative History of the Great Depression*. New York: Henry Holt, 1999. Contains graphic descriptions of the circumstances, events, and people of the depression years.

White, Graham J. *FDR and the Press*. Chicago: University of Chicago Press, 1979. An entertaining book that details FDR's conviction that the press was nearly all against him during most of the years of the New Deal.

ECONOMY AND SOCIETY DURING THE GREAT DEPRESSION

Barber, William J. *From New Era to New Deal: Herbert Hoover, the Economists, and American Economic Policy, 1921–1933*. New York: Cambridge University Press, 1985. Compares Hoover's thought and policies with ideas of contemporary economists. Perhaps the best exposition of Hoover's policies during the depression, and revealing of their coherence.

Bauman, John F., and Thomas H. Coode. *In the Eye of the Great Depression: New Deal Reporters and the Agony of the American People*. De Kalb: Northern Illinois University Press, 1988. Examines the work of reporters commissioned by Harry Hopkins to make a survey describing the hardship of the people.

Bernstein, Michael A. *The Great Depression: Delayed Recovery and Economic Change in America*. New York: Cambridge University Press, 1987. Sophisticated and original investigation of why investment lagged in many industries while recovering in others.

Bordo, Michael D., Claudia Goldin, and Eugene N. White, eds. *The Defining Moment: The Great Depression and the American Economy in the Twentieth Century*. Chicago: University of Chicago Press, 1998. Essays by economists on the major New Deal economic policies and their impact in later years.

Eichengreen, Barry. *Golden Fetters: The Gold Standard and the Great Depression, 1919–1939*. New York: Oxford University Press, 1992. An exhaustive study of the key role the gold standard played in bringing on, worsening, and maintaining the depression in America and abroad.

Friedman, Milton, and Anna Schwartz. *The Great Contraction, 1929–33*. Princeton, NJ: Princeton University Press, 1965. A classic work, arguing that bad monetary policy on the part of the Federal Reserve turned a downturn into an economic disaster after 1929.

Galbraith, John Kenneth. *The Great Crash*. Boston: Houghton Mifflin, 1955. Though somewhat outmoded today, remains an exceptionally readable and lively account of the crash. Argues the crash exposed profound economic weaknesses in the economy and caused the depression.

Hall, Thomas E., and J. David Ferguson. *The Great Depression: An International Disaster of Perverse Economic Policies*. Ann Arbor: University of Michigan Press, 1998. Based on a thorough knowledge of the economic literature. Though written by economists, the book is accessible to others and is one of the most reliable treatments available of the economics of the depression in America and Europe.

Kindleberger, Charles P. *The World Depression, 1929–39*. Berkeley: University of California Press, 1973. An older but still highly useful description and analysis of the depression worldwide.

Stein, Herbert. *The Fiscal Revolution in America*. 2nd rev. ed. Washington, DC: AEI Press, 1996. Traces fiscal policy through both the Hoover and Roosevelt administrations.

Temin, Peter. *Did Monetary Forces Cause the Great Depression?* New York: Norton, 1976. Finds wanting the Friedman thesis that monetary causes were the sole key factor bringing on the depression.

———. *Lessons from the Great Depression*. Cambridge, MA: MIT Press, 1989. Argues persuasively for the importance of the gold standard, and the efforts to maintain it, in causing and worsening the depression. Congratulates Roosevelt's decision to abandon the standard. This is one of the most enlightening volumes on the causes of the depression.

HERBERT HOOVER AND THE DEPRESSION

Burner, David. *Herbert Hoover: A Public Life*. New York: Knopf, 1979. Tracks Hoover's career, ideas, and policies. Based on the research of the 1960s and 1970s that followed the opening of the Hoover Presidential Library and more favorable than previous biographies.

Fausold, Martin. *The Presidency of Herbert Hoover*. Lawrence: University Press of Kansas, 1985. Still the most complete and knowledgeable treatment of Hoover as president.

Hamilton, David E. *From New Day to New Deal: American Farm Policy from Hoover to Roosevelt, 1928–1933*. Chapel Hill: University of North Carolina Press, 1991. Explains how Hoover's beliefs about the workability of associationism and his dread of statism fashioned a farm policy that could not deal with the problem in the midst of depression conditions.

Huthmacher, J. Joseph, and Warren I. Susman, eds. *Herbert Hoover and the Crisis of American Capitalism*. Cambridge, MA: Schenkman Publishing Company, 1973. Four essays by different historians in a book that helped stimulate revisionist studies of Hoover. Ellis Hawley's influential essay introduced the term "associational progressive" in describing Hoover.

Liebovich, Louis W. *Bylines in Despair: Herbert Hoover, the Great Depression, and the U.S. News Media*. Westport, CT: Greenwood Publishing, 1994. The latest and best of the studies that have evaluated and lamented Hoover's unsuccessful press relations as president.

Lisio, Donald J. *The President and Protest: Hoover, Conspiracy, and the Bonus Riot*. Columbia: University of Missouri Press, 1974. A revisionist study of Hoover's role in the events that led to the army's eviction of the Bonus Army from Washington. Much more favorable regarding Hoover than traditional views.

Olson, James Stuart. *Herbert Hoover and the Reconstruction Finance Corporation, 1931–1933*. Ames: Iowa State University Press, 1977. The most detailed study of the subject available.

Romasco, Albert U. *The Poverty of Abundance: Hoover, the Nation and the Depression*. New York: Oxford University Press, 1965. An older, but still useful study of Hoover's associationist ideology and how he applied it during the depression.

Schwartz, Jordan A. *The Interregnum of Despair: Hoover, Congress and the Depression*. Urbana: University of Illinois Press, 1970. Explores Hoover's conviction that inadequate cooperation of the Democratic-controlled Congress spoiled his recovery plan.

Wilson, Joan Hoff. *Herbert Hoover: Forgotten Progressive*. Rev. ed. Prospect Heights, IL: Waveland Press, 1992. Originally published in 1975, Wilson's biography is still useful. Emphatically rejects portrayal of Hoover as a laissez-faire conservative and stresses that his associationism was a new kind of progressivism.

FDR IN THE DEPRESSION YEARS: BIOGRAPHIES

Davis, Kenneth S. *FDR: The New Deal Years, 1933–37*. New York: Random House, 1993. The fourth volume in Davis's four-volume biography, highly regarded for its scope and integration of FDR's life with his times.

Freidel, Frank. *Franklin D. Roosevelt*, 4 vols. Boston: Little, Brown. In four volumes as follows: Vol. I, *The Apprenticeship* (1952); Vol. II, *The Ordeal* (1954); Vol. III, *The Triumph* (1956); and Vol. IV, *Launching the New Deal* (1974). A magisterial biography taking Roosevelt from his earliest involvement in national affairs through the First One Hundred Days in 1933. The standard political biography. Completed by *Franklin Delano Roosevelt: A Rendezvous with Destiny*, listed below, though not at the level of detail originally planned.

——— . *Franklin D. Roosevelt: A Rendezvous with Destiny*. New York: Little, Brown and Co., 1990. The most recent and best treatment of Roosevelt and his policies during the prelude to and during the New Deal years.

THE FIRST NEW DEAL

Biles, Roger. *The South and the New Deal*. Lexington: University Press of Kentucky, 1994. A brief but excellent review of the impact of the New Deal on the South, arguing that it initiated changes that helped lead, with the assistance of the effects of World War II, to the economic growth and social change of the modern South.

Brand, Donald R. *Corporatism and the Rule of Law: A Study of the National Recovery Administration*. Ithaca, NY: Cornell University Press, 1988. Argues, in part, that the NRA codes in some cases had positive benefits.

Collins, Robert M. *The Business Response to Keynes, 1929–1964*. New York: Columbia University Press, 1981. How certain influential business leaders moved during the New Deal years from hostility to support for deficit spending to promote prosperity, a trend that strengthened in the postwar era.

Creese, Walter L. *TVA's Public Planning: The Vision, the Reality*. Knoxville: University of Tennessee Press, 1990. Arthur Morgan, the TVA's first chairman, had an expansive vision; his agency would bring not merely cheap electricity but an array of other benefits to the Tennessee Valley through regional planning. This book details how others constricted and narrowed the TVA's mission.

Funigiello, Philip. *Toward a National Power Policy: The New Deal and the Electric Utility Industry*. Pittsburgh: University of Pittsburgh Press, 1973.

Regarded as the standard overall treatment of the implementation of the Public Utility Holding Company Act.

Galambos, Louis. *Competition and Cooperation: The Emergence of a National Trade Association*. Baltimore, MD: Johns Hopkins University Press, 1966. Study of the Cotton Textile Institute, one of the key trade associations of the 1920s and 1930s, and its role in the formation of the NRA and its policies.

Himmelberg, Robert F. *The Origins of the National Recovery Administration: Business, Government and the Trade Association Issue, 1921–1933*. Rev. ed. New York: Fordham University Press, 1994. Argues that the strongest influence on formation of the NRA was the crusade of trade associations during the 1920s and early 1930s to revise the antitrust laws so as to permit them to suppress competition.

Johnson, James P. *The Politics of Soft Coal: The Bituminous Industry from World War I through the New Deal*. Urbana: University of Illinois Press, 1979. Discusses how coal industry leaders sought to influence government policy in ways that would enable them to "stabilize" their chaotic industry.

Kennedy, Susan Estabrook. *The Banking Crisis of 1933*. Lexington: University Press of Kentucky, 1973. A highly praised, detailed study of the crisis and how the New Deal dealt with it, partly by relying upon ideas and personnel inherited from the Hoover administration.

McCraw, Thomas K. *TVA and the Power Fight: 1933–1939*. Philadelphia: J. B. Lippincott, 1971. Gives a detailed account of the political and legal struggle between the TVA and the utility leaders who tried to block its efforts to provide cheaper electricity to the South.

Olson, James S. *Saving Capitalism: The Reconstruction Finance Corporation and the New Deal, 1933–1940*. Princeton, NJ: Princeton University Press, 1988. Makes a good case for the importance of the RFC during the New Deal as it expanded its operations in many directions not only in an attempt to support financial institutions but also to stimulate new fields in the economy.

Parrish, Michael E. *Securities Regulation and the New Deal*. New Haven: Yale University Press, 1970. A closely focused account of the New Deal securities legislation of 1933 and 1934 and its subsequent implementation.

Rosen, Elliot A. *Hoover, Roosevelt, and the Brains Trust: From Depression to New Deal*. New York: Columbia University Press, 1977. A strongly argued book, highly critical of Hoover. The author discovered highly interesting new material concerning the effort to block Roosevelt's nomination.

Schwartz, Bonnie Fox. *The Civil Works Administration 1933–1934: The Business of Emergency Employment in the New Deal*. Princeton, NJ: Princeton

University Press, 1984. The standard work on the New Deal's first venture into direct federal work relief.

Shover, John L. *Cornbelt Rebellion: The Farmers Holiday Association*. Urbana: University of Illinois Press, 1965. An older book, but still useful, on the organization that caused a stir in 1932–1933 by attempting to prevent farm goods from moving to the market.

Weinstein, Michael M. *Recovery and Redistribution under the NIRA*. Amsterdam: North-Holland Publishing Co., 1980. The best by far of studies that attempt to gauge the effects of the NRA. Concludes that the codes did raise wages substantially but the impact on the economy was deflationary. The NRA retarded recovery.

POLITICAL ALTERNATIVES AND OPPONENTS OF THE NEW DEAL

Bennett, David H. *Demagogues in the Depression: American Radicals and the Union Party, 1932–1936*. New Brunswick, NJ: Rutgers University Press, 1969. The fullest treatment of the subject.

Brinkley, Alan. *Voices of Protest: Huey Long, Father Coughlin and the Great Depression*. New York: Knopf, 1982. A revisionist and highly regarded study of the messages they preached and the groups to whom they appealed. Concludes their appeal was to lower middle class America and was "radical" only in a limited sense.

Cortner, Richard C. *The Kingfish and the Constitution: Huey Long, the First Amendment, and the Emergence of Modern Press Freedom in America*. Westport, CT: Greenwood Publishing, 1996. An excellent study of the reaction to Long's effort to stifle the press in Louisiana.

Gieske, Millard L. *Minnesota Farmer-Laborism: The Third Party Alternative*. St. Paul: University of Minnesota Press, 1979. Treats the Minnesota third party, radical in some respects, with which Roosevelt attempted to cooperate.

Jeansonne, Glen. *Messiah of the Masses: Huey P. Long and the Great Depression*. New York: Harper Collins, 1993. The latest biography of Long. Offers a searching and persuasive argument that Long brought little of positive, lasting benefit to his state and often revealed his ignorance when he went into national affairs.

Lorence, James J. *Gerald J. Boileau and the Progressive-Farmer-Labor Alliance: Politics of the New Deal*. Columbia: University of Missouri Press, 1994. A study of a key figure in this Wisconsin political movement who served in Congress during much of the New Deal and played a major role in the relationship between his party and Roosevelt.

Miller, John E. *Governor Philip La Follette, The Wisconsin Progressives and the New Deal*. Columbia: University of Missouri Press, 1982. Relates the history of La Follette's ambitious attempts to offer benefits to his state, such as work relief, which enhanced the impact of the New Deal programs.

Williams, T. Harry. *Huey Long*. New York: Knopf, 1969. A fascinating and highly readable book that paints a sympathetic portrait of Long, far too sympathetic in the view of most later biographers.

THE SECOND NEW DEAL

Arnold, Joseph L. *The New Deal in the Suburbs: A History of the Greenbelt Program, 1935–1954*. Columbus: Ohio State University Press, 1971. Traces the New Deal program intended to influence the shape of suburban development.

Barnard, John. *Walter Reuther and the Rise of the Auto Workers*. Boston: Little, Brown, 1983. A brief study of this key figure in the rise of the UAW and the CIO.

Bernstein, Irving. *The Turbulent Years: A History of the American Worker, 1933–1941*. Boston: Houghton Mifflin, 1969. A survey that covers the entire history of labor's struggles and triumphs during the New Deal years. The standard source for the period as a whole.

Bindas, Kenneth J. *All of This Music Belongs to the Nation: The WPA's Federal Music Project and American Society*. Knoxville: University of Tennessee Press, 1995. Focuses on the development of the Federal Music Project, emphasizing how it promoted and deepened the popularity in American culture of such American artists as Victor Herbert, George Gershwin, and Philip Sousa.

Brock, William R. *Welfare, Democracy, and the New Deal*. New York: Cambridge University Press, 1988. Explores the role of social workers in bringing about the shift from local and state to national responsibility for unemployment relief during the early New Deal.

Brown, D. Clayton. *Electricity for Rural America: The Fight for the REA*. Westport, CT: Greenwood Publishing, 1980. Stresses the role of the South and southern leaders in creating the REA; interestingly explores the ideological factors that motivated some supporters of rural electrification—they thought it would save and preserve the family farm.

Cannon, Brian Q. *Remaking the Agrarian Dream: New Deal Rural Resettlement in the Mountain West*. Albuquerque: University of New Mexico Press, 1996. Based on oral histories as well as archival sources, portrays rural families that took part in the Resettlement Administration's program to relocate them onto irrigated farming projects in the American West.

Cochran, Bert. *Labor Communism: The Conflict That Shaped American Unions*. Princeton, NJ: Princeton University Press, 1977. Written by a former labor official, this book is quite critical of the role communists played in the formation of big labor in the later 1930s.

Conkin, Paul K. *Tomorrow a New World: The New Deal Community Program.* Ithaca, NY: Cornell University Press, 1959. A highly original book that traces one of the most utopian of the New Deal endeavors, the program that experimented with subsistence homesteads for workers, communal farms for hard-pressed farm families, and planned suburbs for commuters.

Conrad, David E. *The Forgotten Farmers: The Story of Sharecroppers in the New Deal.* Urbana: University of Illinois Press, 1965. The story of the harmful effects of the AAA's policies on southern sharecroppers and the difficulties confronting those who tried to change them.

Fine, Sidney. *Frank Murphy: The New Deal Years.* Chicago: University of Chicago Press, 1979. One of Roosevelt's most loyal political lieutenants, Murphy, as Michigan's governor, played the key role during the CIO's sit-down strike against GM by resisting lower court injunctions requiring clearing the strikers out of the factories.

———. *Sit-Down: The General Motors Strike of 1936–37.* Ann Arbor: University of Michigan Press, 1969. The standard source for the sit-down strike against GM that represented the turning point for labor in the 1930s.

Gross, James A. *The Making of the National Labor Relations Board, 1933–1937.* Albany: State University of New York Press, 1974. A very detailed and complete study of the beginnings of the NLRB under the NRA and its evolution under the Wagner Act.

Grubbs, Donald H. *Cry from the Cotton: The Southern Tenant Farmers Union and the New Deal.* Chapel Hill: University of North Carolina Press, 1971. A sympathetic treatment of this organization that argues it had substantial effect on New Deal policy, for example, the creation of the Farm Security Administration.

Hodges, James A. *New Deal Labor Policy and the Southern Cotton Textile Industry, 1933–1941.* Knoxville: University of Tennessee Press, 1986. Unionism in the southern cotton textile industry failed to take hold strongly during the 1930s, because, argues Hodges, of a conservative "worker culture" and unusually strong and persistent antiunion attitudes among employers.

Huthmacher, J. Joseph. *Senator Robert F. Wagner and the Rise of Urban Liberalism.* New York: Atheneum, 1971. A laudatory but compelling biography of an early, persistent, and sturdy champion of urban liberalism.

Keeran, Roger. *The Communist Party and the Auto Workers Unions.* Bloomington: Indiana University Press, 1980. A revisionist study, arguing that the American communists who played such an important role in the creation of unions during the later New Deal were "good communists" who had the welfare of American workers at heart and were not merely agents of a foreign conspiracy.

Leff, Mark. *The Limits of Symbolic Reform: The New Deal and Taxation, 1933–1939*. Cambridge: Cambridge University Press, 1984. A very skeptical review of New Deal taxation policy, arguing it had very little redistributionist effect.

Levine, Rhonda F. *Class Struggle and the New Deal: Industrial Labor, Industrial Capital, and the State*. Lawrence: University Press of Kansas, 1988. An analysis of the New Deal from a Marxist point of view. Stresses the importance of "intercapitalist" conflict between big and little business.

Lowitt, Richard. *The New Deal and the West*. Bloomington: Indiana University Press, 1984. One of the few books, and a very good one, on the New Deal in the trans-Mississippi West.

Mangione, Jerry. *The Dream and the Deal: The Federal Writers' Project, 1935–1943*. New York: Avon Books, 1972. A scholarly account, written by a participant.

Matthews, Jane DeHart. *The Federal Theater, 1935–1939: Plays, Relief and Politics*. Princeton, NJ: Princeton University Press, 1967. Stresses the democratic impulses behind this branch of the WPA's many-sided relief operations.

May, Dean L. *From New Deal to New Economics: The American Liberal Response to the Recession of 1937*. New York: Garland, 1981. May's thesis is that, though Roosevelt never accepted "Keynesian economics" as such, late in the New Deal era he adopted policies, prodded by Marriner Eccles and others, that amounted to exactly the same thing.

McCoy, Donald R. *Landon of Kansas*. Lincoln: University of Nebraska Press, 1967. A sympathetic biography, attempting to give Landon his due, but has been criticized for not recognizing Landon's political limitations.

McJimsey, George. *Harry Hopkins: Ally of the Poor and Defender of Democracy*. Cambridge, MA: Harvard University Press, 1987. The most recent biography and valuable for the New Deal's relief policies.

O'Brien, Ruth. *Workers' Paradox: The Republican Origins of New Deal Labor Policy, 1886–1935*. Chapel Hill: University of North Carolina Press, 1998. Shows that the Wagner Act was to a great extent the outcome of policies laid down under the Republican administrations of the 1920s.

Poppendieck, Janet. *Breadlines Knee-Deep in Wheat: Food Assistance in the Great Depression*. New Brunswick, NJ: Rutgers University Press, 1986. Details the history of the New Deal's Federal Surplus Commodities Corporation, the agency that distributed food to the needy. Argues its programs were always inadequate.

Quadagno, Jill. *The Transformation of Old Age Security: Class & Politics in the American Welfare State*. Chicago: University of Chicago Press, 1988. Beginning from the premise of the inadequacy of provision for old age under the New Deal's social security system, the author attempts to explain this by reference to factors such as the attitude of labor.

Rose, Nancy E. *Put to Work: Relief Programs in the Great Depression*. New York: Monthly Review Press, 1993. A study of work relief programs during the New Deal. Comments extensively on the tendency of the government's programs to accept the gender and race patterns of the larger society in providing work.

Salmond, John A. *The Civilian Conservation Corps and the New Deal, 1933–1942: A New Deal Case Study*. Durham, NC: Duke University Press, 1965. The standard study of the most popular of the New Deal relief agencies.

Schwarz, Jordan. *Liberal: Adolf A. Berle and the Vision of an American Era*. New York: Free Press, 1987. The first full-length biography of one of Roosevelt's closest political and policy advisors.

Snyder, Robert E. *Cotton Crisis*. Chapel Hill: University of North Carolina Press, 1984. A lively and valuable study of the 1931 movement, propounded by Huey Long and taken up by small farmers everywhere in the South, for a "cotton holiday" to combat the ruinously low prices of that year.

Stepan-Norris, Judith, and Maurice Zeitlin. *Talking Union*. Urbana: University of Illinois Press, 1996. An account of the political battle to elect Stanley Nowak, a union official, to the Michigan state senate and its ramifications for the union movement as a whole, as well as the effort to unionize the Ford Motor Company's River Rouge complex.

Thomas, Jerry Bruce. *An Appalachian New Deal: West Virgina in the Great Depression*. Lexington: University Press of Kentucky, 1998. Traces the impact of the New Deal in the context of one state whose basic industries, such as coal, had become impoverished by the depression. Argues the New Deal's economic effects were limited but did help to reform and open up politics to broader participation.

Valelly, Richard M. *Radicalism in the States: The Minnesota Farm-Labor Party and the American Political Economy*. Chicago: University of Chicago Press, 1989. Shows how the New Deal had the effect of weakening this state party, the best-known and most important of the radical political movements at the state level, by offering an alternative.

Vittoz, Stanley. *New Deal Labor Policy and the American Industrial Economy*. Chapel Hill: University of North Carolina Press, 1987. Written from a perspective that believes the corporate world dominates public policy, the author endeavors to explain how the New Deal's Wagner Act and subsequent labor policy emerged.

Weisiger, Marsha L. *Land of Plenty: Oklahomans in the Cotton Fields of Arizona, 1933–1942*. Norman: University of Oklahoma Press, 1995. In this story of the migrations of Oklahomans to the cotton farms of Arizona, the author argues that the migrant "Okies" were exploited by large Arizona farm operators and found little protection from federal agencies seeking to ameliorate their problems.

White, Graham, and John Maze. *Harold Ickes of the New Deal: His Private Life and Public Career.* Cambridge, MA: Harvard University Press, 1985. An extremely interesting biography written by a historian and a psychologist, which has been much criticized for having too much Freud and too little Ickes. It illuminates Ickes's tortured personality but does not particularly advance our knowldege of Ickes as a leading New Dealer.

Zieger, Robert H. *The CIO, 1935–1955.* Chapel Hill: University of North Carolina Press, 1995. Valuable for interpreting the historical significance of CIO unionism beyond the 1930s, showing how it not only influenced labor conditions in a narrow sense but also issues of participation of blacks and women in the work force.

———. *John L. Lewis: Labor Leader.* Boston, MA: Twayne, 1988. A too brief but excellent treatment of the single most important figure in the labor movement during the New Deal.

POLITICAL AND CONSTITUTIONAL CHANGES

Allswang, John M. *The New Deal and American Politics: A Study in Political Change.* New York: Wiley, 1978. A brief but very useful book that supplies and explains the major changes in voting behavior of the 1930s that led to the "New Deal Coalition."

Best, Gary Dean. *The Critical Press and the New Deal: The Press Versus Presidential Power, 1933–1938.* Westport, CT: Praeger, 1993. An entertaining review of press criticism of FDR, especially by five of the leading columnists, such as Walter Lippmann and Mark Sullivan. Best is so relentless in his hostility to Roosevelt, however, that the book's usefulness is limited.

———. *Pride, Prejudice, and Politics: Roosevelt Versus Recovery, 1933–1938.* New York: Praeger, 1991. A hostile portrayal of FDR and his policies, based to a great extent on what conservative critics of the New Deal had to say during the 1930s. An interesting book, because it provides a thorough review of such criticism, but not a balanced one.

Brinkley, Alan. *The End of Reform: New Deal Liberalism in Recession and War.* New York: Knopf, 1995. Argues that the recession of 1937–1938 gradually shifted the New Dealers' emphasis away from building a stronger welfare state, as planned, toward enlarging consumption through Keynesian tactics.

Coulter, Matthew Ware. *The Senate Munitions Inquiry of the 1930s: Beyond the Merchants of Death.* Westport, CT: Greenwood Publishing, 1997. A valuable revisionist account of the Senate's investigation of the munitions industry in the 1930s.

Cushman, Barry. *Rethinking the New Deal Court: The Structure of a Constitutional Revolution.* New York: Oxford University Press, 1998. A strongly revisionist study, arguing that the Supreme Court's 1937 shift in constitutional interpretation arose less from FDR's attack on the Court than from an internal debate that had been raging within it for over a decade.

Dyson, Lowell K. *Red Harvest: The Communist Party and American Farmers*. Lincoln: University of Nebraska Press, 1982. Presents the history of little-known farmer organizations, such as the United Farmers League, that were communist dominated, and the failed communist efforts to gain control of the better known movements.

Klehr, Harvey. *The Heyday of American Communism: The Depression Decade*. New York: Basic Books, 1984. Though taking account of revisionist views, Klehr nonetheless makes clear that communists were in part directed by Moscow for its own purposes; full advantage of the gullibility of liberals was taken in this respect.

Leuchtenburg, William E. *The Supreme Court Reborn: The Constitutional Revolution in the Age of Roosevelt*. New York: Oxford University Press, 1995. A series of essays on the subject, highly regarded as an important contribution.

Morgan, Chester M. *Redneck Liberal: Theodore G. Bilbo and the New Deal*. Baton Rouge: Louisiana State University Press, 1985. A study of Bilbo as a senator during the New Deal years after 1935 when, unlike most other southerners, he remained loyal to Roosevelt and to the later New Deal's agenda of building a welfare state.

Naison, Mark. *Communists in Harlem during the Depression*. Urbana: University of Illinois Press, 1983. One of the major books that portrays American communists during the 1930s as striving genuinely to help the powerless, in this case by organizing blacks in Harlem to protest for better housing and other causes.

Nordin, Dennis S. *The New Deal's Black Congressman: A Life of Arthur Wergs Mitchell*. Columbia: University of Missouri Press, 1997. A biography of Mitchell, the first black Democratic congressman, which details his undistinguished political career and provides insight into the Chicago Democratic machine's relationship to African Americans in this period.

Patterson, James T. *Congressional Conservatism and the New Deal: The Growth of the Conservative Coalition in Congress, 1933–1939*. Lexington: University Press of Kentucky, 1967. A classic study, with abundant information about many key senators and representatives, and their collective behavior. Describes the beginnings and the growth in power of the "conservative coalition" in Congress.

———. *Mr. Republican: A Biography of Robert A. Taft*. Boston: Houghton Mifflin, 1972. A standard political biography and the best work available on any of the leading Republican figures of the decade.

Plotke, David. *Building a Democratic Political Order: Reshaping American Liberalism in the 1930s and 1940s*. New York: Cambridge University

Press, 1996. Focuses on the creation of the political ideology of the New Deal, what the author calls "progressive liberalism," and attempts a reconceptualization of the political history of the period.

Porter, David L. *Congress and the Waning of the New Deal*. Port Washington, NY: Kennikat, 1980. A detailed study of how the growing tendency toward conservatism in Congress blocked the plans of the New Dealers in the late 1930s.

Savage, Sean J. *Roosevelt: The Party Leader, 1932–1945*. Lexington: University Press of Kentucky, 1991. Sets out to make a case for Roosevelt as wishing from the beginning of his presidency to reshape the Democratic Party as the liberal party and argues he was a strong political leader.

Sundquist, James L. *Dynamics of the Party System: Alignment and Realignment of the Political Parties in the United States*. Washington, DC: Brookings Institute, 1973. Cogently explains the political scientists' conception of the "party system" and delineates the shift to the New Deal system.

Weed, Clyde P. *The Nemesis of Reform: The Republican Party during the New Deal*. New York: Columbia University Press, 1994. The story of the initial impotence of the Republican Party during the New Deal because of its eastern wing's refusal to recognize that circumstances warranted political change, and how the party's fortunes improved in the later 1930s.

SOCIETY AND CULTURE DURING THE DEPRESSION ERA

Alexander, Charles C. *Here the Country Lies: Nationalism and the Arts in Twentieth Century America*. Bloomington: Indiana University Press, 1980. A splendid survey of American writers, musicians, and painters during the depression and how they were affected by the needs of the nation and by its politics.

Alexander, William. *Film on the Left: American Documentary Film from 1931 to 1942*. Princeton, NJ: Princeton University Press, 1981. The story of filmmakers who preferred making documentaries that portrayed contemporary social and economic conditions in the midst of the depression to making films for Hollywood.

Browder, Laura. *Rousing the Nation: Radical Culture in Depression America*. Amherst: University of Massachusetts Press, 1998. Focuses on the writings of three radical writers from the 1930s—John Dos Passos, James T. Farrell, and Josephine Herbst—and the character of political writing during the depression years. Includes interesting material on the "living newspaper" form of drama that developed at this time and found production as a part of the Federal Theater Project.

Brown, Dorothy M. and Elizabeth McKeown. *The Poor Belong to Us: Catholic Charities and American Welfare*. Cambridge, MA: Harvard University

Press, 1997. A study of American social welfare history and Catholic Charities' place at the center of that history.

Cooney, Terry A. *Balancing Acts: American Thought and Culture in the 1930's.* New York: Twayne, 1995. A treatment of the subject that finds the impact of the depression was profound, leading to the introduction of new forms and directions in nearly every phase of thought and culture.

Foley, Babara. *Radical Representation: Politics and Form in U.S. Proletarian Fiction, 1924–1941.* Durham, NC: Duke University Press, 1993. A recent exploration of the proletarian writers, with major emphasis on debates within communist circles concerning its forms and messages.

Harris, Jonathan. *Federal Art and National Culture: The Politics of Identity in New Deal America.* New York: Cambridge University Prress, 1995. Harris finds the arts were somewhat harnessed to their own support by the New Deal.

Pells, Richard H. *Radical Visions and American Dreams: Culture and Social Thought in the Depression Years.* New York: Harper & Row, 1973. A standard work that recounts the tendency of American intellectuals in the early years of the depression to be creative and venturesome in their social thought, a position from which most of them retreated as the decade wore on.

Reiman, Richard A. *The New Deal and American Youth: Ideas and Ideals in a Depression Decade.* Athens: University of Georgia Press, 1992. Delineates the purpose of those who established and ran the National Youth Administration, particularly of its director, Aubrey Williams, and shows that the intention was less to run a work program for young people than to bring about a revision of educational goals and methods in the schools. FDR showed a keen interest in the program from the outset.

WOMEN AND MINORITIES DURING THE DEPRESSION AND NEW DEAL

Greenberg, Cheryl Lynn. *"Or Does It Explode?" Black Harlem in the Great Depression.* New York: Oxford University Press, 1991. Explores the political groups and political persuasions of Harlem during the depression years.

Kirby, John B. *Black Americans in the Roosevelt Era: Liberalism and Race.* Knoxville: University of Tennessee Press, 1980. Few New Dealers felt the need to actively consider and fulfill the special needs of blacks, but people such as Harold Ickes and Eleanor Roosevelt did what they could.

Mettler, Suzanne. *Dividing Citizens: Gender and Federalism in New Deal Public Policy.* Ithaca, NY: Cornell University Press, 1998. Stresses the fact that some New Deal legislation and policies differentiated the protections and benefits they offered by gender, much to the disadvantage of women.

Scharf, Lois. *To Work and to Wed: Female Employment, Feminism, and the Great Depression*. Westport, CT: Greenwood Publishing, 1980. Presents the case that during the depression resentment grew over women working, especially in the white-collar and professional fields, and that this created a social climate that made it hard for women to enter the work force on equal terms after World War II.

Sitkoff, Harvard. *A New Deal for Blacks: The Emergence of Civil Rights as a National Issue*. New York: Oxford University Press, 1978. Although the New Deal offered little specifically to or for blacks, their position nonetheless had improved by the end of the depression decade as American liberals rallied to their cause more enthusiastically than before. By the beginning of the 1940s, blacks were in a stronger position politically and socially.

Wandersee, Winifred D. *Women's Work and Family Values 1920–1940*. Cambridge, MA: Harvard University Press, 1981. Family values changed during this period as Americans came to feel they should live up to the "American standard of living," a standard many families could not attain with one breadwinner. The author explores this and other ways in which the period was a preparation for the wider entry of women into the work force in later decades.

Ware, Susan. *Beyond Suffrage: Women and the New Deal*. Cambridge: Harvard University Press, 1981. A collective biography of twenty-eight women, involved in social reform causes during the previous two decades, who found places of influence in the New Deal and substantially influenced its social legislation.

———. *Holding Their Own: American Women in the 1930s*. Schenectady, NY: Twayne, 1982. Argues that the position of women in society did not decline as badly during the depression as has been thought.

Wilson, Joan Hoff, and Marjorie Lightman, eds. *Without Precedent: The Life and Career of Eleanor Roosevelt*. Bloomington: University of Indiana Press, 1984. A collection of essays by leading scholars in the field.

Zangrando, Robert L. *The NAACP Crusade against Lynching, 1909–1950*. Philadelphia: Temple University Press, 1980. The history of the NAACP's struggle, over four decades, to build an alliance with liberal groups and obtain a federal antilynching law.

VIDEOS

Eleanor Roosevelt. Produced by WGBH-TV, Boston (PBS Home Video, 2000). Includes interviews with relatives and friends in addition to newsreel and home movie footage from the period.

FDR. Produced by David Grubin Productions for WGBH-TV, Boston (PBS Video, "American Experience" series, 1997). A four-part, highly praised biography (two videocassettes).

The Great Depression. Produced by Blackside, Inc., in association with BBC-2 (PBS Video, 1993). A seven-part series covering all phases of the depression years and ending with the defense effort during World War II.

Hoover Dam. Produced by Firstlight Pictures for WGBH-TV, Boston (PBS Video, "American Experience" series, 1999). Regarded at the time as a heroic feat of engineering, the building of the dam is portrayed here through footage and photographs contemporary with the building of the dam.

Huey Long. Produced by RKB Florentine Films (PBS Home Video, 1996). A fascinating biography of the "Louisiana Kingfish."

The Plow That Broke the Plains and, *The River.* Produced by Video Yesteryear. A videocassette release of the famous films made by the Farm Security Administration and the U.S. Information Service during the New Deal, directed by Pare Lorentz with music by Virgil Thomson. Graphically told story of the New Deal's efforts to counteract Dust Bowl and flood conditions.

Riding the Rails. Produced by Out of the Blue Productions for WGBH-TV, Boston (PBS Video, "American Experience" series, 1997). Based on photographs and footage of the mass wanderings of the unemployed on America's railroads during the depression.

The Thirties. Produced by Columbia River Entertainment Group (1997). A four-part video emphasizing social conditions during the early years of the depression decade.

Index

About the Author

ROBERT F. HIMMELBERG is Professor of History at Fordham University. He served as Dean of Fordham's Graduate School of Arts and Sciences from 1993 to 2000. He is the author of *Historians and Race: Autobiography and the Writing of History* (1996), *Business and Government in America Since 1870* (1994), *The Origins of the National Recovery Administration: Business, Government, and the Trade Association Issue, 1921–1933* (1976, rev. ed. 1993), coauthor of *Herbert Hoover and the Crisis of American Capitalism* (1974), and editor of *The Great Depression and American Capitalism* (1968). A specialist in the economic and political history of the Great Depression and the New Deal, he has written numerous papers on the subject.